The Mexican American

The Mexican American

ARE WE GOOD NEIGHBORS?

Alonso S. Perales

ARNO PRESS
A New York Times Company
New York — 1974

Reprint Edition 1974 by Arno Press Inc.

Reprinted from a copy in The Princeton
  University Library

THE MEXICAN AMERICAN
ISBN for complete set: 0-405-05670-2
See last pages of this volume for titles.

Manufactured in the United States of America

Library of Congress Cataloging in Publication Data

Perales, Alonso S   1898-   comp.
  Are we good neighbors?

  (The Mexican American)
  Reprint of the ed. published by Artes Graficas, San
Antonio.
    1. Mexican Americans--Civil rights--Texas.
2. Spanish-Americans in the United States. I. Title.
II. Series.
F395.M5P37 1974   301.45'16'8720764   73-14213
ISBN 0-405-05687-7

Alonso S. Perales

ARE WE
GOOD
NEIGHBORS?

San Antonio, Texas
MCMXLVIII

Dedicated

To the courageous and zealous men and women of the Americas who have labored so long and so well for Christian principles, Americanism, a n d Inter-American understanding and good will.

ALONSO S. PERALES
Attorney and Civic Leader,
San Antonio, Texas

ALONSO S. PERALES. Born in Alice, Texas. Served with the
United States Army in World War I.

Graduate of the Alice, Texas public schools, the Preparatory
School in Washington, D. C., the School of Economics and Government and the Law School of National University, Washington, D. C.,
where he received the degrees of Bachelor of Laws and Bachelor
of Arts.

Has served on thirteen different diplomatic missions for the
United States Department of State, in Washington, Mexico, the

5

West Indies and Central and South America. He was legal Advisor to the United States Electoral Mission in Nicaragua in 1928, 1930 and 1932 and was one of the Attorneys on General John J. Pershing's staff in the Tacna-Arica Arbitration Commission in 1925-26.

He is Consul General of Nicaragua in San Antonio, Texas, and served as Counselor to the Nicaraguan Delegation to the United Nations Conference in San Francisco in 1945.

He is a member of the Texas State Bar Association, the San Antonio Bar Association, the American Bar Association, the Inter-American Bar Association, the American Society of International Law, and the Alumni Association of the National University, Washington, D. C.

He is Director General of League of Loyal Americans, Chairman of the Committee of One Hundred, a Director of the Bexar County Tuberculosis Association, Member of the San Antonio Association of Welfare Workers, a Director of the San Antonio Social Welfare Bureau, member of Alamo Post No. 2 of the American Legion.

He is President, Holy Name Society, San Fernando Cathedral; Member, Advisory Board, National Catholic Community Service of San Antonio; Member, Executive Board, Archdiocesan Union of Holy Name Societies of San Antonio; Fourth Degree Member, Knights of Columbus, Council No. 786, San Antonio; Charter member San Fernando Post, Catholic War Veterans of America; Member, State Legislative Committee, Texas Social Welfare Association; Member, Executive Committee, Bexar County Council on juvenile Delinquency; Chairman, Civics Committee, and a Director of Guadalupe Community Center; President Pan-American Optimist Club, San Antonio; Parlamentarian, Mexican Chamber of Commerce of San Antonio; a founder, Past President General and life member of the League of United Latin American Citizens.

FOREWORD

For sometime the writer has intended to publish the facts regarding the problem of discrimination, particularly against Latin Americans, as he knows them, a problem that vitally affects the interests of our country - the United States of America - and which is crying for solution. The reference is to the discrimination practiced by some, against persons of Mexican or Spanish descent in Texas and other states. At the outset it is only fair to state that not every person, nor every town and city in Texas practices such discrimination. However, the practice by some persons in different towns and cities causes much indignation and ill will among the Mexican and Spanish speaking people in the United States, as well as throughout the Western Hemisphere. For this reason every American citizen who has the interest of our country at heart should lend every effort toward solving the problem.

We have before us a letter written by Mr. Jack Danciger, prominent oil man and outstanding citizen of Fort Worth, Texas, to Mr. Thomas W. Palmer, President of the Pan American Society of New York, dated November 27, 1947, in Santiago de Chile, the capital of the Republic of Chile, South America, which reads partly as follows:

"I read with great interest the enclosed article which appeared in "MERCURIO" of today.

"I live in Fort Worth, Texas, where I have been rather active in trying to stop racial discrimination practiced against Latin Americans in the United States of North America.

"For the past two years I have been travelling all over South America studying conditions and I can assure you, Mr. Palmer, that Latin Americans wherever I have been down here keenly resent these insults and indignities of racial discrimination which brands them all as inferior races.

"I notice in the wording of the parchment given to the President you omitted to mention one of the principal things for which the President is admired in Latin America - namely his firm stand against discrimination or unfair practices against Latin Americans."

We are all aware that the people of Mexico resent this discrimination so deeply that their Government has decided not to permit any more farm workers to come to Texas, or any other state where it is practiced until assurances are given that it has ceased.

The report of President Truman's Civil Rights Commission reveals that there is considerable discrimination, political, economic, and social, in the United States against minority groups. The Commission has recommended both Federal and State legislation to discourage it. Mexicans and Latin Americans constitute the second largest minority group. It requires no great stretch of our imagination to realize the harm that such discrimination does to our country commercially and otherwise.

There are well intentioned, patriotic citizens in Texas and other States of the Union who deplore the existing conditions and who are ready to do something to help solve the problem. Before proceeding, however, they desire to know the facts. There are others who are entirely unaware of the situation who, being good Americans and good Christians, will be aroused to action when they learn the facts and will help to eliminate the evil.

Precisely for these reasons this book is being published, to apprise fair-minded, right thinking Americans of the problem and the urgent need for its solution. It is a factual presentation of a problem that must be solved for the good of our Nation, if for no other reason.

A perusal of this book will disclose to the reader that discrimination does exist, that it is not confined to a few isolated cases as some declare, but that the practice is widespread. The question then arises: What is the solution to the problem?

It is the writer's considered opinion that the people of Texas and of other States where a similar situation exist can end discrimination whenever they determine that it shall end. How?

1. By waging a vigorous educational campaign in the public schools, in the churches and thru the press and the radio calling upon the people to cease to discriminate against persons of Mexican or Spanish descent. In this connection, information regarding the cultural background and the good

8

qualities and virtues of the Spanish speaking people might be conveyed to all listeners.

2. *By ceasing to segregate Mexican children from Anglo-Americans in the public schools.*

3. *By enacting both Federal and State legislation forbidding discrimination against persons of Mexican or Spanish extraction and other descendants of the Caucasian Race.*

Both educational, as well as legislative measures are absolutely necessary if discrimination is to end. To those who argue that one cannot legislate democracy or Christianity, we reply that murder and robbery run counter to the TEN COMMANDMENTS which rely for enforcement only on the appeal to man's heart and reason. Because this has proven insufficient, society has had to enact laws forbidding robbery and murder. It is true that neither medium has proved successful in abolishing crime completely. But we can well imagine what the situation would be if it were not for our schools, our churches, the press, the radio, and THE LAW.

In conclusion, the author wishes to express his deep appreciation to the following distinguished Americans who have so generously contributed with their time, thought and effort toward this factual presentation of one of the most important problems facing the American people to-day:

His Excellency Robert E. Lucey, Dr. Carlos E. Castañeda, Mr. Jack Danciger, Prof. J. Luz Saenz, Dr. J. C. Granbery, Mr. Laureano Flores, Senator Dennis Chavez, Mr. Malcom G. Ross, Mr. Stuart J. Barnes, Mr. L. F. Merl, and others.

ALONSO S. PERALES.

San Antonio, Texas
April, 1948.

His Excellency The Most Reverend
ROBERT E. LUCEY, S. T. D.,
Archbishop of San Antonio, Texas

Due to the untiring and zealous efforts of His Excellency
towards the betterment and welfare of the Spanish Speaking
People of the Southwest, much has been accomplished both
socially and spiritually speaking. For this, and many other outstanding achievements, Archbishop Lucey is admired and respected by both Catholics and non-Catholics.

PART I
THE PROBLEM AS SEEN BY OTHERS

ARE WE GOOD NEIGHBORS?

Opening Address of His Excellency,
The Most Rev. Robert E. Lucey, S. T. D.,
Archbishop of San Antonio

The Conference on
SPANISH-SPEAKING PEOPLE OF THE SOUTHWEST
Incarnate Word College
San Antonio, Texas, July 20, 1943

This is the story of a large minority group in the United States, our Latin-American brothers, generous and warm heart-ed, simple, charming and lovable, yet segregated, persecuted and submerged. It is the story of many Anglo-Americans who have shown stupidity, ignorance and malice in treating their Mexican brethren with injustice, discrimination and disdain. It is not a lovely story; it is profoundly disturbing because it tells of poverty and tragedy, of disease, delinquency and death.

During the past quarter of a century many good citizens of our country sincerely believed that the race question might well be let alone to work itself out to a happy conclusion by the slow, sure formula of peaceful evolution and patient progress. It was a comfortable philosophy and if not very hopeful to the minority groups it largely satisfied the master race.

But the present worldwide and devastating conflict has disturbed peaceful consciences, opened unseeing eyes and posed stubborn questions that simply will not be downed without direct and adequate answers. Some of these questions sound like this: Why did the Burmese natives refuse to fight for England? What truth is there in the Japanese contention that the white races despise the yellow men? Can we keep our self-respect if we demand that the colored American fight for freedom in Africa and deny him freedom at home? Can we make the western hemisphere a bulwark of liberty and law while we maim and mangle Mexican youth in the streets of our cities? Can we condemn our Latin-Americans to starvation wages, bad housing and tuberculosis and

11

then expect them to be strong, robust soldiers of Uncle Sam? Can we tell our Spanish-speaking soldiers that dishonorable discharge from the army will deprive them of civil rights when they never had any civil rights? In a word, can we, the greatest nation on earth, assume the moral leadership of the world·when race riots and murder, political crimes and economic injustices disgrace the very name of America?

These sharp questions are getting under the skin of every decent American and all are agreed that something has got to be done about it.

I take it that in a keynote address the speaker is not expected to cover the whole agenda of a four-day conference. You have gathered here to pool your knowledge and experience of Spanish-American conditions that out of a complete and integrated picture you may draw definite conclusions and recommendations looking to the amelioration of those conditions. For my part I shall confine my remarks to a few broad considerations leading the way to further thought and analysis by the members of this conference.

Before referring to some of the darker details of our subject may I mention that the good effect of the war on the thinking of our citizens is not the only bright spot in a rather somber picture. It may not be generally recognized, and yet it is very true, that during the past half century our ancient Church has stood almost alone in the field of constructive effor n behalf of our Mexican brethren. Unthinking persons, frienuly to our Mexican people, have declared that in the past no one has done anything for them. The truth is that while some counties and some states have contributed generously to the material welfare of our impoverished Mexicans, the Catholic Church, through Diocesan Welfare Bureaus, Chancery Offices and the Extension Society of Chicago, has poured out millions of dollars for both the spiritual and temporal welfare of these children of the Church. I think it is fair to say that the Catholic Church in the Southwest and on the Coast has expended more of Her funds on Her beloved Mexican people than on any other group in our population.

But now we no longer stand alone. The administration in Washington, through the Office of the Coordinator of Inter-American Affairs, is showing an intelligent and helpful interest in these problems. State officials and citizens generally are aroused over the lethargy and mistakes of the past. Now, at long last, we see the dawn of a better day for our Spanish-American people. But this new interest will not automatically lift the burden from the shoulders of this oppressed minority. That interest must be informed and directed to achieve its proper purpose. The proceedings of this conference will contribute greatly to that end.

If I were asked to mention one outstanding problem that weighs most heavily upon our Mexican people, I would say that it is the burden of undeserved poverty. I stress that word *undeserved.* I suppose that among all peoples one can find examples of solemn myths, folklore and bits of popular nonsense. One of the myths seriously entertained by some English-speaking Americans is that Mexican workers are lazy, slow and improvident. He would indeed be an optimist who would declare that no Mexican workers deserve that description. But the same is true of all nationals - a few are improvident but the vast majority are normal, hard working people.

And right here a thought occurs to me which I believe has validity. How hard would an Irishman work if you paid him twenty cents an hour? How much exuberance, vitality and enthusiasm could any people show who had been underpaid, undernourished and badly housed for half a century? If the Mexican is sometimes illiterate, whose fault is it but the fault of those who denied him an education and drove him out to work in the days of his youth? If the Mexican is sometimes diseased and delinquent, whose fault is it but the fault of those who from his birth condemned him to the unwholesome atmosphere of poverty and squalor? If the Mexican is sometimes not a good American, what can you expect from a man who during all his life was socially ostracized, deprived of civil rights, politically debased and condemned to economic servitude? If some Mexicans seem to be inferior it is because we made them so. God gave them rights and gifts like all the rest of us but we have degraded them.

The truth is that the majority of Mexican laborers are honest, industrious and hard working if treated in a civilized manner. Many of them have developed highly technical skills when given the advantage of training. Unfortunately, poverty and race discrimination have robbed many of them of educational opportunities. They are mostly unskilled or semiskilled. In normal times they are given the worst jobs with the lowest pay. Many have been unemployed; others have had seasonal labor with substantial intervals of idleness.

During this conference you will consider conditions among rural communities of Mexicans, the subsistence farmers and the migratory workers in agriculture. You will note that a large number of the agricultural workers are really residents of cities and towns who leave home and church and school to become wandering nomads on the highways of our country. Home life is wrecked, school work is disrupted and parish loyalties are suspended or broken. How fine a thing it would be if these patient, hard-working families could have a little land of their own where they could settle down, earn their bread and save their souls.

To hold this large segment of our population in poverty is false economy. To pay miserable wages to our Spanish-speaking workers is a luxury which our business men can hardly afford. If the purchasing power of this great group of people were equal to their capacity to consume our business men would enjoy the greatest prosperity that they have ever known. If three-quarters of a million of Spanish-Americans in Texas received honest wages the products of our fields and factories would be purchased as never before.

To deny adequate relief to dependent citizens is also false economy. Here in Texas our program of public relief to indigents is pitiful. A very general lack of labor organizations, the absence of good social legislation and the greed of powerful employers have combined to create in Texas dreadful and widespread misery. The evil men who are driving tens of thousands of our poor people into slow starvation will be held to strict accountability by the God of eternal justice.

A third type of false economy is the refusal to employ truant officers for the compulsory education of our children in public or private schools. A study of school enrollment in the city of Dallas was made recently and it was found that 3800 children were not even registered in school. Many of them were Latin-Americans. In this Archdiocese we estimate that there are 10,000 children of grammar school age not enrolled in any school. Most of them are Spanish-Americans. By refusing to employ attendance officers we may save a few hundred dollars annually but we spend all of that and much more to provide jails, juvenile courts and probation officers for delinquent youth; and the loss in social values is beyond estimation.

From all of this it will be seen that poverty walks hand in hand with a host of spiritual and physical tragedies-bad housing, poor education, crime and juvenile delinquency, disease and early death, loss of religious loyalties and the crushing of the human spirit. But we English-speaking people are also the losers for we are deprived of the music and laughter, the art and culture, the skills and achievements of a people who could add so much to the richness and fullness of our lives.

It is passing strange that we should consider these Spanish-Americans as aliens and foreigners in this great Southwest. They are natives to this land. It was theirs alone when this vast region was the distant border of the Spanish empire. It was theirs be-

14

fore Columbus and before Cortés. It was theirs when Junipero Serra established the old missions of California. It was theirs when the Alamo was the center of a community in a circle of missions along the winding river of St. Anthony. They and their ancestors were here before the Spaniards brought them the cruel burden of western civilization, but brought them also the saving grace of Christ. They have named our Cities Santa Fe, Los Angeles, San Diego and San Antonio. They have named our rivers Rio Grande, Guadalupe, San Pedro and Colorado. This is their country.

These people are our people. They are the most numerous body of Catholics in the whole Southwest. They are God's children created to His image and likeness. All of us, English and Spanish-speaking Catholics, have been blessed with the same heritage of Christian faith. We receive with them the same sacraments, at the baptismal font, at the altar, in the tribunal of repentance and the last anointing on our bed of death. With them we believe, we pray, we are governed. With them we strive for salvation in a blessed immortality.

But there is another tie that binds us to them; all of us are Americans. The Spanish-speaking were here first. We, in a certain sense, merged with them. This is their country and ours. God gave these pleasant fields and lovely rivers to all of us. Unfortunately this whole Southwest lives an unstable existence. But our Spanish-speaking brothers suffer from its instability worst of all. There are poor English-speaking people here-poor Germans and Czechs and Poles; but none are so numerous, none have so suffered as those whose forbears were here before Coronado and Columbus. Completely to cure the insecurity of the Mexicans means curing also the basic insecurity of this whole area. It is a difficult task, but not impossible. Without delay we must devise ways to save them from the worst features of this insecurity.

I would be unfair to truth if I did not add another word. We of the ancient Church must develop leaders among our Spanish-American brothers and we must persuade their ablest men and women who have achieved a measure of prosperity not to abandon their own brethren. Through our Catholic Action organizations we should be able to develop leaders among our Spanish-Americans and perhaps in time we may win back those who could have made a contribution to their own race but who in an evil day separated themselves from their ancient culture, their traditions and their people.

If in the past our English-speaking Catholics have not seemed to cooperate intimately with our Latin-American brothers it surely was not entirely their fault. Worthwhile inter-American relations require leadership, action and organization. If these have not always been available we intend to supply them now. Our Anglo-Catholics must give to our non-Catholic fellow citizens a good example of sincere, wholehearted cooperation with Spanish-Americans here and throughout the hemisphere.

Before concluding I wish to make three definite recommendations. Organization is needed here in the Southwest to solve our basic problems of insecurity. It would be ideal if a statewide or even an interstate organization could be formed to analyze and attack our problems of industry, agriculture, relief, housing, race discrimination and such like. If this ideal is not now feasible we should support existing organizations and create new ones when possible.

Here in Texas Junior Chambers of Commerce are studying inter-American relations. The Coordinator's office in Washington is setting up a statewide advisory committee to help solve these problems. Here in San Antonio a planning committee is being organized to coordinate the social welfare programs of our community. A statewide legislative committee for better social legislation is also under way. Our Mexican people have a stake in all of these forward looking movements. We must not refuse our cooperation.

My second recommendation has already been mentioned. We must labor in season and out of season to develop loyal, intelligent leaders among the Spanish-Americans themselves. And my final word is this. All of us, Catholics and non-Catholics, must think and plan and live like Christians. I am convinced that the present worldwide conflict was caused in part by the sins and the lethargy of part-time Christians. And doubtless here in the Southwest if we shall only live as Christians we shall witness less of tragedy and a larger hope.

I bid you welcome to this conference and I thank you for your coming. May your deliberations be rich in God's blessing and fruitful in achievement.

THE SECOND RATE CITIZEN
AND
DEMOCRACY

By
Carlos E. Castañeda, Ph. D.
Professor of History
University of Texas

The desire to hide from the public certain unpleasant conditions that exist in Texas and the Southwest has grown in intensity in recent years. At the same time the tendency to appeal to the primitive· instinct of race pride - more accurately race prejudice- to maintain the *status quo,* ignoring the social, economic, and political injustice on which it rests has become more general and widespread.

There are many in high places who feel strongly that the subject of discrimination must not be discussed. If one needs mention it, the only thing that one can say with decorum is that the practice has become a thing of the past. It existed, yes; but fortunately it has been eliminated by the good neighbor policy. Here is a truly dangerous trend for the effective practice of democracy.

A prominent educator and economist recently called attention to the increasing insistence on the denial of truth. He pointed out that in every age the real danger arises from ignorance of the facts by the public, and that this is greater when the community becomes afraid of the truth. In a democracy it is not truth but ignorance that is dangerous. The result of the prevalent attitude in regard to this matter today is obvious. Ignorance has become a virtue, the truth, something that can be admitted only in private.

Because of historical factors, language differences, and cultural patterns that set it apart, there is a group in Texas and the Southwest whose members have become for all intents and purposes second rate citizens in a democracy. Not a pleasant fact to admit. It proclaims the existence of an anomalous condition incompatible with democracy.

17

DR. CARLOS E. CASTAÑEDA, Ph. D.,
Professor of History
University of Texas.

DR. CARLOS E. CASTAÑEDA Ph. D., Professor of History of the University of Texas and outstanding civic leader, who has done much for the progress and welfare of the inhabitants of Mexican descent of the United States as well as toward the strengthening of relations between the peoples of the United States and Mexico.

The Mexican, constituting the second largest minority in this region, while not officially classed as "colored", has generally come to be designated as "non-white". Discuss the component parts of our population, or of any meeting, or audience, and you will find yourself facing three classes in the mind of the average citizen: White, Colored, and Mexican, or White, Colored, and Non-White. Thus the Mexican may not be considered "Colored" but he certainly is not "White" either, in the opinion of the man on the street.

Now, then, since there is but one group against which the pattern of segregation - with all its implications of inferiority - may be applied in the South with the full sanction of the community, it follows that the tendency to accord the Mexican the same treatment has become general. It is as unfair in one case as in the other. It assumes in either case the existence of a second rate citizen.

Why the insistence on a practice that is undemocratic, un-american, and un-christian? It is not pleasant to admit the basic cause of such a practice. If the question is analyzed, the obvious and logical conclusion is the same in both cases: economic exploitation. A second rate citizen, member of a group admittedly inferior, cannot render services equal in value to those of the superior group. Consequently, his remuneration and his opportunities for advancement in employment are limited. As long as the community brands him as inferior by the treatment accorded him, the employer can continue to exploit him with a clear conscience. What are the consequences? His economic exploitation and the denial of equal opportunities for improvement will continue to deprive him of the means of eradicating the external justifications of discrimination: clothing, health, low standards of living, poor education. The truth is bitter. Why deny it? Admission of equality would imply equal economic and educational opportunitites.

Under the term "Mexican" are included those who have recently come from Mexico and those who have lived in Texas and the Southwest for generations, those who are American citizens by nationalization or birth and those who are citizens of Mexico; those who speak English without an accent and those who speak nothing but Spanish. In the mind of the average citizen the Mexican is a "Mexican" regardless. The term has come to imply more than national origin, or language, or citizenship. It has come to imply in the most intimate recesses of the mind "non-white", consequently "non-equal", a person inferior in every respect. Have to admit it? Yes; embarrassing, to say the least. But the best proof

19

of this inescapable conclusion is the general practice of using the term "Spanish" to designate a member of the group who has been admitted on a basis of equality. The frequent use of the term "White Mexican", now becoming general, implies the existence of Mexicans who are not to be considered "White".

This false conviction gives rise to frequent acts of discrimination and the adoption of practices that are humiliating to members of the group and embarrassing to good Americans. Such acts are a denial of the emphatic professions of good neighborliness. Cooperation between the peoples of the Americas cannot be developed under such conditions. Democracy becomes a travesty if a single citizen is denied equal rights. Hence the easy solution to the resultant embarrassment has been found in glossing over concrete examples of discrimination. In imitation of the ostrich, there are those who prefer to dig their heads in the sand and declare that everything is rosy while the storm rages. Such a policy will inevitably destroy confidence in democracy; more than that, it will destroy democracy itself.

"The real enemies of the present order of society are those who refuse to allow its ills to be examined", recently declared a distinguished student of economics. The time has come for frank dealing, for the examination of the facts in the case, for the presentation of the ungarbled truth. A hush, hush policy, like appeasement of totalitarian states, can end only in disaster. The insatiable appetite of dictators and world conquerors is only whetted by the concessions of peace loving nations. Failure to reveal the true facts in regard to our second rate citizens can lead only to the ultimate destruction of the basic principles of democracy. If we admit the damning theory of racial superiority implied in such a condition, we are no better than the nazis.

On the main building of the University of Texas are deeply carved the words "Ye shall know the Truth and the Truth shall make you free". The people of Texas and the Southwest want the truth, the whole truth, and nothing but the truth. The concrete cases of discrimination against Mexicans presented in this volume illustrate many phases of the problem and the extent of the malady. They do not constitute the whole picture, but they are an authentic part of the whole with which patriotic Americans need to be acquainted. The social conditions they reveal must be remedied if our democracy is to survive. Radical ailments require radical cures. The time has come for making our pledge to the flag of our country a reality: one nation indivisible, with liberty and justice for all.

STATEMENT ON RACIAL DISCRIMINATION

By Jack Danciger

Santiago (Chile), November 15th, 1947.

Mr. Alonso S. Perales,
Suite 308-309 International Bldg.,
510 W. Houston St.,
San Antonio, Texas

Dear Mr. Perales:

I was astonished when I recently read an official statement in October 10th, 1947, issue of the magazine *"TIEMPO"* of Mexico City, by Honorable Hector Perez Martinez, Secretary of Gobernación, and a member of the Cabinet of President Miguel Alemán, outlining in detail the position of his government on racial discrimination practiced against his people in Texas, as set forth in a letter he sent to Governor Beauford H. Jester on September 2nd, 1947.

The predictions made that after World War II the grave problem of racial discrimination would be solved have not come true as, in fact, this problem now seems to be more serious than ever.

As I have been away from Texas travelling in South America for nearly two years, I do not know what action Governor Jester has taken to solve this vexatious problem definitely, but, as he is a good and brilliant man, I have hopes that he will fearlessly attack this problem and soon find a satisfactory solution, because the indignities and insults aimed at our Latin-American friends in certain places in Texas by a relatively few ignorant, thoughtless men, could well have repercussions transcending the temporary disagreements now existing between two border countries. I believe that the great nation of Mexico is right in maintaining her thesis of equal treatment for the Mexicans.

As you know, the Demographic Congress was held in Mexico in 1943, presided over then by Honorable Miguel Alemán, now President of Mexico, and that Congress passed a Resolution to bury the bad habit of racial discrimination in this Continent. Later at the Chapultepec Conference, and then at San Francisco and finally at the Assembly of United Nations, concrete declarations were made relative to this offensive practice against the dignity and honor of certain social groups who were labeled as inferior races.

It is a lamentable paradox that, after the worst war of all history, racial arrogance is being reborn to create discourtesies

21

JACK DANCIGER,
Prominent Business and Civic Leader,
Fort Worth, Texas.

MR. JACK DANCIGER is an outstanding business man and civic leader. Deeply interested in inter-American affairs, he has traveled widely in Latin America and has contributed much toward continental friendship and solidarity.

between those who were allies and loyal collaborators during the armed conflict.

This tends not only to weaken our "Good Neighbor Policy" but also places some in a position to question the right of the United States of America to assume postwar leadership, unless they change their attitude on racial discrimination.

Therefore, I say that every honorable and well-intentioned person in every part of this hemisphere should strive to awaken the nobler sensibilities of all our people to solve forever this bad situation which works openly and undercover against a better understanding between our countries.

Mr. George Messersmith, one of our greatest Americans, in an address made in New York City on October 13th, 1947, before the American Foundation for the most outstanding contribution to Inter-American relations by a North American during last year, stated:

"I learned the problems of the simple man who is the backbone of the life of our country. I learned that the life of a small community does not differ much from the relationship between States, and that practically all the problems with which we have to deal in international relationships are found in their essence in relationships of the people comprising a small community. Relationships between States and peoples are a two-way street, and anyone who does not have deep human understanding and sympathy, is in no position to adequately interpret developing events to his own government, nor is he in a position to make recommendations as to policy which have their basis in the long range interest of the two countries . . ."

"Men in responsible positions in our country are not smaller, less competent than in the past. The tasks are greater and infinitely more complicated. There are times when those of us who have had intimate relationships with problems of government, whether internal or external, feel that the tasks are beyond human capacity."

"We can no longer think of other American states as backward countries, but as undeveloped countries which require our sympathetic and understanding assistance. . ."

"No country can pursue a healthy and progressive life unless the government is such as to maintain the initiative and self-respect of the individual citizen."

"We do know that none of us would put our confidence in anyone who has not shown that he can keep his own house in order. If we do not show in the United States, that we know how to keep our house in order, and do keep it in order, we shall not have

23

demonstrated our power to carry through our obligations of leadership . . ."

"We cannot neglect a friend and keep him as a friend."

"We are increasingly realizing that good relations are a two-way street. We must all be forbearing with each other and this is very easy if we only do a little thinking before we do a lot of talking. We must all stop throwing stones."

This is wise advice from a man who has won his spurs as a recognized authority in fomenting friendly relations among countries in this hemisphere, and should be heeded by all servants placed in high position everywhere through the votes of the people of our country.

Having had the honor of representing two Latin-American countries as their Consular representative, namely Mexico for about seven years in Missouri and Texas, and the Dominican Republic for nearly 17 years in Texas, I have had to deal with racial discrimination in all of its many phases during these years, and have given much time and thought just as you have, to find a solution to this problem fraught with great danger to the future well-being of our own country as well as other countries of this continent; and before closing this letter I will give you some of my ideas on this important matter of racial discrimination practiced so openly against our Latin-American friends in certain parts of the United States, as well as some opinions of others on this subject:

1) Racial discrimination against Latin-Americans is unquestionably one of our most serious problems and must be solved quickly and satisfactorily. This practice is prevalent in the United States, especially in Texas. It is harmful, incivilized, shameful, pernicious, abominable, sinister, unfair and un-Christian.

2) The Legislature of Texas passed a Resolution condemning racial discrimination against Latin-Americans, and this was implemented by our great Governor of Texas, Mr. Coke Stevenson in an open letter to peace officers of the State. In this open letter the Governor stated:

"Texas enjoys more than one half of the extent of the common boundary between the Republic of Mexico and the United States of North America."

"If for no other reason we have in this fact alone a predominant part to play since we constitute a proving ground of the policy of Good Neighbor which has been accepted unanimously by the citizenry of this great Nation."

24

3) Mr. Don E. Weaver, publisher and managing editor of the Fort Worth Press (Scripps-Howard Chain of Newpapers) now editor of "The Citizen" of Columbus, Ohio, published the following statement in the *"PRESS"*:

"Texas is the chief place in all the Americas where Latins and Anglo-Saxons are neighbors, living side by side. What happens, good or bad is magnified out of all its possible small significance in the press of Latin-America."

"Instances of respectable Mexicans being insulted or mistreated by ignorant proprietors of small restaurants and the like get immediate attention in the press and also in the Consulates of Latin-American countries. We have a big job of education to do, not only along the border, but to a great extent throughout our country."

4) It is claimed by some well-meaning people that the problem of racial discrimination; insults and indignities against Latin-Americans, can be solved entirely by education and that no legislation of any kind is necessary as an implement in solving this problem, as they claim you cannot legislate good manners or decency into people.

I do not agree with this theory, and while I agree that a Campaign of Education during the next one hundred years will do much to help to solve the problem, I contend that the enactment of a law such as proposed in the "Spears Bill" is absolutely necessary.

I contend that racial discrimination is a crime in the same category of other crimes and violates our National Constitution and that laws with heavy penalties should be passed to curb such practices. The States of New York and New Jersey have recently made a good start in enactment of such laws.

5) If an American citizen of Latin extraction, or a citizen from Mexico or Latin-America desires to send his children to our public schools without discrimination; dine in a public restaurant or hotel; purchase soft drinks at a drug store; rent or purchase a home of his choice, or attend a movie or theater and is flatly not permitted to do so, at the risk of personal violence, I contend we need a law to protect the safety and lives of these citizens and guarantee them these rights which no fair minded person would want to deny them.

6) When newspapers in the United States, especially many of those printed in Spanish, such as the great daily newspaper *"LA PRENSA"* of San Antonio, Texas, *"LA OPINION"* of Los Angeles, California, *"LA PRENSA"* of New York published detailed reports of all kinds of discrimination and indignities practiced against

Mexicans or Latin-Americans in Texas, these articles are repro-
duced in the newspapers and magazines in all the countries of
Latin America and often enlarged upon, doing great damage to the
prestige of all North Americans thus engendering a bad feeling
that will take decades to overcome. Can we North Americans afford to have such a shameful situation continue any longer?

I say certainly not. All good patriotic North Americans
should demand wise and adequate State and Federal laws with
severe sanctions, to put an end to every type of racial discrimination against Latin Americans, and also call for International
Treaties to stop such abuses practiced against the nationals of their
countries, who reside in the United States of North America.

Possibly this serious matter will be on the agenda of the
Conference to be held at Bogotá, Colombia, in January 1948. If
not, it should certainly be discussed at some other future International Conference.

7) Edith Alderman Guedry, well known columnist states:

*"We, that is, some of us forget that Latin-Americans are of the
same Caucasian race as we are. We forget that they belong to a
land as proud of its people and its traditions as we are of ours.
We forget that they posses an old culture that equals anything of
which we can boast. They could, if they would, look down upon a
culture as young as ours."*

*"Or can we say our people who show racial discrimination against
Latin-Americans do forget? Isn't it that they are ignorant? But
ignorance is no excuse."*

*"We, Texans,, who are residents of the state which can do more
than any other in the nation to cement better relations between the
United States and all Latin-Americans, particularly our nearest
Latin neighbors, the Mexicans, should not be guilty of such
ignorance any longer. We should inform ourselves about how we
can foster better relations."*

*"We can not do it if we do not permit Mexican children to attend
our public schools. We can not so long as certain regions do not
permit Mexicans to travel in cars set aside for "white persons".
We can not so long as we refuse them entrance into hotels, theaters
or restaurants. We can not so long as we refuse to let them live
in whatever areas fit their economic position. As it is, too often
we push them into our slum areas."*

*"The Mexicans, a sensitive, proud people, may feel just as keenly
our slights, but they don't demand apologies. That is no reason*

26

RACIAL DISCRIMINATION

By J. Luz Saenz

(A synopsis of The Number One Problem in Texas. It might look Red-Hot due to the spirit that moves us to express it, but there is nothing of Red-Communism in it as our enemies might presuppose or imply.)

Racial discrimination toward the members of the Mexican race in Texas and other states in the Union, is the most unfair distinction and treatment because we are as good American citizens as the best, and we have the right to demand fair and complete respect for our inalienable rights and equal share of all privileges and prerogatives granted to other citizens of our country.

It is not difficult to trace the origin of racial hatred or simple misunderstanding, as many would like to call it, here in Texas between the Anglo-Saxon and the Mexican people. First, we want to make clear that when we mention Anglo-Saxon race we specially mean that individualistic group, a very limited and undesirable designation, of European descent, who flocked to west America in search of a peaceful place to make their homes and who now despise and ruthlessly antagonize citizens of the original stock in Texas. The victims are members of the Mexican race, of course. By Mexicans we mean all Indo-Americans or Amerindians regardless of whatever other blood may run now in their veins.

Second explanation is in order at this time. In the so-called New World there were never INDIANS only Aborigines. The virgin wilderness of America were inhabited by people that nobody knows where they came from or when. Any fifth grader knows that Columbus did not find India or the Indians he was looking for. The idea supported by the Genoese navigator was either a deliberate mistake or a conventional lie to keep receiving

29

PROF. J. LUZ SAENZ,
Educator,
McAllen, Texas

PROF. J. LUZ SAENZ, native Texan, public school teacher for over a quarter of a century, veteran of World War I, saw service overseas and knows the sting of discrimination at first hand.

help from the Spanish rulers. This historical mistake should have been corrected long ago.

"There is nothing in a name", and yet . . . "Indians" made feasable the early conquest of Mexico and South America by the Spaniards; "Indians" made profitable the stay of the French in Canada and on the Mississipi Basin; "Indians" saved the Puritans from sure starvation and helped other colonies to survive and paved the way for the birth of the Great Republic. How were the "indians" paid for all this and more that they did in order that western European civilization should not perish in the Americas?

Spain destroyed the most advanced people and their civilization, took possession of their land, and killed countless members. Those who survived were brutally forced to labor for three hundred years; France exploited them likewise; the English, after grabbing their land, adopted the policy: "The only good Indian is a dead Indian". Is it strange that the final outcome of all this might have been mutual, eternal hatred, distrust, and everlasting resentment between Europeans and aborigines?

Returning to the subject that moved us to write this, we wish to limit ourselves to racial discrimination in Texas, THE LAND OF FRIENDSHIP, as suggested by the name of TEXAS. We want to repeat that the "indians" were the first inhabitants of this land. Then came the Spaniards and still later the mestizos or Mexicans.

Accidentally the French stumbled on Texas soil, but their stay was a disastrous failure. Then came the Anglo-Americans in the XIX century, bringing with them colonists of German extraction who settled in New Braunfels, Fredericksburg, etc. Now we can name these places and others, such as Uvalde, Ozona, Goliad, Rosenburg, New Gulf for ferocious hostility to Mexicans regardless of their citizenship or social, intellectual, and economic standing. Many of these immigrants were adventurers, wanderers, filibusters, soldiers of fortune, or expansionists. They found their way into Texas in search of a place to make their homes. They implored acceptance, first, from the Spanish government and after its downfall from the Mexican Government. No more generous inducements were ever offered to immigrants than those offered by the Mexican government to these home-seekers. They were given the privilege to choose the best land in Texas for their colonies. It did not take very long to find that many of them came with the well premeditated intention of settling and working to win its independence, to annex Texas to their Fatherland. A historical past needs no proof now. The record of many was not clear in their own country. Some of these found the

31

topsy turby state of affairs in Texas propitious to become heroes and win fortune and renown in the pages of History. We have nothing against them. They had the right and it was their duty to rise, prosper, and pursue life and happiness here, something they were unable to do in their own homeland because of adverse circumstances.

Racial discrimination is the deplorable form in which European rivalries has come down to us. It has had its high and low ebb, but it appears to rise invariably after a war. After the Texas Revolution and its annexation to the Union it found expression in the most violent and barbarous antagonism against the Mexican people. The Texas History written then, when racial feeling was high and events were seen through a lens of hatred, was taught in Texas public schools until recently. The negative results gathered from such teaching is beyond calculation. That history said little or nothing about the part our forefathers took in the struggle for Texas Independence. Instead, our people were misrepresented and exposed to hatred before the eyes of the world.

In the Civil War between the North and South we had also representatives who fought on the Confederate side. Our ancestors suffered and underwent all privations and miseries created by war. No recognition was shown in any way for our efforts. The organization of the Ku Klux Klan appeared. Klanism did not confined itself to hostilize ex-negro slaves. It revived the dormant hatred to the Mexican people.

In the war with Spain in 1898, our brothers fought in San Juan Hill and in the Philippines. The duration of that war was so short that the persecution of Mexicans, bandits or no bandits, by the famous Texas Rangers was not interruped or lessened. The Cortinas, Catarino Garza, and Gregorio Cortez incidents are well remembered yet.

In 1910 when unfortunate events of the Mexican revolution burst, the effect of such calamity trespassed our frontiers and greatly embittered our already bad civil and political condition in Texas. Numerous abuses were perpetrated on members of our race such as lynchings, persecutions, etc. Time there was when international relations were very acute and in consequence worse was the animosity for those of our racial element. During this time came the birth of the short term, badly equipped, neglected shacks and the undemocratic segregated schools for Mexican children. The fruit of such schools is evident everywhere today. Despised and abused many American citizens of Mexican extraction became "slackers". They found in this the best expression of their just resentment for unfair treatment, and lack of due recognition

32

for their loyalty. Some of us volunteered to replace those who had evaded military service. We were accepted, but during our entire military life, we felt a humiliating load of distrust on our shoulders, a kind of suspicion and enmity, never free to discharge our duties as soldiers well disposed to defend our national honor and our Flag to the end. Why? We knew under what conditions we were fighting. It was 100% prejudice. Once an officer stated this before me in clear cut words: "I know these greasers well. We will never get anything out of them. Once a Mexican always a Mexican". He was questioning me about the SAN DIEGO INCIDENT of which I knew nothing. He could not see why I had volunteered my services when hundreds of racial brothers had evaded service.

This was our status thirty years ago. We have passed the Second World War. This time my family contribution was three boys for the army and navy and a girl as cadet nurse. After demobilization from service in World War I it took only three days after we had received our Honorable Discharge to throw us out from restaurants and deny us service as human beings. During this monstrous atomic war that has just ceased, it did not take that long. Many of our boys in full uniform and bemedaled as heroes that they were, returning home on furlough, or to serve as models to others, were thrown out of BLUE MOON dancing hall. We need not say a word of how some of their relatives were treated while they were fighting in behalf of democracy.

While contending against these disgusting problems, it is encouraging to know that our racial element has advanced much in all fields of progress and culture. Perhaps, this is the reason why we resent now, more than ever, insults and unfair recognition, after we have loyally performed all civic and patriotic duties that can be demanded from any loyal citizen. We protest against the undemocratic segregated schools for our children. There is no reason to justify their existence. Worse still is the denial to serve us in public places such as barbershops, restaurants, and theaters, etc. Such attitude more than insultant is cowardly and debasing. We need the support of our fellow Anglo-Saxon citizens. their cooperation that we may fight in peace to defend the same sacred ideals we defended against foreign foes. Openly, we are beginning to have this cooperation, but we need yet a more solid front, not only to eradicate unamericanism from within but to prevent any other foreign ISMS from permeating and undermining our solidarity on which rests the security of our cherished American way of living and our love for Justice and Freedom.

Signed

J. Luz Saenz

McAllen, Texas, November, 1947.

RACIAL DISCRIMINATION

A Number One Problem of Texas Schools

By J. Luz Saenz

SOMEONE had to start it. We are glad that someone was the proper party. Our school superintendents of the Lower Rio Grande Valley have talked, and talked in earnest, toward correcting a transcendental evil or problem. Transitory children of migratory working people have been a problem in our regulated public free schools. Problems, because we have wished that every child should have an education here in Texas. The truth is that in many cases these unfortunate children have never demanded any school at all. All they ask is to be with their parents and free access to work which is for the good of many other children. They are not to be blamed. They are victims of inevitable circumstances prevailing at their homes or in their country. Let us thank our God for our advantages.

Here they are the square peg in the round hole. In our public standardized schools, these children retard the regular advance of classes, with their meager irregular attendance. The school work is planned for a nine month period and children attending four of five months can not do the work in a satisfactory manner. Poor attendance on the part of these children, and selfishness and narrow-mindedness on the part of other children and parents have created the well known and much disgusting discriminating racial problem, known in Texas as the "Mexican Child Problem in Texas Schools". Other states have this problem and may call it whatever they wish. Causes and results are the same.

Summing up the whole situation, it has given us in the Valley of the Lower Rio Grande the retarding undemocratic segregated schools for children of Mexican extraction. In other sections of Texas these schools are still worse. The finished product from such schools has been stubborn and malicious misunderstanding between Anglo-Americans and Mexican-Americans. Administrative and pedagogical reasons may have a right place in the problem, but the main and true reason can be traced to historical and racial prejudice fostered in the minds of children at school and in their homes. Much of this cause is fading away, but the segregated schools remain to keep alive, as long as they continue to exist, hatred, remorse, and just resentment on the part of offended parties. Many persons claim that there are not segregated schools, only "separate schools". These are the same. A great number of our children never go beyond these segregated schools. Can you imagine what is the result? Those who never go beyond them either accept in their minds the pernicious notion of "Inferiority complex" or lose faith and trust in American ideals and the American people. Those who go through high school, and even taste college, learn from first hand information that "intellectual superiority" does not exist just because of the color of the skin.

Very little credit has been rendered us for fighting for flag and country. We have done this. We are doing it. We shall keep doing it. Till when? How? We have done this, not because we might be contented with "democracy, liberty, equality, and justice" as practiced toward so many of our race in Texas, but because we are intelligent enough to know the things that man must fight for. Do not take our loyalty for servilism.

Parallel to providing schools for transitory children is the problem of providing a high school, here in our country, for colored children and a university for colored students and colored GI's who are demanding it. In our city we do not think it wise to construct a high school to accommodate half a dozen colored children, or in the state to construct another university for colored students. A room and a few teachers in our school (and theirs) will solve that problem. Why should McAllen taxpayers be burdened with more taxes to support racial prejudice? Colored citizens travel on passenger trains and buses, work as cooks in homes and hotels, and daily we see them riding in the same cars with white people as chauffeurs, etc. Why not do the same in educational institutions? And even in American Legion Posts? Are they not Americans? Have they not done their part in fighting for flag, country, and our democratic public free schools?

Should there be those who are blind to justice? Think first that we are now living in a new postwar world where compulsory readjustment is unavoidable. We destroyed or are trying to destroy Hitler's racial theory. Why not do the same thing with Bilbo and his imitators here in Texas, or in any other part of our union? This is the right thing to do if Christian civilization and democratic principles mean anything to us.

To educate transitory children is an altruistic, democratic, and American policy. Give us a chance to contribute our part in this meritorious program. We are worth very little, but allow

35

us to place at disposal for this cause, should our spare time be deemed of value, our thirty-seven years experience dealing with and trying to contribute toward the solution of the problem of "Mexican children in Texas public free schools".

("THE TEXAS OUTLOOK", December, 1946, Published By Texas State Teachers Association.) November, 1947.

ARE WE DEALING FAIRLY WITH THE "MEXICAN"?

By John C. Granbery

It is the privilege of thousands of Anglo-Americans to visit Mexico for pleasure or business. It has been my good fortune to make many such visits, and I never tire of that fascinating country. I have been treated uniformly with courtesy and kindness. We Anglo-Americans go to the best hotels and restaurants, and freely make use of facilities for travel, communication, and sight-seeing.

Similar hospitality is expected for Mexican visitors to this country. Such, I hope, is the rule, and instances of its violation bring a sense of mortification to right-thinking people.

In this connection there are two groups to be considered and carefully distinguished: citizens of Mexico and citizens of the United States of Latin origin. With regard to the former it is the right and the duty of the Mexican Government to protect to the limit its citizens travelling in this country, and we should give Mexican officials full cooperation and encouragement.

The average Anglo-American makes little distinction between citizens of Mexico who are in this country and Spanish-speaking citizens of the United States. Recently I was on the Border, and was surprised to discover how sharply the line is drawn. Here in San Antonio there are many Latin-Americans who have never been to Mexico, but I found persons on the Border, hardly able to speak English, who had never crossed the Rio Grande into Mexico. To them Mexico is a foreign country, and should they cross the River, they are immediately spotted as Texans. I learned a new word, "pocha", slang in Mexico for a Latin-American girl from Texas. On the other hand, Texans who have lived long on the Border can identify immediately real Mexicans from Mexico itself, often without hearing them utter a word.

A silly remark is sometimes heard to the effect that "Mexicans" should use their own public facilities, parks, swimming pools, and the like. The so-called "Mexicans" are citizens of the United States,

37

born in Texas, and their parents and possibly grandparents were born in Texas. What then do we mean by "their own"? The parks and swimming pools and other services provided for the people are "their own."

The whole history of Texas on down thru the second World War bears indisputable testimony to the loyalty and heroism of our Latin-American citizens.

Some years ago I had a humiliating experience in visiting Seguin in the company of a U. S. official interested in racial justice. We found it to be true that the magnificent park for which that town is famous is closed to Latin-Americans. If the President of Mexico were to visit the place, he could not put foot in the park. Ever since that revelation it has been burning in my heart as a kind of collective sense of shame. Whether this insult to Mexico and to our Latin-American people has been corrected, I do not know.

Anyone who alleges that there is little or no discrimination in Texas is either unfamiliar with the situation or is self-deceived and unwilling to see what is before his eyes.

To my mind it is plain what should be done. Fair-minded Anglo-Americans can see that no injustice is done without due protest and reparation. Participation in any group, society, or event that makes the discrimination should be refused. Self-respecting Latin-Americans worthy of special honor should be accorded the standing and recognition they merit, while every individual, whatever his race, is treated as a human being and child of God.

The solution of the problem is, however, chiefly in the hands of Latin-Americans themselves. A bearing of dignity and self-respect will usually find recognition. No member of the group should ask for political preferment and favors on the basis of his race, but if he has the qualifications in a free field, he should offer his services and in a dignified manner present his candidacy on its merits. "Caudillos" and "jefes" who put up their services for financial considerations and attempt to round up their friends in the interest of this and that candidate discredit their own people. Reputable leaders who stand for principles and who are not for sale will one day win the respect both of their own people and of the community in general. Bargaining and trading and swapping belittle the cause and the individuals who engage in such practices. Again, Latin-Americans should know who are their real friends among Anglo-Americans. When they scrape and bow and bootlick before windy politicians who profess friendship but whose only fundamental interest is their own glory, they accept a position of inferiority. A poor fellow was selling something on the streets, and a passe,-by said: "I am sorry, brother, but I do not have any change at the moment." "You do not need to buy anything or pay me anything," was the reply, "for you have called me 'brother' ".

The solution is to be found in education, better incomes, a higher standard of living, improved housing, sanitation, good citizenship, self-respect, unselfish service to the community, which is intrinsic worth.

John C. Granbery
November, 1947.

Dr. John C. Granbery, College Professor, retired, life long student of sociology, stout defender of social justice, publisher, speaker, and friend of the poor.

DISCRIMINATION IN TEXAS

By *Laureano Flores*

Racial discrimination in Texas unfortunately, is an undeniable fact in spite of self-inflicted blindness on the part of a few. That it should exist in a country whose very birth and subsequent greatness and achievements as a world power are based precisely upon the radically opposite principles of democracy, equality for all, and freedom in the pursuit of one's own happiness, is not only inconsistent but obviously a negation of such principles. One would wonder how such an aberration could be explained were it not for the realization that some blind never-do-wells trample the name and prestige of our great State under their feet, just for the sake of politics, in absolute disregard of present day trends of civilization and the teachings of bloody wars. The world realizes that such a condition is no longer tenable. They know that their cause is lost because it is contrary to reason and logic and justice, but they are still unmoved; their minds refuse to grasp the meaning of the transitions which have taken place within the past 120 years. They are still back there watching the pageantry of years of civilization pretending not to understand what it is all about. They are still blind, unconscious, sphinx-like.

How could it be explained that in this great country of ours so few ever dared to raise their voice and put the case consistently and squarely up to the people of our State? Why is it that most of the newspapers whose God-given mission is to enlighten the people, to properly and honestly try to forge and shape their opinion in the right direction never have seen fit consistently to take up so obviously just a cause, to erase a macula and a stain that for years has unjustly blurred the prestige and reputation of our State? Why do they not try to bring about a frank and sincere understanding and create a sincere, frank and genuine friendship with our neighbors to the South, especially our next door neighbor? I mean of course, the kind of friendship and understanding that wealth cannot buy, the kind that is born down deep in the bottom of the hearts of people where grudge and hatred cannot grow?

Have we forgotten that Hitler's war cry of "race superiority" came near burying civilization and culture in his own Germany and the world itself under the debris of a catastrophe, which will take generations to remove? In the face of such catastrophe: hospitals full to capacity with boys groping around blind, walking on crutches, or still lying in bed; hundreds of thousands of fresh graves scattered all over the world, how could we under such circumstances still support, indeed, encourage such crass stupidity as "race superiority", more so when we should realize that only a solid racial front, made up of an amalgamation of people saved the world from utter destruction and slavery? How in all sincerity, could we frankly, honestly and conscientiously call upon all these peoples to join us again should another emergency arise? How could we invoke full hearted, voluntary co-operation from certain peoples, especially our neighbors to the South, whose friendship, understanding and cooperation we have found so useful in times of grief and national tragedy and emergency, but so obnoxious in times of peace?

Money, it is true, can buy acquiescence, smiles and bouquets or orchids; but let us not kid ourselves, a sincere friendship and understanding (and I wish to underline these words "Sincere friendship and understanding") takes like specie in exchange and nothing else. What can be said otherwise is sheer nonsense and stupidity.

Some of our politicians pretend to believe and make believe, that in our case, and I am talking for my own people, there is nothing radically wrong that education and time could not correct, implying, of course, that our people need all the educating and the time and understanding. A childish pretext to prolong the situation! Stalling lest their friends will be disturbed and their own position made insecure! I often wonder what our politicians are, anyway, leaders or followers. My concept of an honest politician is one who because of his education and patriotism should qualify as a leader, one who should have the interest and welfare of his people and his country uppermost in his heart and in his conscience, one who is willing to do what he honestly and conscientiously thinks is the best for the community he serves.

Supporting and encouraging discrimination is obviously wrong. In doing so, is he trying to please his friends? Is he honest to himself? If he is endeavoring to please his friends, just for the sake of his position, he is certainly cheating his community and his country by trying to undermine the most sacred principles of democracy and freedom upon which our great country is founded. At best he is just a leech.

41

If he is in reality, honest to himself, then he has no vision and no foresight. He is unquestionably, by any logic or line of reasoning, on the wrong side of the fence. He is incapable of being a real leader, but he is a potential cheap, dangerous agitator. If he is incapable of recognizing a good cause that would benefit his community, he should be ousted. How could there be a sincere understanding, friendship and assimilation if discrimination only engenders repulsion and hatred? Discrimination then is, in the minds of honest people, clearly the root of the evil and it should be eradicated at once. The prestige of our State and our nation so demands it.

Some pretend to believe that discrimination is only confined to a few ignoramuses. This is hard to believe; a naive excuse I should think, intended to shield the truth or to assuage a few. When so they talk, they refer to certain restaurants, barber shops, theatres, skating rinks, etc. some of them in large cities, some in small towns, where Mexicans are neither served nor admitted, or at best, served only in the section reserved for negroes; in a number of these establishments our people are told to go elsewhere. Does this reflect the personal feeling of the proprietor? In some instances, it certainly does. In others, in many others, it reveals the feeling of the patrons and the business-like desire of the proprietor to please his clientele. I cannot conceive the owner being such a big fool as to try to antagonize his customers. He knows what they demand and like any business man, he is willing to accommodate them. Who is, then, responsible? I would say that both proprietor and patron are responsible, both are accomplices in the perpetuation of the deed.

Now, let me say this, we Mexicans individually are not trying to force anybody's friendship or sympathy; we are not individually courting anybody's love. Far from it. We recognize everybody's right and privilege to associate with whomever he or she may desire, regardless of racial lines. That, I repeat, is his individual right and privilege. As to public places, my views, however, are different. Public places, schools especially, should be compelled by law if necessary to serve the public, at least to those who under the state constitution are supposed to enjoy equal rights and privileges. It may appear rather strange to advocate a law to enforce the constitution, but this, I believe, is the only solution. When a license or permit is issued for some to operate a public place, the applicant should know that the law would require him to draw no racial lines in his establishment, that the state constitution does not draw. That's all we want.

The situation, as it is now, is far more serious than most people are inclined to believe. It is not local but international in

42

scope; it does affect not only American citizens of Mexican or Spanish extraction and their children, who will necessarily develop a complex of inferiority that will cripple them for life, but will also affect Mexican citizens from Mexico as well as from other Latin-American countries.

But let us look at the situation from a more concrete and realistic standpoint, from a business standpoint if you will. Suppose for a moment that Mexico took a notion to retaliate; a rather farfetched and remote possibility as it may seem; what Mexico could do if such a situation might develop?: (1) Mexico could if it so desired, apply very effectively at that, a retaliatory custom house tariff against reactionary, rebel states, such as Texas, for instance, who insist on discriminating its nationals. (2) Mexico owns and operates the railroads of the country. Freight tariffs could be made to reinforce the custom house tariffs. To make it profitable and advantageous for the Mexican buyers to purchase outside of Texas, the tariffs could be manipulated and adjusted so that it would be cheaper to buy in, say, St. Louis, Kansas City, Chicago or New York, than to buy at even Laredo, Texas, or San Antonio. (3) Mexico could go all the way out to frankly and openly boycott Texas goods originating in or being shipped from Texas. (4) Finally, let us add another possibility. Suppose now, that Latin-American countries for reasons of solidarity, or I might say, self-protection, or pride if you will, would join Mexico in its retaliatory efforts against discrimination. What will happen then? What sort of publicity and financial losses, what would be the repercussions and how long would it be before we could recover? Let us not forget these possibilities. Let us not forget that Latin America is not now what it used to be. Let us not forget the changes that the world situation has brought about. Let us not forget our own situation which originated and gave birth to the much talked-about Good Neighbor Policy. If we insist on discriminating against Latin Americans on racial grounds and a situation such as I have described should develop, would we call upon the Federal Government to help us settle the matter on other than the basis of equality implied by the Government's own Good-Neighbor policy? Let us think it over.

It seems, however, that the United Nations are creating a machinery designed to deal with problems of this nature and it seems to me that some of our reactionary newspapers, our politi-

43

.cians, and our people ought to see the situation in the light of the present day trends and civilization, in the light of the 20th Century and spare an embarrassing situation to our State and to our great country.

Laureano Flores.
November, 1947.

Mr. Laureano Flores is a nationalized American citizen. He studied in the best schools in Mexico and attended schools in England. A public minded and active member of his community he has given much thought to the problem of discrimination.

San Antonio, Texas, March 25, 1947

Hon. Alonso S. Perales
Attorney at Law,
San Antonio, Texas

Dear Mr. Perales:

I want to commend you on your untiring effort and resolute campaign spearheaded by you to extirpate the wide prevalence of racial and religious prejudice so rampant in the world today. It is my sincere hope your efforts will bear much golden fruit. Conditions like this cannot exist anywhere without bringing certain retribution. A French poet once said: *"Man never fastened one end of a chain around the neck of his brother, that God's own hand did not fasten the other end around the neck of the oppressor"*. We have seen this in our own time.

Some of the recent incidents chronicled by you and also appearing in the daily press, is a definite challenge to the deep sense of fairness and the intelligence of our right thinking people. Especially has the recent unfortunate occurence which took place in a neighboring town brought forth a volley of caustic comment, and justifiably so. As reported by the press, here several cultured and refined Latin American ladies were refused customary catering service based solely on their racial status. This incident shows definitely how far some folks, and communities too, have ventured into the morass of mental bias and prejudice. Acts like these not only stultify the perpetrators themselves, but the communities as well. It is safe to say that the early Spanish and German colonizers of a century or two ago did not maintain a "back door" service for anyone. But on the contrary extended the hand of good fellow-

44

ship to those coming from foreign shores to join in their combined efforts to build an empire which we now so abundantly enjoy—an empire built by ambitious, Godlike men and women of several races, of varied customs and beliefs, but free from the present day streamlined prejudice, hate and confusion. Is it too much to hope that the "good neighbor" policy of a century or more, will yet become a present day reality? Why should not the progressive, aspiring, cultured and well-meaning Latin-Americans among us be universally respected and receive the same conventional courtesies extended all individuals of merit, culture, composure and decency?

Throughout the ages men, of all races and nationalities, have chosen their own associates and friends and selected human contacts of their personal preferment. Men and women of christian principles, good breeding and character recognize intuitively and respect character, culture and human intelligence irrespective as to origin, and WITHOUT prejudice. It is to such people we must look to for the tempering of, and eventual recession of the many prejudices existing today. To hinder the peaceful evolution of universal social progress of a Godly endowed humanity by spurious means is contemptible, to say the least. The heart of man must be set right by a deeper faith and cognizance of the teachings of the "Prince of Peace"; the doctrine of the "Fatherhood of God and Brotherhood of Man", and the personal application of the Golden Rule.

In conclusion, I give you two quotations which, in my opinion, are very apropos to the matter under consideration. The first is this: *"The man who has not anything to boast of but his illustrious ancestors, is like a potato—the only good belonging to him is underground".* There is no ceiling on this kind of potato. The other quotation reads as follows: *"We must not blame God for the fly, for man made him. He is the resurrection, the reincarnation of our dirt and carelessness".* Neither was prejudice made by God. I still have faith in the American people and, that the good that is left in all of us, will yet some day assert itself into a militant force for the rebirth of universal peace, human understanding, love of humanity and world justice.

Yours very truly,

L. F. Merl.

Mr. L. F. Merl, educator, fair-minded citizen, who believes in practicing democracy.

45

PART II

THE PROBLEM ON THE NATIONAL LEVEL

DEMOCRACY AND CHURCH-RELATED SCHOOLS

Jubilee Address by Archbishop Robert Emmet Lucey, D.D., S.T.D. at Our Lady of the Lake in San Antonio, Texas, College Golden Jubilee Exercises, April 21, 1948.

Democracy as a form of political economy is defined as government by the people; in a broad sense it means the belief in or practice of social equality; the absence of snobbery. With us, sovereignty resides in the people and is exercised by elected representatives.

Government by the people is only a form or structure of political life; it is not necessarily good government. Elected representatives may be presumed to be a fair cross section of the citizenry. It follows that the quality of government in a republic depends upon the quality of the governed. A people who are just, peace loving and civic minded will provide themselves with good government, they will elect to public office men and women whose conduct will reflect the virtues and mores of the people. When, therefore, on patriotic occasions inspired orators extol the glory of America as the land of the free and the home of the brave they are exulting not so much in a political philosophy or in an ideal structure of civil power but rather in the historic fact that good citizens here have created good government. To view the picture from another angle one might say that democracy can be bad; monarchy and benevolent despotism could be good. The form of government, while important, is not decisive; it is the substance that counts.

When thoughtful people speak of dangers to our democracy I do not think they have in mind that some tyrant, foreign or domestic, is about to take over the White House or that commissars or conquistadores will soon be substituting for the Congress. In spite of political campaign speakers to the contrary I think that free elections will be with us for a long time. On the other hand anyone can see that widespread and long continued exploitation of the people brings on revolt.

When, therefore, we speak of dangers to our democracy we do not have in mind an imminent change in the structure; we refer rather to those weaknesses, those inconsistencies, those injustices and discriminations in everyday American life which ought to be removed, first because they are wrong and, secondly, because they might conceivably grow worse and definitely weaken the foundations of the structure itself. All of this might be summed up as follows: the monarch who gives his people peace, liberty and justice has nothing to fear; the democracy which denies those blessings to its citizens has cause for anxiety.

A salient truth seems to emerge from this discussion, namely, that the enemy of democracy is not monarchy, or aristocracy, or oligarchy or any form of government; the enemy is neglect of the people, injustice and exploitation. Thus we come to the field of morality. It is the democratic way of life which is decisive; the structure of government is only a form. We believe that our form is the best in the world but it isn't a function or an operation, it is only a machine.

The democratic way of life requires faith and good works; faith that all men are created equal and that they are endowed by their Creator with certain inalienable rights; good works in the sense that we make that faith effective in all the departments of life.

All men are created equal; they possess natural rights from God, not from government. This is the credo of the American people. We believe that every human being is a creature of sublime dignity and surpassing destiny; we hold that human personality is inviolable, that every citizen has a right to life, liberty and the pursuit of happiness. With us, people are important because they were made to the image of God.

In recent years the American credo has been challenged; the result is a tremendous conflict which has spread across the world. All that we hold dear depends on the outcome. We who still cling to at least the shreds of Western culture hold that people are important, that limited power should be entrusted to the government, that the citizen must have liberty under law. Our adversaries would give all power to the government and slavery to the people. In their eyes the citizen is not important.

We said a moment ago that the danger to our democracy is from within; it is neglect of the people and their exploitation, but in the next breath we pointed to a peril from without, a world-wide conflict of ideas regarding man in which we support human dignity while our adversaries deny it. Are there then two present dangers to our democracy, one from within and one from without?

Philosophers love to draw distinctions and the answer to our question is simply this: if the American people, always and every-where, consistently support the idea of the grandeur of man as man, a foreign ideology which debases man cannot harm us; and by the same token, if we give aid and comfort to the enemy by exploiting and despising any substantial number of our fellow citizens the battle may be lost from within and from without. In a word, the challenge is in America, the challenge is in the minds and hearts of our people to make the democratic way of life effective, to practice sincerity, to extend liberty and justice to all.

And speaking of sincerity would it not seem that many of our citizens in the past have been something less than sincere? They chose to enjoy the peace and security of Christian civilization without being full-time Christians. They admitted the grandeur of the human spirit if the skin of the man was not brown or black. They claimed that all men are created equal -- with a few ex-ceptions. They echoed the old refrain about liberty and justice to all, but kept one third of our people in poverty. They insisted on the value and necessity of universal suffrage and denied the ballot to a large segment of our population. They plugged for free enterprise in a free economy and kept working people in economic servitude. They sang the praises of political democracy while denying to the masses the innate right of industrial democracy. A godless foreign government has now called the bluff of these alleged Christians. They are challenged to be sincere.

Yes, the peril is from within; there it is a question of fundamen-tal morality. It is not sufficient to proclaim high ideals; we must also make them effective; we must practice what we preach. Since we stand before the world as the defenders of human dignity we must in fact defend it. And when we debase a man or a group of men we delight the Communists, because, in spite of fair words to the contrary, they do not believe in the rights of man. When they speak of democracy they do not mean what they say; when they talk of freedom their words have no meaning. They cannot believe in man because they will not believe in God the Author of our being and the Source of all our rights. They hold that men are animals and must be treated as animals. They employ the language of liberty and justice but their words are false and hollow.

To defend their own indefensible record the Communists say that we are the ones whose words are hollow. They claim

48

that we pay lip service to the dignity of man and to the democratic process, the while we debase men and make a mockery of democracy. They point an accusing finger at us and declare that elections here mean nothing because most of the people don't vote and many are not allowed to vote. They say that we use a special device to discourage them.

These charges are serious and if they are true the evils ought to be corrected. And while we are at it let us inquire if the Communists have any other complaints against us? They seem to have plenty for they claim that we lynch people whom we don't like and the murderers are never punished. They say that we talk about democracy for all the people and four governors go to Washington to kill a civil rights program. These governors are not humorous, they are only grotesque.

We claim to enjoy the highest living standards in the world and tens of thousands of citizens right here in San Antonio and millions throughout the country live in unspeakable shacks and hovels. We enact child labor laws for the protection of children and many thousands of them work all day in the burning Texas sun. We believe that a good education is necessary for every American child and Dr. George I. Sanchez, Professor in the Texas University, has just declared that one half of the children of Texas who have Spanish names do not spend even one day in school throughout the year.

Our adversaries say that this all adds up to insincerity; that we want to give democracy to the world, but not to our own. If the peril to our way of life is from within we may not safely ignore these and similar charges.

This, then, is our American democracy. Most excellent in form and structure; revealing undeniable weaknesses here and there in function and operation. Since destiny has bestowed upon us the moral leadership of the world every citizen has an obligation to live up to the highest ideals of our nation. In spite of our blundering and our weakness we do have ideals. The American tradition in its finest concepts is something to emulate.

We have said a good deal about democracy; where does the Church-related school enter the picture? More than ever before the Christian school is needed to protect the foundations of the democratic way of life. I am not prepared to say that a secular school could not teach the excellence of the form and structure of democratic government. By the light of reason we can discover the advantage of permitting citizens to rule themselves by freely chosen representatives, but I have tried to make it clear that the form is not of the essence of good government; peace, justice and prosperity can be procured for the people by any reasonable form of civil authority. It is the behavior of the government that counts and, by the same token, the behavior of the people.

Good government involves questions of conscience and morality under God. The civil power finds the proof of its authority in religious truth; the obedience which the citizen owes his government is sustained only in the field of religion and the respect which he must extend to his fellow man is a supremely spiritual concept unless we wish to stipulate that the penitentiary is the noblest sanction of the state.

For such an audience I need not recount the contribution of the religious school to the idea of the democratic form of government and most especially to the democratic function and process. You all know that God created men as social beings in the sense that to achieve the richness and fullness of life they must live in society under a civil government. The public authority therefore exists by the will of God. Sovereignty resides in the people and the civil power, whatever be its form or structure, must recognize the innate rights of citizens, their marvelous dignity and sublime destiny as children of God. The citizen must respect and obey the just decrees of government because all power is from God and government functions by the will of God. The citizen must also respect the rights of his neighbor as a brother in Christ made to the image and likeness of God.

The civil power, therefore, finds the best explanation of its existence, authority and function in the truths of religion. I do not see how a secular college can teach these truths because they are theological. Secular professors are not theologians and in any event are not permitted to teach religion in our public schools. It may be that even the name of God may not be mentioned in our tax supported institutions.

The secular approach to the essence of public authority and law observance is a pitiful thing. When God and religion are removed from the picture, the citizens become a herd of animals and their government is a group of trained animals. The laws of this animal kingdom do not bind in conscience because there is no conscience. The highest motivation of the citizen is to avoid the jail and thus the majesty of law is destroyed; the civil authority has only police power, the sanction of force. The slogan of the citizen may well be: "Do what you like but don't get caught".

It may be objected by the materialist that even without God we have the conventions of civilized society, the approved mores of the people and the sacred traditions of the past. Furthermore, in a secular state, the government is more than a policeman pro-

50

tecting law and order; the civil power, without thought of God, can provide for the common good, maintain peace and pursue justice and prosperity.

By way of reply we might observe that civilized society received its culture from the Church and secular states today are living on the shreds and remnants of a Christian past. But leaving all that aside it is still true that there must be an absolute in human life or everything will be relative. In Soviet Russia, Yugoslavia, Czechoslovakia and wherever materialistic Communism rules, honor, justice and truth, are relative; everything depends on the will of the dictator; his word is right, his word is law. There are no absolutes there save only absolute tyranny.

Society cannot live on relative morality; the conventions of society change, the mores of the people may be good or bad. For peace, stability and justice there must be something absolute and that absolute is God. Without a divine legislator there is no test, no standard, no measure of right and wrong; everything is futility and frustration. The basic principles of morality must be immutable and that postulates an unchanging God.

Such is the contribution of the Christian college to democracy. It describes government by the people as being in harmony with the nature of man; it calls upon the state to respect the innate rights of the individual and to procure the common good; it instructs the people regarding the sacred character of public authority and forbids them to revolt without just cause; it teaches men to love their neigbor, their country and the people of all nations; it inculcates in public officials and citizens generally the virtues of honesty, sobriety, justice and charity. The Christian college gives meaning and purpose to life.

If all of this is true, and I know that it is, something somewhere has gone wrong. If for twenty centuries the Church has been teaching these high ideals of Christian citizenship in school and pulpit why do we stand today in a restless and wretched world? Has the Church lost her influence in public and private life? Has the Christian school failed to achieve its purpose of building better men in a better world? In part, the answer is a regretful yes. Any thoughtful person can see that in recent centuries Christian principles as proclaimed by Church and school have not taken hold in the market place. Certainly the voice of the Church has not been clearly heard in the fields of government, industry, public education, literature and international relations. These important departments of human life leave much to be desired so far as Christian principles are concerned. And just as the Church has been ignored by a secularist world so also the Christian school has failed to achieve some of its noblest objectives.

51

Let no one think that the principles of the good life as enunciated by Church-related schools have had no validity. Being immutable they are valid in every century but I am inclined to think that many of the graduates of religious schools in recent centuries have not carried their ideals effectively into the market place; rather, they have permitted themselves and their principles to be absorbed and submerged in a reckless and thoughtless world. What they learned was excellent but it did not produce abundant fruit.

An evil old era is passing and in the midst of world-wide tension and tragedy I think we can see the faint dawn of a better day. The friends of God are more alert and dynamic today than they have been for centuries. The powers of darkness have gained many a victory but now at long last, the children of God are on the march. We have a world to reconstruct and who shall be the builders but the graduates of such a college as this? You have the tools to rebuild a broken world -- faith, courage, vision, determination and a knowledge of the things by which men live and struggle and conquer. With this equipment you cannot, you must not fail.

THE SPANISH SPEAKING PEOPLE OF THE UNITED STATES

An introductory statement by Rev. John J. Birch, Executive Secretary of the Bishop's Committee for the Spanish Speaking, San Antonio, Texas. Statement made in a public hearing before the President's Committee on Civil Rights, May 14, 1947, Washington, D.C.

In setting up the President's Committee on Civil Rights, President Truman stated that freedom from fear, which comes from the preservation of civil liberties, is the duty of every government, state, federal and local. He further stated that in some places and at some times, this freedom from fear has been gravely threatened. It is my understanding that this Committee has heard in public hearings, evidence to show that many minority groups in the United States are victims of this fear at this very moment. That this fear is real, actually existing, all of us know. I speak to you about one minority group—the Spanish Speaking people, largely of Mexican extraction whom I am convinced are the greatest victims of this fear. From personal experience I can testify that there is no group in the United States more susceptible to fear than the Spanish Speaking. The Latin by his very nature and culture is a highly sensitive person and discrimination, exploitation and mistreatment hurt him deeply. This fact can be attested to by all who work with and for the Spanish-speaking people. It was brought out very strongly in a book recently published, entitled, "Not With The Fist", by Ruth Tuck; it was emphasized in another recent publication, "The Latin Americans in Texas" by Pauline Kibbe, Executive Secretary of the Texas Good Neighbor Commission, and it was stressed further in Robert C. Jones' pamphlet, "Mexican War Workers in the United States", published last year.

It is conservatively estimated that there are in the United States, approximately three million people who belong to the Latin American minority. Ninety percent of them are by birth or extraction, Mexican. The greater part of these people reside

53

in Texas, California, Arizona, New Mexico, Colorado and Michigan. The problems they face and the problems they have created, follow practically the same pattern in every region where they are found. It is safe to say that the over-whelming majority of these people are American citizens. Consequently, our government has the obligation to take all possible measures to see to it that they enjoy the civil liberties guaranteed to all American citizens under our democratic form of government.

The vast majority of the Spanish Speaking people in the Southwestern part of the United States will be found to be in the lower economic group. For the most part, they or their parents have been the victims of exploitation at the hands of un-scrupulous employers. The result has been one grand vicious circle. It is necessary for all members of the household who can, to work a full day in order that the family may obtain the bare necessities of life. Un-biased observers like Agnes Meyer in her series of articles in the Washington Post bear testimony to this fact. When families are so poor that even the children must work, it becomes impossible to secure even the minimum education for these children. A man without education (and as in the case of the Spanish Speaking with a language handicap) has no other choice than to become a common laborer. If he is a common laborer and is badly housed, without water or sewer facilities; and if he is forced to live in a colony at the edge of town always "across the tracks" or "on the other side of the river", it is asking him to lift himself by his boot straps when you tell him that he ought to better his condition. Complicating the problem is the fact that, "Mexican" neighborhoods in most cities and towns are without playgrounds or playground facilities; poorly lighted or with no lights at all; hounded by unsympathetic law enforcement officials and worst of all, with inadequate school buildings and badly trained teachers.

I have already stated that wide-spread discrimination is practiced against the Spanish Speaking in the Southwest. Most of this discrimination is due to a deep-seated prejudice against the Spanish Speaking people on the part of the majority group. It is difficult for one of these people, an American citizen who has served his country honorably during the World War (750,000 served according to available records) it is difficult, I say, to feel like an American when he is refused service in a restaurant; is not permitted to attend a certain theatre; when he is told that he cannot join the local American Legion Post or belong to a civic club; and when through such humiliations he is constantly being reminded that he is considered inferior, solely on racial grounds. At the same time we must admit that it is difficult if not impossible,

54

to legislate out of existence such deep-seated prejudice as is found in the majority group in the Southwestern part of the United States. Yet unless the very fear of discrimination is removed completely from the hearts of the Spanish Speaking people, they will always remain a people apart, and a serious problem, through no fault of their own, to the communities and states in which they reside. In Ruth Tuck's book, already referred to, she makes the statement that practically every Spanish-speaking person she has ever met has been the victim, one time or another in his life, of discrimination, and that those who have not actually met it, live in constant fear of encountering it sooner or later. The demoralizing effect of this fear is known to all who work with this minority group.

Legal discrimination against the Spanish Speaking is much more subtle than social discrimination. The law, for example, states that all citizens, regardless of race or creed, must be given equal opportunities for jury service. The Spanish Speaking and the Negro in the Southwest will find their names on jury lists proportionate to their membership in the c o m m u n i t y but they are practically never called for jury duty. When one hears complaints from Latin Americans about an alleged mis-carriage of justice against one of their members, and asks, "Why didn't you protest, why didn't you fight it?", he will be told inevitably, "What chance has a Mexican got with a prejudiced judge and an Anglo jury?".

At a meeting of the leading educators of the Southwest held at the University of Texas last year on the subject, "The Education of the Spanish Speaking People in the Southwest and West", it was pointed out that segregated schools, over-crowded schools, inadequate facilities, poorly paid and incompetent teachers seem to be the rule rather than the exception in practically every state. Yet the Spanish-speaking children, because they must speak Spanish at home and English at school, need *more* help and *better* facilities than the other children. The attitude of many school boards is tantamount to saying that you cannot teach the Spanish Speaking people anything, so why try? Yet, unbiased observers know that given equal educational opportunities, the Spanish-speaking boy or girl makes a very apt student.

In practically every city and town of California, Texas and Arizona, there are residential districts where persons of Mexican extraction, regardless of wealth and social position, are not permitted to reside on the ground that they are not "white". In some of the larger cities there is an un-written law to the effect that Latin Americans must never be given opportunities to buy real estate in any section of the city except in the colony reserved for this minority. Furthermore, it is to be questioned whether our government, through its housing authority has done as much in the field of federal housing for the Spanish Speaking who reside for the most part in sub-standard dwellings, as it has for the less privileged English speaking groups.

It has been estimated that some 60,000 Spanish Speaking workers migrate to the sugar beet fields of Michigan annually. The plight of these migratory workers is a very unhappy one. Every year in late April and early May the highways from San Antonio north are filled with truck-loads of human beings, packed like sardines, who are being shipped to the Michigan beet fields. Grandparents, parents, children, including babies make this long and difficult trek in order to supply our tables with sugar. According to a socio-economic survey made by the City Health Department of San Antonio, the family income of these people for six months work will average $580. To earn this amount everyone must work, including the little children. As low as these earnings are, they are better than the family would earn if it stayed in Texas to pick cotton; for their earnings then would only be $191.00 on a three months basis.

This Committee might be interested in knowing that two years ago the Catholic Bishops of the Southwest united in order to be able to make a more effective fight against the evil conditions which I have described. A regional office has been set up for the first two years in San Antonio, Texas, and will move from region to region as the program grows. This office has attempted to develop and encourage native leadership among the Spanish Speaking people; to supply educational opportunities through student-aid funds; to build and equip centers, clinics, and athletic fields; to form councils consisting of outstanding Spanish and English speaking citizens and through the use of such means as lectures, inter-group activities, the press and the radio, it has attempted to break down prejudice. Our earnest but limited efforts have been greatly handicapped by the weight of discrimination.

If I may be permitted I would urge the Committee to support these recommendations.

1. Practically every problem faced or created by the Latin American in the United States finds its basis in economics. Before anything else is done, the earning power of the Spanish Speaking people must be increased. I would recommend, therefore, that this Committee do all in its power to bring about a law which would eliminate unfair employment practices.

2. Since large numbers of Spanish Speaking people in the United States are employed in agriculture and most of them earn less than a decent living wage, I would recommend a minimum wage for un-skilled agricultural laborers. Our government has recently completed an agreement with the Mexican government permitting more than 100,000 Mexican laborers to work in the United States at the prevailing wage of 25c an hour. According to present day conditions it is impossible to live with a minimum of decency on less than 60c an hour.

3. With a view to removing fear, I would recommend a clarification and strengthening of the law so as to enable the Department of Justice to prosecute effectively, the violation of civil rights.

4. My fourth recommendation concerns housing. Any fair study of the housing conditions of the Spanish Speaking in the Southwest will demonstrate the wide-spread need for more Federal Housing for this minority group.

5. That the Federal Government undertake a socio-economic survey of the states in which the Spanish Speaking are found in large numbers. No such survey has ever been made and as a consequence no orderly plan of assistance has ever been presented to agencies who are attempting to aid in the solution of this minority problem.

THE PRESIDENT'S COMMITTEE ON CIVIL RIGHTS

1712 G Street NW., Room 208, Washington 25, D. C.

Robert K. Carr,
Executive Secretary

———

April 29, 1947

Dr. Carlos E. Castañeda
Professor of History
University of Texas
Austin, Texas

Dear Professor Castañeda:

The President's Committee on Civil Rights is very much interested in the status of the Mexican-American minority in this country. It is concerned about the dangers to the civil rights of this group and would like to have more specific information on this subject. Accordingly, the Committee staff is engaged in the preparation of a memorandum. You have been suggested to us as a person who has been much interested in the civil rights of Mexican-Americans and as one who would perhaps be willing to provide us with valuable information.

I am wondering whether you would be willing to prepare a confidential statement on the subject for our use. I understand that you have been particularly interested in the nature and extent of discrimination against Mexican-Americans in employment. I very much hope that you will be willing to make particular reference to this problem in your statement, although I will be happy to have you touch upon other phases of the problem as well.

The Committee is working under a rather rigid time schedule and it would be helpful if you could let us have your statement by May 15. I realize that this doesn't give you very much time, but it is my thought that you can perhaps give us the benefit of your accumulated knowledge and information without much need for further research.

The President's Committee will be very grateful to you for your assistance.

Sincerely yours,

Robert K. Carr

May 9, 1947.

Mr. Robert K. Carr,
President's Committee on Civil Rights,
1712 G. Street NW,
Room 208,
Washington, D. C.

Dear Mr. Carr:

It affords me pleasure to send you herewith attached a brief statement on the problem of discrimination in employment as it affects the Latin American or Mexican throughout the Southwest from Texas to California.

More than twenty years of work in behalf of the Latin American in the Southwest has convinced me that at the base of the various forms of discrimination suffered by them in the political, social, economic, and educational fields, lies the economic. This is, in my humble opinion, the real root of the evil.

Refusal to give the Latin American citizen equal opportunities for employment and advancement, and the denial of the same wage for the same type of work to members of this group have condemned this segment of our population to a substandard level of living that forms the basis for all other forms of discrimination by which the economic exploitation itself is justified.

Briefly, the Mexican, be he an American citizen or not, is generally refused employment except in certain types of undesirable unskilled jobs. Furthermore once employed, he is refused advancement, generally speaking, regardless of his ability. Thus his income is restricted and held below that of the average citizen. As a result, he and his family are forced to live in homes that lack every comfort and sanitary devices, they are ill dressed, ill cared for, and ill fed. They are unable to keep their children in school. Consequently their physical appearance and their education are substandard. The community concluded that in a country of equal opportunities a group that remains in this condition is considered inferior, and, consequently, an inferior wage and inferior field of advancement are justified.

Sincerely yours,

Carlos E. Castañeda
Professor of History

STATEMENT ON DISCRIMINATION AGAINST MEXICAN-AMERICANS IN EMPLOYMENT.

By Dr. Carlos E. Castañeda,
Professor of History, University of Texas.

The Mexican American has been and is the victim of discrimination throughout the Southwest from Texas to California to such an extent that in many instances and in many localities within this area, his condition is inferior to that of the Negro in the deep South. At the basis of these discriminatory practices lies the economic status to which he is condemned as a result of discrimination in employment, wages and opportunities for advancement.

During the war the writer was assistant to the chairman of the President's Committee on Fair Employment Practice as regards cases of discrimination against Mexicans through the United States. He had an opportunity at that time to investigate numerous cases in Chicago, the states of Texas, New Mexico, Arizona, Colorado, Utah, and California, and more particularly in the Los Angeles–San Diego area. As a result of the efforts of the President's Committee on Fair Employment Practice the condition of the Mexican both in industry and agricultural employment was greatly improved; in the latter case by the indirect effect which the insistence on the principles of fair employment had on large scale farm employers.

It was not until 1943 that the Mexican labor supply was first tapped and the Mexican throughout the Southwest began to be integrated into our industrial plants. The shipyards, the air-

59

ship factories, the oil industry, the mines, the munition factories; and the numerous military and naval installations slowly, reluctantly, and with much misgivings, began to give the Mexican American a trial in semiskilled positions, and eventually in some skilled jobs. Investigations in the mining, oil, ship and aircraft industries in 1943-44 revealed that in a good many cases Latin Americans were given employment but only as common laborers. In few instances they were being employed in semiskilled labor, but in both, the first and the second case, many of those who were classified as common laborers and semiskilled workers were in fact performing skilled jobs at the lower rate of pay.

A summary of the conditions that prevailed during the war, when a number of factors contributed to break down prejudice and necessity forced the fuller utilization of our labor resources, is found in the reports made before the hearings held by the Labor and Education Committee of the Senate. It is not necessary to restate here the facts presented at the time. Your Committee has access to the *Fair Employment Practice Act hearings before the subcommittee, 79th Congress, 1st session; on S. 101 and S. 459;* May 12-14, 1945; and to the *Hearings* held by the same Committee *To prohibit discrimination in employment, 78th Congress, 2nd Session, on H. R. 3986, H.R. 4004, and H. R. 4005,* November 16, 1944. Of value also in the work of your Committee is the *Final Report of the Fair Employment Practice Committee,* June 28, 1946, recently issued by the U. S. Printing Office, in which the numerous cases of discrimination in employment of all minority groups are summarized.

When the United States Employment Offices were turned back to the States last November an effort was made through the Secretary of Labor to demand of the States the observance of a minimum of basic principles that would guarantee the continuation of the practices instituted during the War as the result of the Fair Employment Practice Committee. This effort proved fruitless and the employment offices now under the administration of the states have relapsed to the discriminatory practices in general use before the War. This is true of the Southwest, where Mexican Americans who register for employment in skilled jobs for which they became fit during the War, either in industrial employment or while serving in the armed forces, are, as a general rule, never referred to the employers calling for such skills. Frequently, all too f r e q u e n t l y, the Mexican American, regardless of his skill, when he attempts to secure a job through the former U. S. Employment Service is told that there are no openings in his special skill, but there are common

60

labor jobs to which they can refer him. Faced with unemployment, the candidate decides to accept the unskilled job until something better turns up.

Many of the men in the employment service said to the writer during the years of the War that when it was over the Mexican American would be *put in his place.* His integration to the industry was deeply resented by those who had come to consider him as an inferior worker. They suffered his advancement and his improvement in wages as a necessary evil, but resolved they would return him to his "proper place" on the first opportunity. The time came when the Employment Service was returned to be directed by the state governments without any stipulation as to their operation. A number of those who have been deeply interested and much concerned over the denial of equal rights to all Americans felt, and still feel, that if the Federal Government furnishes a good portion of the money for the operation of this basic service, it has the right to demand that the employment offices perform their functions without discrimination of race, creed, color, or national origin.

The wages paid to Mexican-Americans and the opportunities offered for employment are, in the final analysis, plain and simple exploitation, based on the assumption that the Mexican is inferior to the Anglo-Saxon in ability and in physical endurance. Yet, he is employed in skilled jobs, which he performs well, at common labor wages; but he is employed in the hardest and filthiest type of work in the industry and in the agriculture fields, in spite of the allegation that he is too weak to do a good day's work. He is, therefore, paid an inferior wage for hard work that no one else will do for that or any other wage.

Concretely, the fruit growers in the Lower Rio Grande Valley in Texas have declared recently that the prevailing wage in the industry is 25 cents an hour. The fruit growers in California, who have to compete on the open market with Texas fruit, can afford to pay, and do pay, 60 cents an hour for the same type of work. The agreement just had between the Mexican and the American governments with regard to Mexican laborers in the United States provides that they shall be paid the prevailing wage. Consequently, Mexican alien labor will be used, and is already being used, to force Mexican American citizens, who pay taxes and are citizens of this country, to lower their standard of living and work for 25 cents an hour, or else they must remain unemployed.

There is no federal or state law setting a minimum agricultural wage. As a result the employers in the various regions and areas are left to determine what the prevailing wage is - the wage they think best to pay and the Mexican Government's representative declares it the minimum wage for its citizens in the designated area, thus making it the official minimum wage for all agricultural labor in the area.

What is the effect of such practices? The Mexican American in Texas is now taking to the roads in dilapidated cars, going to California, to Michigan, to Colorado as migrant labor to secure temporary relief and earn a decent wage. But at the same time he is increasing the housing, the school, the feeding problems of the areas into which he is forced to move in search of a living wage. When winter comes and seasonal employment is over, many of them will return to their former homes with little or nothing left; while many others will remain in the fields to become public charges of the communities who lured them by a wage which in itself is low, but which compared to Texas wages appears a princely one.

Economic discrimination, or, rather, EXPLOITATION of the Mexican American in the payment of an inferior wage and by the denial of equal opportunities for promotion and improvement, will retard and make impractical the operation of American democracy in the Southwest. Half starved, half clothed, disease afflicted citizens cannot but lower the standards of the community through no fault of theirs. Unable to take advantage of such opportunities as are offered for the education of their children, they, as well as their families, will continue to swell the ranks of the illiterate through no fault of their own. Ignorant, miserable, discontented, they will fall an easy pray to the enemies of democracy who will *play* upon their sufferings to turn them against the American way of life.

When it is recalled that over three-quarter million young men from the Southwest fought and bled, suffered and died for the maintenance of democracy in the recent holocaust just past, which in proportion to the number of men in the armed forces there were more Latin Americans who received the Congressional Medal of Honor, and that these people have a deep and abiding faith in democracy, the situation becomes tragic, a real travesty on democracy. These citizens, like all others, have an inalienable right to the enjoyment of equal rights and opportunities to improve their standard of living to better enjoy life.

Economic discrimination, a term used to cover the uglier word of exploitation, can be eliminated through the adoption of federal legislation that will set up machinery similar to that of the Fair Employment Practice Committee. Its work during the war proved conclusively that economic discrimination can be eliminated, but

62

it necessitates eternal watchfulness and a federal law that will command respect throughout the nation. The establishment of a minimum wage for agricultural laborers is a need that has long been neglected. When minority groups are given equal opportunities for employment and advancement regardless of Race, Creed, Color, or National Origin, the externals on which discrimination is based will disappear. Given a decent wage and equal opportunities with all others to advance and improve himself, the Mexican American, as well as the members of every other minority group, will raise his standard of living, and in proportion as he gains in welfare and education he will become a better American citizen and a stauncher defender of a democracy that is a reality.

Austin, Texas. May 9, 1947

Carlos E. Castañeda
Professor of History
University of Texas

November 10, 1947

Mr. Robert K. Carr,
President's Committee on Civil Rights,
1712 G Street NW.,
Room 208,
Washington, D. C.

Dear Sir:

The Report of the President's Committee on Civil Rights is excellent, and the Committee deserves the highest commendation indeed. It is exactly what was needed to bring our Nation to a realization of the shameful situation existing in certain parts of our country. Now let us hope the "famous" Southern Block will not filibuster to death every bill introduced pursuant to the Committee's recommendations.

If you will send me a copy or two of the Committee's Report, I will appreciate it very much.

Thanking you in advance, I remain

Yours very truly,

Alonso S. Perales

Director General,
Committee of One Hundred, The League of Loyal Americans.

OUR PERSONAL RELATIONS WITH MEXICANS.

By Malcom Ross

This paper was presented at the eighth annual Conference on Science, on Philosophy and Religion in their Relation to the Democratic Way of Life held at the American Philosophical Society, Philadelphia. Mr. Ross is university editor, University of Miami, Florida; formerly he was chairman, President's Fair Employment Practice Committee and previously director of information, National Labor Relations Board.

The theme of this Conference was, "How Can Scholarship Contribute to the Relief of International Tensions". Seventy-eight scholars presented papers which, as in the case of the preceding Conferences, will be published together in a book by Harper & Brothers. Mr. Ross's paper will also be used as a chapter in his book, "All Manner of Men", to be published in January by Reynal & Hitchcock.

In the Copper Queen Mine at Bisbee, Arizona, where I worked a long time ago as a mucker, one steady amusement underground was the feud between the Cornishmen and the Welshmen. Why they should fight with each other eleven hundred feet deep in the earth of a foreign country five thousand miles from home was never made clear. There was no creed involved nor economic advantage nor any other visible chip on shoulder.

A squat, mustached firebrand of a Cornishman was a car-pusher partner of mine for a time. We would each put a shoulder to the end of a loaded gondola, free hand holding an acetylene lamp, and down the drift we heaved her to the switch where the donkey engine waited. On one trip we made exceptional speed, the result, I found at the finish, of my having held the flame of my lamp on the seat of my partner's pants. He rubbed his rear and roared. I deserved to be socked for my stupidity but a quid of tobacco settled accounts. He sat in a pool of blue copper sulphate water to cool off and I queried him about Welshmen. If a Welshman had held a lamp to his pants would he have fought? Sure. Why? Because the man would have been a Welshman and so would have had to be licked.

This was pure tribal hostility of a high order, the essence of the paler variety which makes the Dodgers good sports copy or Los Angeles a byword in San Francisco.

American, Welsh, Cornish or what not, we underground miners were a clan all our own. We were "Anglos" in so far as the Mexican miners were concerned. They were not allowed to work underground.

The Mexican's stint was to blast and load on the open hillside where rock slides killed or maimed several of them to every one of us Anglos.

Curiously, the danger of the work was in inverse proportion to the wages. My daily rate as a novice mucker topped that of skilled Mexican miners who had worked in the dangerous trade for years.

THE WAY IT WAS IN THE BISBEE

It was not easy to know whether a man was a Mexican national or an American citizen of Mexican origin. Both were there but we Anglos never mixed with either in Bisbee. The only ones with whom I had even a nodding acquaintance were in the saloons of Naco across the border where everybody grinned, chinked glasses and pledged each other in strange tongues. Bisbee itself kept us apart, we Anglos in the boarding houses and cabins on the hill slope, the Mexicans in their quarters up Brewery Gulch where the flash floods occasionally crumpled huts.

The Mexicans meant no more to the real miners than they did to me, a kid fooling around after college. There was no union in the mines then. Each man lived to himself.

The fact that there are a couple of million Americans of Mexican origin living among us as second-class citizens never occurred to me until many years after. I had missed the chance in Bisbee to know some of them at close range.

Anglo city dwellers, even in a city such as Los Angeles with its three hundred thousand Latin-American population, live their own lives in their own part of town without much concern about their local foreign quarter. Excitement over a zoot-suit riot flares and dies. Politicians cultivate Latin-American counter-parts at election time. Hospitable citizens take visiting friends for luncheon in a little Mexican side street rigged up with adobe stalls, painted earthware, scarlet peppers and Mexican cooking al fresco. It is pleasant to sit and listen to foreign patter and to let the sun step up the hot fragrance of Mexican dishes. But let it stop there. Do not offend your nose with the smell of poverty in ten thousand

65

hovels behind this showplace. Do not spoil the foreign atmosphere with sudden realization that these are American citizens, children of the City of Angels, whose darker skins condemn them to the short end of the stick in politics, law, wages and common courtesy.

It was not always so. These second-class citizens are kinfolk of the adventurers who named Los Angeles, Santa Fe, San Diego and San Antonio. It used to be the Anglo who stepped deferentially into the cool patio of the Latin and who reckoned the stages of his ride north by the asylum he could find at the monastery cloisters.

How in a hundred years did the Anglo of the southwest learn to paraphrase the southern doctrine for Negroes, into: "All Mexican-Americans shall be subservient to all Anglo-Americans"?

This rule of conduct the Anglo has learned very thoroughly, from his press, from his white schools and from churches where God speaks Spanish only in the last three pews.

When President Roosevelt and President Camacho of Mexico met in the spring of 1943, The Houston Post celebrated the event with the following editorial:

THE BATTLE OF SAN JACINTO

"As for the San Jacinto Day association, the two presidents may feel that the anniversary of the battle in which Texas licked Mexico is a delicate subject for comment at a time when the two countries are fighting together. However, if Winston Churchill or Anthony Eden should land in America on the Fourth of July and meet the President, we imagine they would say something about our Declaration of Independence which led to our whipping England. While President Roosevelt visited San Jacinto battleground in 1936, the centennial year of the fight, it is conceivable that neither he nor Camacho recalled that battle in their conversation Wednesday. But a Texan cannot help but feel that they might have taken cognizance of the great occasion."

This is an historical gap which needs to be filled, and I propose to fill it in the manner in which the editorial writer evidently supposes the conversation would have run:

ROOSEVELT: "Well, here we are, Camacho, right on the very spot where the Texans licked hell out of the Mexicans. Pretty place, too."

CAMACHO: "Yes, Mr. President, begging your pardon, sir, it is a pretty place . . . Now maybe can't we let by-gones be by-gones . . ."

ROOSEVELT: "Santa Ana was a scurrilous cur . . ."

CAMACHO: "He was a very bad man, but . . ."

66

ROOSEVELT: "Bad, Camacho? Do you remember the Alamo?"

CAMACHO: "Oh yes, Mr. President! We are never allowed to forget it. But Mexico is now your ally. We are fighting side by side . . ."

ROOSEVELT: "About time, too. Not that we need you. We Texans whipped you, we whipped England, we can whip Germany single handed, we can whip the United States . . wait a minute, where am I?"

This stirring dialogue, otherwise appropriate to the heads of two friendly countries, has the one flaw that it supposes Roosevelt and Camacho as ignorant of Texas history as the editorial writer on the Houston Post.

Carved on the walls of the battle monument at San Jacinto, by Texans more ready to ackowledge a debt, is this inscription:
"The early policies of Mexico toward the Texas colonists had been extremely liberal. Large grants of land were made to them, and no taxes or duties imposed. The relationships between the Anglo-Americans and the Mexicans were cordial."

Covered wagons from Ohio brought the first Anglos to San Antonio. The old Spanish town welcomed this first wave of emigrants and the many more who kept rolling across the prairies, eventually patrolled by riders in United States Cavalry blue.

A REBELLION OF MEXICANS

The revolt against Santa Ana was a joint one of Texas-Mexicans and Texas-Anglos. It originally started as a rebellion of Mexicans who wanted a return to the liberal Constitution of 1824. Only after Santa Ana, "the Napoleon of the West", had crushed these Mexican patriots did he tackle the like-minded patriots of Texas. There he found Mexicans among the Texan dead on the bloody floor of the Alamo and later felt the steel of an all-Mexican troop in the battle of San Jacinto.

The names of martyred Mexicans are there on the walls of the Alamo and on the battle monument of San Jacinto, side by side with Texan brothers, exactly as they appeared during World War II in the daily casualty lits of every Texas newspaper.

As for its Anglo-fighters, the army of Texas liberation was made up of men from such well known Texas counties as Kentucky, Arkansas, Alabama, Michigan, North Carolina, Massachusetts, England, Ireland, Scotland and a few more up in the Panhandle too trifling to mention.

Most Texas drugstore and hotel clerks have listened more to Statehood Week oratory than to the quieter voice of history.

They are continually infuriating Mexican consuls and South American notables by giving them the same bum's rush they daily extend to Mexican shrimp shuckers and migrant farmhands. The latter, in point of fact, probably have sharper appetites to be disappointed than do visiting diplomats.

One of these cola-counter patriots in the spring of 1946 refused service to a Mexican-American in uniform. In the fracas the soldier was delayed in arriving at a luncheon given to celebrate his decoration by the president of the United States with the congressional medal of honor.

THE INFLUX OF PEONS

Our bad manners toward Latins began in the nineteenth century when we began to import tens of thousands of Mexican peons to ballast railroad tracks, mine copper, chop cotton, pick beets and shuck pecans at four cents an hour upward, but not very far upward. The ripple of profits from these operations have long since crossed the broad pool of American wealth and disappeared. The peons remain here and remain peons. They keep coming. During the war fifty thousand Mexican workers were loaned to us to help fill our labor shortage, on condition they would return after the war. But in addition there was the regular flow of "wet Mexicans", those who swim the Rio Grande and vanish into the human stream of migrants bound for San Fernando and Denver. In the winter they come "home" for three months in Texas, Americans now by census count.

Archbishop Robert E. Lucey of San Antonio has his residence in an open field on the Mexican side of town. His neighbors like him well enough to cross that difficult gulf between their hovels and the elegance of a clerical establishment. The archbishop is an alert and vigorous man with a highly unclerical lack of reticence in secular affairs. He lectures business men (bulwark of his archbishopric) for paying miserable wages to Latin-American workers. He sends telegrams to congressmen and daily persuades the meek that they will inherit heaven just as easily on ten cents an hour more.

WHAT CAN YOU EXPECT?

"How hard would an Irishman work if you paid him twenty cents an hour?" Archbishop Lucey asked a 1943 gathering. "How much exuberance, vitality and enthusiasm could any people who had been underpaid, under-nourished and badly housed for a half a century?" "If the Mexican is sometimes not a good American, what can you expect from a man who during all his life was socially ostracized, deprived of civil rights, politically debased and condemned to economic servitude?"

This fiery talk comes from a man angry at the fact that nearly ten thousand Spanish-American children of grammar school age in his archdiocese are not enrolled in any school. In his gentler moods the archbishop can regret that Anglo-Texans are deprived of the music and laughter, the art and culture of a people they do not care to meet.

Archbishop Lucey is only one of many in Texas who work hard at improving the relationships between Anglos and Mexican-Americans. The state officially works at it through its Good Neighbor Commission, established by Governor Coke Stevenson in 1943. The University of Texas at Austin has for years been seeking the cure within Texas of the displays of prejudice which so offend the pride of the nation with which the state shares hundreds of miles of common boundary.

These Texas gestures of friendliness are well reported in Mexican newspapers; the people south of the border know a great deal about Texas. They respond warmly to any show of friendliness. I have before me a copy of "Hemisferio", published in Mexico City in Spanish and English and designed to report how things are going with the neighbor to the north. There is a picture of Sumner Welles. He is described as "revered by all Latin-American peoples" and the quotation chosen to accompany this praise was Welles's statement that "humiliating and wounding discriminations create lastings resentments which no eloquent speeches by government officials, or governmental policies, however wise, can hope to remove".

Sharing honors with Welles in "Hemisferio" is a picture of Jack Danciger. He is a prosperous oil man but it is not why the government of Mexico has made him its honorary consul at Fort Worth nor why "Hemisferio" suggests that the insignia of the Aztec Eagle should adorn his bosom.

Jack Danciger spoke only Spanish during his New Mexico boyhood. He maintains an office in Fort Worth where Mexican-Americans bring their troubles and his lawyer is available to take the cases to the courts. He gets offers of aid, signed "Tom", from his fellow Texan, Attorney General Tom Clark. He likes to give advice to American tourists of how not to throw your weight around below the border.

The G. I.'s who came back to finish up at the University ot Texas take a dim view of discrimination against fellow G. I.'s of Spanish ancestry. Editorials in the college paper have blasted those Austin landladies who have turned them away from their rooming houses.

Texans are working at this thing, and why should a damn yankee put in his oar to say how it might be helped along?

There is a key to this door, I brashly think a key which may have been overlooked in the attempt to crawl under the door or knock it down. It is this: social discrimination is strongest where there is a large body of Mexican-Americans working at wages less than Anglo workers will accept.

Not a new or profound statement but let's see how it applies to Texas's problem.

All the efforts to stop "social discrimination" end in surface cures. Remove a sign: "Mexicans will Not Be Served Inside" and you will get: "Mexicans Will be Served in the Kitchen Only." You may persuade the city fathers to take down: "This Park is for Whites, Mexicans Keep Out" but the chances are that an unwritten sign will still reserve all the park benches for Anglos. Decide not to huddle sixty Mexican-American children in a small frame shack under one low-paid teacher. Those of them who are admitted to a "white" school will still have separate classes, separate drinking fountains and be allowed to play in the school yard only when the Anglo children are through with it.

These practices run in well-worn channels. The Good Neighbor Commission can correct abuses but the mere doing of that will not change opinions. Jack Danciger can fight a few cases successfully in the courts. Should Texas in one sweep abolish discrimination in restaurants, swimming pools, residential districts and schools, the old habits would still persist. The change must come from within the people themselves. The surest way to effect that is through the conventions which make people accepted—the conventions of being affable, neat, assured, clean, healthy. A babbitty standard? Sure, but it works.

Texans are used to seeing Mexicans in old clothes, old jalopies, earth-floored shacks and menial jobs. The only basic cure is to see them in decent clothes and clean houses, walking with heads erect and without either the abject or angry eyes which poverty inspires. Skilled jobs, good wages and money in the bank are powerful ways of winning neighborly respect. Pedro and Juan will see the signs taken down in restaurants windows only when their pay envelopes match the Anglo's for equal work. Maybe not until a generation of such pay envelopes have put enough meat on their kids to resist tuberculosis, inspired them to learn English and let them laugh with Anglos without feeling self-conscious.

70

COLD FACTS ON BAD MANNERS

The Mexican-Americans have the beginnings of that economic strength which is their surest hope as the Texas Good Neighbor Commission should know. For it owes its existence to the refusal of the Mexican government to send workers into Texas until something should be done about discrimination. In the first report of its investigation the Commission heard some cold facts on how bad manners toward Mexicans can affect Anglo pocketbooks.

At Lubbock, the report said, seven thousand immigrant field hands, come to pick the cotton, spent $13,000 in the town's business places over one week-end. So far, score the Anglo with a nice profit. But here is how it works on the debit side as told in the Good Neighbor Commission's report:

"There is no place provided where they may park their trucks, take a bath, change their clothes, even go to the toilet.

The result is that the laborers come into the nearest big town on Saturday, having had no facilities on the farms for bathing. Naturally they are dirty and because there are no facilities available to them in the towns, they remain dirty and are refused entrance into or service in public places."

A CERTAIN FARMER IN HOCKLEY COUNTY

"A certain farmer in Hockley County, who lived near the town of Ropesville was badly in need of a large crew of pickers. The farmer contacted this agent and late one evening the agent took a crew leader and two or three laborers out to the farm from Levelland. They found a good crop of cotton, acceptable housing, agreed on a price and the crew promised to come out from Levelland to work the next day. On the return trip, passing through Ropesville, the agent and the laborers stopped at the only cafe in the town that was open. It was about eight o'clock on a cold night and they wanted a cup of coffee. There was no one else in the cafe. The owner came up and said: 'What do you want?' The agent replied: 'I want a cup of coffee. I don't know what the other boys want. They may want sandwiches.' The owner said: 'I don't serve Mexicans.' The agent said: 'Well, now, these boys have come out here to help the farmers harvest their crops. They have just agreed to come out tomorrow to work for Mr. So-and-So. I don't see anything so elegant about your cafe and I don't see why you can't serve us a cup of coffee'. The owner said: 'I'll serve you, but I don't serve Mexicans'. The agent said: 'No, you can't serve me either, and they walked out. Naturally the laborers were angry and the result was that they did not return to the farm the next day and the farmer failed to have his crop picked."

There were other stories such as that of the constable who flagged down all trucks and told the migrants to keep on moving through town under threat of arrest. The report comments:

"They didn't even stop in Howard County and the farmers who had their cotton picked in Howard County were very few indeed. On this trip we passed hundreds and hundreds of acres of cotton that have never been touched and never would be touched, the farmers realized that the position of the migrant must be recognized with tangible improvements. Of the one million persons of Mexican extraction in Texas, eighty per cent are citizens of the United States, most of them citizens by birth. They are our people, and their problems are our problems. We must solve them not for the benefit of the Mexican government but for our own benefit."

Here is a good, round, forthright admission that cotton drying on the stalk costs more than decent accommodations for the migrant workers. The offended migrants could move on. They had something of value to withhold. In doing so they took the first step in improving the manners of their Anglo fellow citizens.

A PROFESSOR FROM THE UNIVERSITY OF TEXAS

The FEPC Regional Director for Texas, Dr. Carlos E. Castañeda, came on loan from the University of Texas, to whose faculty he has now returned. He is a naturalized citizen, born in Mexico. In the college and capitol town of Austin he walks the streets as free from insults as any man. His complexion happens to be fair. He travels anywhere in the southwest without embarrassment but many of his friends of Spanish descent—lawyers, business men, Mexican consuls have been turned away from public doors. They do not like it. They get mad, write letters, form committees. With one accord they came to its support when Dr. Castañeda opened an FEPC office in Texas and this letter tells why. It was written in appreciation of Dr. Castañeda's work by a San Antonio Lawyer, Alonso S. Perales.

"Before the committee came into being, Latin-Americans were grossly and unjustly discriminated against in government camps and in shops and factories doing work for our federal government. They did not receive the same pay received by Anglo-Americans for the same kind of work and they were not given any promotions and as far as a Latin-American becoming a foreman or supervisor, that was out of the question. All that has changed considerably, thank the Lord. We thank God that He gave our President Roosevelt the courage to come right out and order that such discrimination cease. If all of us Americans thought and acted like President Roosevelt on this particular question, we would be in a much better position nationally and internationally. Then we would have not only an absolutely united America (U. S. A.) but real Pan-American solidarity as well."

GREAT EXCLAIM OVER A SMALL PAY RAISE.

Why this fervent thanks to his Maker because a few Mexican-Americans got raise in pay? Perales is well enough off. What is it to him - to Castañeda, Galarza or Senator Chavez? Why should Archbishop Lucey declaim about a ten cent an hour raise as though it was an article of salvation?

Each sees, I think, the link between the pay envelope and human dignity. I attended a dinner in San Antonio where the guests of honor were four Mexican-Americans whose pay had been raised to match the work they were doing. The dollars involved were few; the spur to their pride enormous. They were accepted skilled workers among the Anglo skilled workers. A man could go on from there . . . .

The prosperous San Antonio Mexican-Americans who staged this dinner for the four upgraded workers, themselves made speeches celebrating the triumph. I have forgotten the texts but this impression sticks: their group interest was strong because their personal interests were deeply involved. Their tidy bank balances, their pleasant homes, their confidence in their own abilities could not make them fully citizens of the United States so long as the great mass of their people were set apart and kept in squalor.

This is a valid motive. It is not peculiar to Latins or Anglos. The hope for personal security and peace of mind may very well underlie most of the efforts which men make to better the living conditions of people whom they do not personally know and whose miseries they do not share. It may have moved Teddy Roosevelt to swing his Big Stick as it probably did his distant cousin Franklin.

To scoffers it is "do-goodism"; yet it is dangerous to swing that generality by the tail. The cotton planter who puts in showers and toilets and pays a higher wage than his neighbor in order to get his cotton picked is buying personal security and peace of mind. The old do-gooder!

When the British, miserable in their 1947 blizzards, shared coal and food with Germany, they were buying (or hoped they were) security against having their sons killed in battle twenty years hence.

A Mississipi friend of mine told me, with a gleam in his eyes, that the planters of that state during the postwar decade

73

will solve their Negro problem by putting skillful Negroes on tractors, flama cultivators and mechanical cotton pickers. These Negroes will be well paid. The other two-thirds of the Negro field hands will have to go elsewhere to find work, probably in the north.

There was no malice in his mind. He is a man who worries about the poverty of the Negroes of Mississippi. He had taken the rap of listening to outside criticism and had borne the strain of being a conscientious man in a homeland where civil rights are denied. It would give him a sense of personal security and peace of mind to know that those Negroes who might remain in Mississippi would be well fed, well clothed, well housed. It may be forgiven him if his eyes lighted at the thought that it would be the Yankees to whom the unneeded Mississippi Negroes might flee for food, clothing and shelter.

The hourly wage rate is a pretty good index of how things stand in racial relations. I have tried to illustrate what seemingly remote reactions are caused by it in the case of Mexican-Americans. If the thesis holds by them, it is equally true for Negro workers.

Frank P. Graham, president of the University of North Carolina and during the war a public member of the Labor Board, is a man who does not feel that official papers must be read as though they had been dehydrated and kiln dried. He likes to let himself go. For the War Labor Board he wrote the Southport petroleum decision, the one which abolished the distinction between "colored laborer" and "white laborer" and reclassified both simply as "laborers" with the same rates of pay for all who do the same work. Literally applied, that decision would reshape the southern economy. It was only a wartime decision, no longer having authority. Its interest now lies in the mental processes of a great Southerner.

I do not know Frank Graham's inner motives any more than I know (except by deduction) the minds of those others I have cited as coming to the aid of the ill-used out of their own compulsion to build a world in which their hearts and minds can be at peace. I do assert, though, that Frank Graham's Southport petroleum opinion is logical in its statement of what tremendous issues hang on so simple a thing as paying a man fairly for work done.

"The world", he wrote, "has given America the vigor and variety of its differences. America should protect and enrich its differences for the sake of America and the world. Understanding religious and racial differences makes a better understanding of other differences and for an appreciation of the sacredness of human personality, as a basic to human freedom. The American

74

answer to differences in color and creed is not a concentration camp but co-operation. The answer to human error is not terror but light and liberty, under the moral law. By this light and liberty, the Negro has made a contribution in work and faith, song and story, laughter and struggle which are an enduring part of the spiritual heritage of America . . . "

A TEST OF OUR WORLD WAR II AIMS.

"Whether as vigorous fighting men or for production of food and munitions, America needs the Negro; the Negro needs the equal opportunity to work and fight. The Negro is necessary for winning the war and, at the same time, is a test of our sincerity in the cause for which we are fighting. More hundreds of millions of colored people are involved in the outcome of this war than the combined populations of the axis powers. Under Hitler and his master race, their movement is backward to slavery and despair. In America the colored people have the freedom to struggle for freedom, hope, equality of opportunity and the gradual fulfilment for all peoples of the noblest aspirations of the brothers of men and the sons of God without regard to color or creed, religion or race, in the world neighborhood of human brotherhood."

Once in a while a newspaper columnist bursts loose in his own emotional voice. The importance of what he has to say is too much for him. You would not expect a staid military analyst, writing in The New York Times, to break out in a rash of colorful metaphors. But it happened to Hanson W. Baldwin one day in the spring of 1947. If Vanderberg or Austin had said it, you would have paid attention. It still remains true and important.

"Heavy are the responsibilities of power," Mr. Baldwin began, "and never heavier than in this age of dissolution and decay of old values and the emergence from the dust of dead empires of a new world order.

"THE RAMPARTS OF TRADITION" ARE UNDERMINED.

"Today, the torrent of history is seeking a new channel. The forces of the surging waters are conflicting and convulsive, broiled and troubled; they tear at the dam of the past and undermine the ramparts of tradition.

"They will not be stayed but they can be guided. The United States today lies squarely in the stream of history; it can guide that stream or be swept away by it. The new is inevitable; change is certain but that change can be either malevolent or salutary. The United States, far more than any other single factor, is the key to the destiny of tomorrow; we alone may be able to avert

75

the decline of western civilization and a reversion to nihilism and the dark age."

There are many ways to win or lose that opportunity. My neighbor, Edward C. Acheson, is a professor of monetary theory and naturally supposes that the interest rate is the key to the door of destiny. The United States really assumed responsibility in 1914 when the British pound gave way in world trade to the American dollar. Today the lowering of a decimal on the interest rate of that mighty dollar can move ships, feed the hungry, start dynamos, support political policies . . . all this is persuasive to a layman especially since my learned neighbor underlines his fiduciary jargon with the idea of the moral responsibility which goes with the power to make and break nations. From 1919 to 1928, we supported Europe by loans, then-as whimsically as a father cutting off the allowance on which his son had come to rely, we started a run on the treasuries of Europe by demanding repayment all at once. That we collapsed ourselves in the following year is the moral kicker to the story.

Congress, too, is the keeper of keys to the doors of destiny. A loan to Britain, raising the immigration quota, withdrawal from China, instructions to our U. N. delegates - every direct move is at once a practical step in our world stewardship and a measure of our moral stature. Uncle Sam as trustee for the world's widows has to show himself a very upright agent.

Interest rates are specific. An international loan is so many dollars and no more. But how shall we measure the practical effects of so nebulous a thing as respect for other races and other religions?

Let's have a look at the possible impact of intolerance on world affairs.

We have Senator Austin's word for it that world security rests on the "oaken beam" of western hemisphere solidarity. The best way to attain unity on this side of the world, he suggested, is through regional pacts among the American republics. As a foot note to his remarks, President Truman in that same week in the spring of 1947 won the affection of Mexico by laying a wreath on the graves of the cadets who died bravely at American hands in 1848.

A SIMPLE ACT OF FRIENDLINESS.

Mr. Austin's pacts may be exactly what is needed to unite the hemisphere in working agreements but they will never stir the emotional fervor which Mr. Truman's simple act of friendliness sent throughout Latin America.

76

We need both attributes — the skill to set up security pacts, the sense to keep on good terms with the peoples who support them.

Mexico is the bellwether for a large part of Central and South America. Her government has a special prestige as the one nearest the powerful "Americanos del Norte". We need Mexico's friendship to make an oaken beam out of that western hemisphere with which Mr. Austin hopes to impress the rest of the dispirited world. Yet for decades we have treated Mexicans as though our interest lay in goading them into hating us.

God watches the sparrow's fall no more closely than governments watch over their own people in foreign lands. When Japanese slapped the faces of Britishers in Hong Kong, the empire trembled. When an American G. I. was held by the Russians, our headlines screamed. Why then should we forget that Mexico City watches the insults offered her people above the Rio Grande?

During the war the Mexican Congress appointed a committee on discrimination, that is, on American discrimination against Mexicans. Texas was cut off the list of those states to whom Mexico sent workers to maintain roadbeds and harvest crops. That was at the peak of our war manpower shortage. It was then that Governor Stevenson appointed his Texas Good Neighbor Commission. But Mexico was not sufficiently impressed to withdraw the ban. Official Texas could not at one stroke cure the bad manners of her people. Drugstore and hotel clerks, used to tossing out anything Latin, made the mistake of insulting Mexican Consuls and visiting notables from other South American countries. These incidents are remembered south of the border.

Tolerance (good manners, absence of active prejudice, mutual respect or whatever name you wish to give it) has its measurable effects. New Orleans, which rests its hopes of prosperity on being the great port of entry for South American trade, may find its balance disturbed by some witless act of an irresponsible Anglo in San Antonio or Los Angeles.

The niceties of diplomatic usage soft pedal these incidents. But they are syndicated in the Latin American press. The people know. Those gringos!

American delegates to the United Nations have watched racial and religious issues bedevil the cause of world peace. Arab against Jew. Hindu against Mohammedan. And the white nations, nearly always, at loggerheads with the colored. The fight for economic survival cannot alone account for the fanaticism of national positions.

Shall we hush these things? — leave their solution to the gradual processes of education between nations?

The lid refuses to stay shut. The brew simmers over in unexpected places. The great internationalist, General Smuts, suddenly breaks out in a quarrel with India over South Africa's treatment of Mohammedans and in the course of it reveals that his country's views on white supremacy are a notch tighter than Mississipi's.

Shall we admit that world-wide intolerance is an incurable disease of the human spirit?

The only answer, I think, was given by Sumner Welles to Hitler. In a prewar interview, Welles received from Der Fuehrer the usual taunt about American treatment of Negroes in response to Welles' question on Hitler's policy toward Jews. The difference, Welles replied, lay in the fact that nazi policy evidently favored discrimination against Jews while American national policy was in favor of fairness toward Negroes.

You cannot condemn a country which is honestly making an effort to cure its own prejudices. The Good Neighbor Policy could stand up under individual insults to South Americans if it were accepted that we as a people dislike bad manners and mean to correct them.

No people in the world is insensitive to affronts. We, the most polyglot and the most powerful nation in the world, have the problem of prejudice on our hands along with all the other baggage that goes with the responsibility of power.
Year 1947.

BITTERNESS ON OUR BORDER

By Stuart J. Barnes

Editor, Speakers Magazine, Tacoma Tark, Washington, D. C.

Throughout the southwest portion of the United States the word "democracy" is becoming a mere mockery. In our great Southwest, including the states of Texas, New Mexico, Colorado, Arizona and California, are well over a million American citizens of Mexican descent. Against these people, American citizens, are being perpetrated incidents of the worst kind of persecution and discrimination. Long stifled prejudices are coming to the surface in outbreaks of violence and bloodshed.

In all these border states, there is growing a deep feeling of bitterness on the part of the numerous Mexican-American citizenry. This bitterness has arisen from the diverse ways in which Mexicans have been the object of social and economic discrimination. Wherever one travels in this area, he cannot escape the evidence of prejudice. "NO MEXICANS ALLOWED", "WE DON'T SERVE MEXICANS — THIS MEANS YOU." Virtually the only jobs that an ordinary Mexican-American can obtain and hold are the low-paying jobs, the "dirty" jobs, and these for wages which are by no means on a parity with the costs of living. Neither are the wages on a parity with the pay received by Anglo-Americans performing similar duties.

Sergeant Macario Garcia, of Sugarland, Texas, holder of the Congressional Medal of Honor, entered a restaurant in Richmond, Texas, and asked for a cup of coffee. He protested when informed that the restaurant did not serve "Mexicans". An Anglo-American chased him out with a baseball bat.

In Fredericksburg, Texas, (the home of Admiral Nimitz) three Mexican-American soldiers were refused service at a Main Street Cafe, unless they "went around to the back."

In Ozona, Texas, Pvt. Tomas Garza was refused refreshments at an Ozona Drug Store. He protested that his money was as good as anyone else's, whereupon the city Sheriff, pistol in hand, ordered Pvt. Garza to leave the drug store. Pvt. Garza attempted to call his Captain and report the incident but was refused a telephone connection. This same drug store had also refused refreshments to Pvt. Arturo Ramirez and his wife. Pvt. Ramirez was killed in action in France.

A worker in McCamey, Texas, has to travel 45 miles to Fort Stockton in order to get a haircut, because there is no barber shop in McCamey that will cut the hair of a Mexican.

At Big Springs, Texas, the commanding officer of the army field had to declare the Mexican area "off limits." "Any soldier who considers himself white shall not go into the Mexican district of Big Springs, Texas", was the order.

For a Fourth of July celebration at Lockhart, Texas, several city blocks were roped off for dancing. Mexicans who joined their neighbors in celebrating the Fourth were humiliated by the following announcement by the master of ceremonies:

" I have been asked to make this announcement: that all Spanish people gathered here must leave the block. (This was received with many cheers and hurrahs.) Since this is an American celebration, it is for the white people only. (More applause and cheers followed.)" A similar situation occurred at Poteet, Texas, during an Armistice Day celebration.

A source of embarrassment has been the humiliation of Latin-American visitors, citizens of Honduras, Venezuela, Colombia, and the other republics. It is difficult for them to understand, inasmuch as American tourists in Latin-America receive every consideration and courtesy. Two Mexican government officials' were recently denied service at a restaurant in Pecos, Texas.

In many Southwest industries Mexicans have been refused employment in other than common labor classifications, regardless of their qualifications or training in higher skills. The oil industry, its unions, the railroads and their unions, the mining industry, military installations employing civilians, public utilities, have been the chief offenders. Generally, only the aircraft and shipbuilding industries have offered the Mexican equality in employment and promotion. There has been no distinction made between the treatment of Mexican nationals and Americans citizens of Mexican extraction. If his name sounds Spanish the worker is considered to be a Mexican and is treated as such.

This practice is not confined only to our Southwest. There have been similar instances in Chicago, where a holder of the Purple Heart was turned down for a job with the street-car company on the grounds that "you are from a minority group and we don't know whether that would work so well."

Similar discrimination has been reported in connection with housing of Latin-American and Negro war workers. Many minority group workers were required to travel from 30 to 80 miles per day to and from the industries in which they were employed, because of restrictions which compelled them to live in designated areas. Abnormally high rates of absenteeism and tardiness, and an accompanying low efficiency rating, were traced to this very cause.

These incidents and countless similar ones, were brought out in hearings of a Subcommittee of the Senate Committee on Education and Labor in connection with a proposed bill to continue the work of the Fair Employment Practices Committee, a wartime agency designed to prevent employment bottlenecks due to discrimination in employment for racial considerations.

In addition to the instances of discrimination are the actual outbreaks of violence against the Mexicans by the native "Texans". On the increase throughout Texas are youthful "vigilante" groups whose sole purpose in existence is to "teach the Spiks where they belong."

In San Angelo, Texas, an organized gang of young Texans have been beating up Mexicans in a small-scale "reign of terror". In early September they beat up a Mexican veteran; he had to be hospitalized. The young Texans were all acquitted by the County Judge.

San Antonio, Texas, was the scene of a fight between two bands of boys, one Texan and one Mexican, in September. One of the Anglo-American boys had armed himself with a gun and killed one of the Mexican boys while the latter was running away. Tried as a juvenile, he was acquitted by the jury.

All through Texas, New Mexico, Colorado, Arizona and California, it is the same story. Soldiers, returning veterans, heroes, come home to find that their communities have turned traitor to the cause for which they fought and bled. They have returned only to be "put in their place" - that place being, of course, on the bottom rung of the Southwest's social and economic ladder.

DISCRIMINATION IS ECONOMIC

The entire situation is basically an economic one. The Mexicans constitute a formidable economic group competing for labor against the Anglo-Americans. There is no real competition. The Mexicans have for generations been accustomed to low standards of living and can work for wages which no Anglo-American can live on. The Mexicans will work in the citrus fields, accept household and service employment, work as common laborers, in general, do the "dirty work" of an industry or community. They do not ask, and would never get it if they did ask, more than a fraction of the pay that an Anglo-American would require.

Talk to the average Texan. . Texans do not like the "Mexes". They will tell you so. Some will try to justify their hatred and discrimination. The majority do not bother. For the most part it is an intense, blind, unreasoned prejudice which admits of no questioning, no argument.

"Mexes" and "Whites" (an ethnologically fallacious distinction) are separated by the same social and economic barriers which exist between all large social groups. The Mexicans live poorly, do menial labor for low wages, rear large families. They are solidly and devotedly Catholic in a region of Pope-haters. Many of the older Mexicans speak little English; the younger generation speaks both languages. This is true primarily of the so-called "low class" Mexicans.

Among them is a substantial prosperous element, landowners, merchants, professional groups. Most of these are from old Texas or California families and maintain their position and culture

81

with dignity and grace. On the whole, however, the living standard among Mexicans is low.

Texans regard them as lazy and untrustworthy. The Texan will tell you of the Mexican's contempt for work, his propensity to "goldbrick", and his general inefficiency and lack of application to the job. "You gotta watch 'em all the time", he will tell you.

In many instances this is all too true. The Mexicans are not at all satisfied with the type of employment they are forced to accept, and they realize the futility of expecting reasonable advancement. Confronted with a distasteful job, they follow the normal human inclination to make the job as undemanding as possible. They are offered little incentive to be efficient. They try to do as little as possible for the little they receive.

The notion that Mexicans are not capable of other than common labor deserves attention. A statement by a personnel officer of a California shipbuilding corporation said in part:

"Generally speaking our Mexican workers for the most part have come to us in recent months. The Mexican-Americans are not only capable, but the variety of jobs at which they can be utilized is limitless if employers, managers, and general management simply will make a point of using them. Production records indicate that they have an equal aptitude with other groups or other individuals. They are definitely on a par. There is no difference."

Other statements by personnel officers indicate that the Mexican, properly trained, is perfectly capable of performing skilled jobs.

Delinquency is regarded as being high among the Mexicans. Actually it is no greater than among any Anglo-American group on the same social, cultural and economic level. Prostitution is quite prevalent in almost all Mexican communities. It is supported to a large extent, however, by Anglo-American indulgence. The children are on the streets almost from the time they are able to walk. They shine shoes, beg for pennies, and too often learn the ways of the petty thief. Fights and knifings among the older element are common.

In most communities the Mexican children and the Anglo-American children are segregated in the public schools. Many Mexican children receive their education in the numerous parochial schools. Their devotion to the Catholic church and faith is high. Mexican language and customs tend to be perpetuated perhaps more than is healthy for a young Mexican who must live among people so virily "American" as the average Texan.

Until the war, the Mexicans accepted their status more or less passively. Soon a high proportion of their numerous sons went into the armed forces. They fought, bled, died beside their Anglo-American comrades. They absorbed the torrents of high principled speeches and declarations concerning freedom, tolerance, world-wide security, our condemnation of racial and religious prejudice. They, too, learned "Why we Fight." Perhaps some of them wondered why we concerned ourselves with establishing the "freedoms" across the ocean, while our own back yard is still cluttered with bigotry, intolerance, racial discrimination and underprivileged classes. *Whatever their thoughts, they fought on and fought well.*

These same sons are coming back now — those who can come back. They are coming back to be kicked out of restaurants, beaten by "vigilantes", refused decent, well-paying employment. How will they accept this status?

The probability is that they will not like the situation. Many of the returnees among the Mexicans are becoming quite bitter about the discrimination. They feel that they fought for democracy abroad only to lose it in their own home towns.

The problem has its international aspect. We are trying to build something solid in the way of peace, understanding, cooperation, a "community of nations". We are trying desperately to atone for our former sins in Latin America. We have achieved conspicuous success in this undertaking. Many of these same Latin Americans are asking, however, if our intentions towards them are any better than our intentions towards and treatment of their racial cousins — American citizens — within our own borders. We still enjoy something less than the complete trust and confidence of our Latin American neighbors. Our fight to establish democracy and social justice abroad may well be seriously hamstrung by our indifference to our own internal inequalities.

Senator Chavez, of New Mexico, submitted the following in a report from the Committee on Education and Labor in May:

"At this critical stage of world history, America cannot afford to say to the world that it intends to resume within its own borders, practices of racial and religious discrimination in employment and still expect its exhortations of equality and freedom of opportunity for all to be received without skepticism by the hundreds of millions of people that constitute the United Nations. It would seem expedient and practical to prove to the entire world that we have the capacity to deal justly and amicably with people in our midst without regard to differences of faith and ancestry."

We cannot effectively use our influence to direct the democratic growth of other nations while we permit a large proportion of our own citizens to remain under-privileged. We still have to apologize for our "Negro problem." Now, in our border states, a similar problem is beginning to reach dangerous stages.

Our Southwest is a potential danger spot. The violence which has begun to flare up in isolated communities may very well break out into wholesale fighting and extensive bloodshed. Feeling on both sides is running high. We cannot afford to delay in our recognition of the gravity of the situation and in our determination to do something about it.

It is quite obvious that there is no single solution to this pressing problem. Too many factors are involved. As with any economic maladjustment the difficulties of alleviation are legion.

Let it be said that the national government is not to blame; under existing laws the responsibility rests upon local and state governments. With the exception of the beatings, no laws are being violated. We have no statutes against discrimination. Legislation in itself cannot erase deep-rooted prejudices. A government may remove as far as possible the basic inequalities which are the product of prejudice. It is then confronted by the fact that the very prejudice which opposes equitable wage scales, fair employment practices, better housing, relief and educational facilities, is merely deepened by the attempt to enforce the new conditions. Thus governmental action, while essential, is halting and ineffectual in reaching the seat of the problem.

ACTION NEEDED

Three main steps are necessary. They involve a basic change in both local and national governmental policy, which has been prone to ignore the situation. The "hands off" attitude has the sanction of political expediency.

First: The extent and quality of educational facilities must be increased. The entire problem must be recognized as a problem, and intelligent use of the educational facilities can help immensely both to modify and to eliminate prejudices and to prepare for concerted ·democratic action to bring about a settlement.

Second: Continued regulation on the part of state and national governments seems necessary to dig up and expose the seats of discrimination. In this connection the continuance of the Fair Employment Practices Commitee as an agency for eliminating discrimination in employment attitudes is essential. Additional legislation is required to reduce instances of prejudice and discrimination in other fields.

Third: There must be limitless publicity directed to the issues involved. Everyone concerned should understand the entire situation and be informed as to what action is being taken and as to what action he should take individually to bring about a settlement.

A statement of Mr. Eduardo Quevedo, President of the Coordinating Council for Latin American Youth, of Los Angeles, California, is noteworthy:

"We want to assume all our responsibility and obligation to Government; we want to do our duty by Government. We do not want any special privileges whatsoever. We do not even want a job, or feel that we are entitled to a job, just because we happen to be of a certain racial extraction. But inasmuch as we accept our duties and responsibilities as Americans, even to the extent of losing our lives as Americans, we do not want to be deprived of a job on account of our ancestry or national origin or race. We desire an equality of opportunity and to have some dignity as citizens."

No settlement can be expected overnight. The solution involves time and human emotions. There is nothing as tenacious as prejudice. Years will be required to uproot it, years of education, firm regulation and limitless publicity. First, however, must come the desire to tackle the problem. (Texans appear ready to do this, but they have seized the wrong method). They cannot do it with clubs, with terrorism, with additional discrimination. Soldiers from our Southwestern states have been unsurpassed in valor in the struggle for world security. The great Southwest can be equally stalwart in forbearance and tolerance in pursuit of our democratic ideals.

EUGENIO LOPEZ
By Stuart J. Barnes

What was it the speaker had said
Of soldiers both living and dead
    Who bled for democracy?

"The debt of a nation is due
To valorous heroes like you,
    Who saved our democracy."

Eugenio, beaming with pride,
At home with his medals and bride,
    Believed in democracy.

"Tonight we shall dine and be gay,
And dance those grim mem'ries away,
Enjoying democracy."

The voice of the waiter was clear:
"We do not serve Mexicans here!"
Disgraced is democracy.

Washington D. C.
December, 1945

FAIR EMPLOYMENT PRACTICES ACT HEARINGS

before a
SUBCOMMITTEE OF THE
COMMITTEE ON EDUCATION AND LABOR
UNITED STATES SENATE
Seventy-Eighth Congress
Second Session
on S. 2048

A BILL TO PROHIBIT DISCRIMINATION IN EMPLOYMENT
BECAUSE OF RACE, CREED, COLOR, NATIONAL ORIGIN,
OR ANCESTRY
August 30, 31, September 6, 7, and 8, 1944.
Afternoon Session
(The subcommittee reconvened at 2:35 p. m., pursuant to
the recess.)

Senator CHAVEZ. The committee will come to order.

The testimony adduced before the committee up to now
has been in reference to the discrimination against the Negro
population of the country, and against the Jewish population
of the country. It is the purpose of the committee this afternoon
to listen to testimony with reference to discrimination against
other classes of minorities in the United States.

Before we call the witness that is to appear next, I would
like to have the clerk of the committee read into the record a
letter received by the chairman of the committee from Alonso
S. Perales, of the Committee of One Hundred of San Antonio,

86

Tex. I happen to know the witness personally and I am sure it would be quite a contribution to the information before the committee.

Before reading the letter, I would like to have inserted into the record this statement with reference to Mr. Perales' qualifications.

(The statement referred to follows:)

Perales, Alonso S., Lawyer, legal adviser to the United States electoral mission in Nicaragua, 1932. Born in Alice, Tex., October 17, 1898. Married. Graduated from public schools of Alice, Texas., and preparatory school, Washington, D. C. Attended School of Arts and Sciences, George Washington University; graduated from the School of Economics and Government, National University, A. B; and from National University Law School, LL. B.; admitted to Texas bar September 1925. Served with the United States Army in Texas during the World War; 2½ years in the Department of Commerce, Washington, D. C. Served in the Diplomatic Service of the United States as assistant to Hon. Sumner Welles; personal representative of the President of the United States in the Dominican Republic, 1922; assistant to the United States delegation, Conference on Central American Affairs, Washington D. C., 1922-23; assistant to Inter-American High Commission, Washington, D. C., 1923; attorney and interpreter, United States Delegation, Plebiscitary Commission (Gen. John J. Pershing, president), Tacna-Arica arbitration, 1925-26; special assistant to United States delegation to Sixth International Conference of American States, Habana, Cuba, 1928; attorney with agency of the United States, General and Special Claims Commission, United States and Mexico, 1928; attorney, United States electoral mission .in Nicaragua, 1928; special assistant to United States Arbitration, Washington, D. C., 1928-29; special legal assistant, Commission of Inquiry and Conciliation, Bolivia and Paraguay, Washington, D. C., 1929; assistant to United States delegation, Congress of Rectors, Deans, and Educators, Habana, Cuba, 1930; legal adviser to the United States electoral mission in Nicaragua in 1930. At present engaged in the private practice of law in San Antonio, Tex.

Mr. BADGER (reading):

COMMITTEE OF ONE HUNDRED
A Strictly Political Organization
San Antonio, Tex., September 6, 1944.

Hon. DENNIS CHAVEZ,
Chairman, Senate Committee on Education and Labor.
Senate Office Building., Washington, D. C.

MY DEAR SENATOR CHAVEZ:

We are indeed very sorry that because of our inability to secure a plane priority, we shall be deprived of the privilege of testifying before your honorable Committee pursuant to your kind telegraphic invitation. However, we wish to avail ourselves of this opportunity to voice the hope that the President's Committee on Fair Employment Practices may be made permanent by our National Congress at the earliest possible date, in fairness to all the minority groups in the United States, including Latin Americans, and for the good of our Nation as a whole.

There is a great deal of discrimination in the economic field in Texas, Arizona, Colorado, and California. There are quite a number of public establishments where persons of Mexican and Hispanic descent generally are not employed, and where they are employed they are not paid the salary or wage that Anglo-Americans receive for the same services. The Committee on Fair Employment Practice has relieved the situation in Government camps and in factories and shops where work is being done for the Federal Government, but in establishments, factories and shops over which said Committee has not jurisdiction, the situation remains the same. Should our National Congress see fit to make the Committee a permanent one, it would serve as a living example to private employers.

We understand Dr. Carlos E. Castañeda will testify before your committee on the 7th instant, and in this connection we wish to state that everything he is going to say to you gentlemen regarding discrimination against Latin Americans is true, and, furthermore, that he enjoys the confidence and respect of the 3,000,000 inhabitants of Mexican descent in the United States.

Referring to the social phase of discrimination in Texas, we are prepared to prove that discrimination exists against persons of Mexican and Hispanic descent, including members of the armed forces of our Nation, in 249 out of 254 counties in the State, and that said discrimination consists not only of slights and humiliations in restaurants, theaters, barber shops, and other public places of business, but also segregation in public schools and residential districts. Not only persons of Mexican lineage are victims

88

of such discrimination. Venezuelans, Hondurans, and Argentinians, some of them members of the Armies of said countries, have also been discriminated against.

For the past 4 years we have been asking the Texas Legislature to pass a law forbidding the humiliation of Mexicans and Hispanic people generally in this State, but it has absolutely refused to do so. Among the legislators who have actively opposed the enactment of such a law are Senator R. A. Weinert, of Seguin, and Representative Frank B. Voight, of New Braunfels. Seguin and New Braunfels are two German-American communities of Texas that have always distinguished themselves for their anti-Mexicanism.

There are some people who opine that the solution of this problem rests in waging an educational campaign among the Anglo-American element designed to show them the merits and qualities of the Mexicans and of the Hispanic race generally, but the overwhelming majority of us contend that in addition to such an educational program there is need for a Federal law prohibiting the humiliation of Mexicans and persons of Hispanic descent generally in any part of our country. A Federal law is necessary in order to put an end to this painful situation immediately. The educational program is useful, but it is very slow, and we have no time to lose. We are at war and in order to win it, we need unity among the peoples of the Americas. The best way to show all the inhabitants of Hispanic America that they are respected in our country is to pass a Federal law making it unlawful for anyone to humiliate them here. The citizens of Venezuela, Honduras, Argentina and the other Hispanic American Republics feel just as deeply hurt as the citizens of Mexico when they learn that there are places in the United States where members of their race, and above all their fellow-citizens, are humiliated; more so at this moment when more than a quarter of a million soldiers of Mexican descent are giving their blood for democracy. The resentment of these sister Republics of ours has reached the point where Mexico, for example, has become quite firm in her resolve not to send more workers to Texas until an end is put to these humiliations.

The writer has just returned from the Congress of the Inter-American Bar Association held in Mexico City from July 31 to August 8, at which the matter of racial discrimination, in all its phases, was thoroughly gone into, and you should have seen the attitude of the Hispanic-American delegates upon the subject. All of the Latin-American Republics, except three, were represented, and 47 bar associations from the United States were likewise represented. There were 450 delegates from the Western Hemisphere. The Congress went on record, unanimously, as condemning said discrimination, and they passed a resolution recommending to the Governments of the American Republics that a treaty be entered into by them to the effect that no country will permit the citizens of the other American states residing within its territory to be humiliated by any corporation, institution, society, organization, or person because of race, creed, color, or national origin, and, further, that the states of the Americas establish adequate penalties, through Federal legislation, for all cases in which the provisions of said treaty may be violated. It is thus seen, Senator Chavez, that the problem has become an international problem insofar as the Western Hemisphere is concerned, and one that should be settled by the Federal Government; and the sooner our Government takes the necessary steps to end the shameful situation existing in our country the better it will be for our Nation. We need the cooperation and good will of all the Hispanic American peoples not only now that we are at war but in the days of peace that are to follow. However, we shall never have their good will and cooperation until we learn to treat them and respect them as our equals. At present our governments are united, but the peoples of the Americas are not, precisely for that reason.

As regards the thousands of American citizens of Mexican descent who are fighting in the battle fronts, the best way to encourage them to continue fighting with enthusiasm is to pass a Federal law that will assure to them that our Federal Government does not intend to permit anyone to humiliate them or any member of their families, either in Texas or in any other State of the Union, merely because they are Mexicans by blood. Incidentally, it might be said in passing that the casualty lists published in the local newspapers show that from 50 to 75 percent of those from south Texas who are falling, either dead or wounded, are soldiers of Mexican descent. Our Federal Government owes it to these boys to make sure that when they return to the United States they will find the kind of democracy that they have been given to understand they are fighting for. It would be a great disappointment to them, to say the least, to find upon their return that they could not secure employment or that if they found it they could not receive equal wages for equal work merely because of their racial origin, or that the owner of any restaurant, barber shop, or theater could continue to humiliate them as he saw fit just because they were of Mexican descent. In this connection, permit us to cite a paragraph from a letter which we received recently from a young United States Army officer of Mexican descent who took part in the invasion of Normandy:

"The assault boat I was leading was sunk several hundred yards from the beach, but all of my men managed to swim safely ashore. It was a veritable hell. Sniper bullets, machine-gun fire, mortar and artillery shells, and personnel mines, took their toll of victims. I saw many of my close friends—officers and men - get shot right through the head by deadly sniper fire.

"When I think of the men left behind dead on the beaches, I wonder if the people at home understand this tremendous sacrifice. I wonder particularly if those who are charged with the responsibility of framing the peace to come fully realize the cost of victory. I pray, that, when the fighting is all done, our boys can go back with the utmost assurance that they can live and work in peace and that America still remains the symbol of liberty, justice, and freedom. I have sworn that if ever the combatants of this war are cheated of the things for which they risked their lives, and for which thousands of their comrades gave their lives, I shall take the stump loud and strong and shall not cease in my condemnation of such fraud."

In conclusion, allow us to emphasize, Senator Chavez, that it is most urgent that our Government make the Committee on Fair Employment Practice a permanent organization forbidding discrimination on account of race, color, creed, national origin or ancestry. This, in fairness to all the minority groups in our country, and as a token of friendship and respect for the people of the Hispanic-American Republics.

You may read this letter to the other members of your committee and you may incorporate same in the record of your hearing, if you wish.

Again thanking you for the invitation extended us, and regretting our inability to be present for the reason already stated, we remain

Sincerely yours,

Alonso S. Perales
Chairman

FAIR EMPLOYMENT PRACTICES ACT HEARINGS

before a
SUBCOMMITTEE OF THE COMMITTEE ON
EDUCATION AND LABOR, UNITED STATES SENATE.
Seventy-Ninth Congress
First Session on S. 101

A BILL TO PROHIBIT DISCRIMINATION IN EMPLOYMENT
BECAUSE OF RACE, CREED, COLOR, NATIONAL ORIGIN,
OR ANCESTRY
AND S. 459

A BILL TO ESTABLISH A FAIR EMPLOYMENT PRACTICE
COMMISSION AND TO AID IN ELIMINATING DISCRIMI-
NATION IN EMPLOYMENT BECAUSE OF RACE, CREED,
OR COLOR
March 12, 13, AND 14, 1945

STATEMENT OF DR. CARLOS E. CASTAÑEDA, SPECIAL
ASSISTANT ON LATIN-AMERICAN PROBLEMS TO THE
CHAIRMAN OF THE PRESIDENT'S COMMITTEE ON FAIR
EMPLOYMENT PRACTICE, BEFORE THE SENATE COM-
MITTEE ON LABOR AND EDUCATION IN THE HEARINGS
HELD SEPTEMBER 8, 1944, ON S BILL 2048, TO PROHIBIT
DISCRIMINATION BECAUSE OF RACE, CREED, COLOR,
NATIONAL ORIGIN OR ANCESTRY.

For more than twenty years I have been interested in the
problems arising from the various forms of discrimination against
the Spanish-speaking people of the Southwest. I have been an
active member of the League of United Latin-American Citizens,
Loyal Latin-American Citizens, the Catholic Association for International Peace on its Committee on Inter-American Relations,
The Southwestern Committee on Latin-American Culture, The
Inter-American Bibliographical and Library Association, and other
national and international associations interested in the promotion of better relations and understanding between Anglos and
Latin-Americans.

I was appointed Senior Fair Practice Examiner in Region X, comprising the states of Texas, New Mexico and Louisiana, on August 23, 1943, and was made Acting Regional Director in charge of the Dallas Office until December 17, 1943, when I was made Special Assistant to the Chairman on Latin-American problems, in which capacity I have served the Committee since that time.

Our Spanish-speaking population in the Southwest, made up almost entirely of American citizens of Mexican extraction and Mexican nationals are ill-dressed, ill-fed, ill-cared for medically, and ill-educated, all because of the low economic standard to which they have been relegated as the result of the general policy of restricting their employment and utilization to the lowest paid, least desirable, and most exacting jobs from the physical standpoint. Not only have they been restricted to the lowest bracket jobs, but even in these jobs they have been paid wages below the minimum of sound and tested going rates in all the various industries in which they have been employed.

In the investigation of complaints filed with the President's Committee on Fair Employment Practice involving discrimination against Spanish-speaking Latin-American citizens of Mexican extraction and Mexican nationals, I have visited the states of Arizona, California, Colorado, New Mexico, and Texas and I have had an opportunity to study conditions at first hand. I have gathered statistics that reveal the magnitude of the problem insofar as it affects what is the largest underprivileged minority group in the Southwest.

In the State of Arizona, according to the 1940 census, there is a total population of 449,261, of which about 30% are persons of Mexican extraction. Of the 160,000 Spanish-speaking persons of Mexican extraction, only 24,902 are foreign-born Mexican nationals. The mining industry in Arizona normally employs between 15,000 and 16,000 men. The percentage of Mexicans, that is American citizens of Mexican extraction in the main, is over 50% on an average and in many mining centers it runs as high as 80%. In round figures there are between 8,000 and 10,000 persons of Mexican extraction employed in the mining industry in Arizona. Their employment is restricted, however, very largely 'o common labor and semi-skilled jobs and even the urgent need of Manpower as the result of the war has not broken down the prejudice which bars large numbers of skilled laborers from promotion in order that they might be utilized at their highest skill and thus contribute more fully and more efficiently to the total war effort.

The total population of California, according to the 1940 census, is 6,907,387. The number of persons of Mexican extraction according to the same census is 457,900, of which 134,312 are foreign-born, or Mexican nationals. In the Los Angeles area with a population of 1,673,000, the persons of Mexican descent number about 315,000, or approximately 20%. As late as the summer of 1942, more than six months after Pearl Harbor, only 5,000 persons of Mexican extraction were employed in basic industries. This figure was ascertained in a survey conducted by the CIO in November, 1942, among whose membership there are over 10,000 Mexican-Americans.

Equally revealing as regards the failure to utilize more fully the Mexican labor supply along the West Coast of California are the figures given in a study made by the War Manpower Commission as late as April 13, 1943. Out of the 315,000 persons of Mexican extraction, only 10,000 were being employed in the Southern California shipyards, 2,000 in the San Diego aircraft industry, and 7,500 in the Los Angeles aircraft industry, making a total of 19,500 employed in essential war industries in the area included between Los Angeles and San Diego. Much better utilization was being made of Mexican labor in the San Francisco area where, with a total population of some 30,000 persons of Mexican extraction, 8,000 were engaged in basic war industries. In percentage, 22% of the Mexican-Americans were being employed in San Francisco, while only 6% had found employment in basic war industries in the Los Angeles and San Diego area.

The failure to utilize the available Mexican labor supply in California, traceable in a good measure to prejudice, was not limited to essential and war industries. In an institute sponsored by the Los Angeles City and County Schools and the Southern California Council of Inter-American Affairs to discuss the problem of "What is the Vocational Future of Mexican-Americans", held on February 19, 1944, Mr. Sid Panush, Personnel Examiner for the Los Angeles County Civil Service Commission, stated that out of 16,000 employees, about 400 were of Mexican extraction; that is, a 2½% of the total amount. Mr. John F. Fisher, Director for the Los Angeles Civil Service Commission explained, at the same time, that out of the 16,500 civil service employees in the city government about 450 were of Mexican extraction, which makes the percentage the same as that in the County.

The population of Colorado, according to the 1940 census, is 1,123,296. The number of foreign-born Mexicans is given as 6,360. In the southern part of Colorado, where the larger portion of the Mexican-Americans reside, many of them descendants of the first settlers in the area, there are approximately some 50,000 Spanish-

94

speaking Latin-American citizens of Mexican extraction. In Denver, in Pueblo, and in Trinidad itself these Mexican-Americans are restricted in their employment to common labor jobs in the main. The number of Mexican-Americans employed in the steel industry, in Civil Service jobs, in military installations and in other war and essential industries, is less than 6% of the available Mexican labor supply. Mexican-Americans have been refused employment in clerical and office positions, and they have been denied promotion and upgrading in accord with both seniority and ability in private industry and by military installations in the area.

In the State of New Mexico, with a population of 531,818, there are 8,875 foreign-born Mexicans according to the 1940 census. The number of Mexican-Americans is about 40% of the total population. In the southwestern corner of the state there is a large mining area between Santa Rita and Silver City. Investigation of complaints by Mexican-American citizens in this area has shown that from 40 to 60% of the men employed by the mining companies are of Mexican extraction; that they are barred from promotion into certain departments and that they are refused upgrading into skilled jobs because of their national origin.

Texas, with a population of 6,414,824, has approximately 1,000,000 Mexican-Americans. According to the 1940 census there were 159,266 foreign-born Mexican nationals in the state, or about 1/6 of the total number of Spanish-speaking persons of Mexican descent were Mexican nationals. Less than 5% of the total number of persons of Mexican extraction in Texas are employed at the present time in war and essential industries. Such industries as have given employment to Mexican labor have restricted them to common or unskilled labor jobs largely, regardless of their ability, training, or qualifications. In the oil, aircraft and mining industries, in the numerous military installations, in the munitions factories and shipyards, and in the public utility corporations, such as gas, light, and transportation companies, their employment has been limited and their opportunities for advancement restricted.

The prevalent idea or belief among employers for the various industries, personnel managers, officials of military installations, and various government agencies in the Southwest is that the Mexican-American is incapable of doing other than manual, physical labor; that he is unfit for the type of skilled labor required by industry and the crafts. Back of this belief is prejudice.

Mr. A. O. Anderson, Personnel Department, Lockheed Aircraft Corporation, has stated that in the company's two Los Angeles plants, 10 to 15% of the employees are Mexican-Americans;

that 80% of these are women; that they work principally in detailed assembly, general assembly and riveting. He added:

"Mexican-American women workers have shown that they are capable of adapting themselves to difficult job conditions more readily than others; that this is, they are less bothered by physical discomfort, fumes, and varying temperatures.

"We have many Mexican-Americans who now perform some of the more complicated assembly jobs and others who assumed supervisorial responsibilities."

This statement, repeated by all those who have had the courage to give the Mexican-American an opportunity to work at other than manual jobs, shows that the Mexican-American can be integrated into American industry and that the failure of the Mexican-American to enter the ranks of industry has been largely due to prejudice. This fact is borne out of Mr. Floyd L. Wohlwend, Member WMC Management-Labor Committee and Personnel Officer in the California Shipbuilding Corporation, one of the largest employers in the Southwest, who stated:

"Generally speaking our Mexican workers for the most part have come to us in recent months . . . They just lately began to filter in and our majority of Mexican employees have come in the last 18 months . . . The Mexican-Americans are not only capable, but the variety of jobs at which they can be utilized is limitless if employers, managers, and general management simply will make a point of using them . . . Production records indicate that they have an equal aptitude with other groups or other individuals . . . They are definitely on a par . . . there is no difference."

That the Mexican-American, if given an opportunity, is capable of performing any job in industry was affirmed by Mr. Robert Metzner, President, Pacific Sound Equipment Company, who stated that his company had begun to employ Mexican-Americans in 1942 as the result of the increasing shortage of labor in the Los Angeles area. He declared that:

"As the result of training, Mexican-Americans qualified for skilled jobs, inspectors, both Class A and Class B, radio repairmen, machinists, Turret lathe operators, spot welders and leadmen."

When the Mexican-American asks for equal economic opportunities he is not asking for a favor or privilege. Dr. C. D. Trillingham, Superintendent of the Los Angeles Schools, stated their case well when he said during the Institute at Los Angeles on February 19, 1944:

96

"We are not being asked to grant something to the Mexican-American out of our benevolence if you please, but to grant them that to which they are entitled along with us, certain inalienable rights as human beings . . ."

The belief held by some that certain racial or national groups have different mechanical aptitudes, a conviction that is at the bottom of the prejudice held against Mexican-Americans, is completely unfounded in fact. Mr. Richard Ibañez, Member of the City Council of Upland, California, who is also a member of the Board of Governors of the California Housing Association, was merely repeating what is well known by students of anthropology, when he said:

"Any one who has taken an anthropology course knows that the Gods gave their skills equally to those of dark skin and light skin."

The urgent need of manpower, in view of the increasing shortage of labor, forced industry to give the Mexican-American an opportunity, but not without the greatest reluctance and misgivings. Wherever he has been given an opportunity he has shown the ability to learn and produce with the same efficiency as members of any other group. To what extent has the President's Committee on Fair Employment Practice enabled war and essential industries to utilize more extensively this neglected pool of labor and given an opportunity to the ready and willing Mexican-American to contribute more fully to the war effort is shown by the following statistics on cases involving Mexican-Americans handled by the President's Committee on Fair Employment Practice during its first year of operation.

In Region X, comprising the States of New Mexico, Texas and Louisiana, 124 complaints were filed and docketed. These included complaints against oil companies, shipyards, public utility companies, Government agencies, military installations, mining companies, and chemical plants. These different agencies and industries had either refused employment to qualified workers, or denied them proper classification and adequate upgrading in accord with their seniority, experience and ability, or paid them a differential wage scale because of their national origin. Of the 124 complaints, without having to recur to a public hearing, through interviews and conferences with employers, 68 were settled; that is, 54.9%. The settlement of these complaints resulted not only in the correction of the individual complaint but in bringing about a relaxation of general discriminatory policies which resulted in the fuller utilization of available Mexican labor by the industries and agencies involved. The 124 complaints filed, represent about 37% of all the cases docketed in Region X involving other minority groups.

In region XII, comprising the states of California, Nevada, and Arizona, out of 279 cases filed and docketed, involving discrimination, 63, or 22.6% were complaints by Mexican nationals and Mexican-Americans. Some of these have been settled, but the majority are still being processed.

Bill S 2048, being considered by your Committee to prohibit discrimination in employment based on race, creed, color, national origin or ancestry will enable three million Mexican-American citizens throughout this country, from California to New York and from Illinois to Texas, to secure equal economic opportunities in employment in the post-war era. The President's Committee on Fair Employment Practice is a war agency, designed to secure equal participation in the total war effort by all Americans regardless of race, creed, color or national origin. During its short period of operation it has done m u c h to integrate Mexican-Americans in war and essential industries and in Government employ. Mexican-Americans have generously responded to their responsibility in the present world struggle for the victory of the democracies. They have unstintingly made the last sacrifice on a world-wide battle front in order that all peoples may enjoy the blessings of freedom and peace. Equal economic opportunities, the right to work and earn a decent living on a par with all other persons regardless of race, creed, color, national origin or ancestry, is a basic principle of American democracy which will be safeguarded by the establishment of such an agency as Bill S 2048 proposes.

------·••◆┃┃◆••·------

STATEMENT OF
DR. CARLOS E. CASTAÑEDA, REGIONAL DIRECTOR, FAIR EMPLOYMENT PRACTICE COMMITTEE, REGION 10, SAN ANTONIO, TEXAS.

Dr. CASTAÑEDA. I am Dr. Carlos Castañeda, of San Antonio, Texas, regional director for F. E. P. C., region No. 10 former professor in the history department of the University of Texas, where I have taught for 17 years, and I am now on leave of absence to work for the committee.

Senator CHAVEZ. Have you a statement that you care to make before the committee?

Dr. CASTAÑEDA. Yes, Senator, I have a statement which

98

I would like to present at this time.

Senator CHAVEZ. All right.

Dr. CASTAÑEDA. Eighteen months of investigation in connection with complaints filed with the President's Committee on Fair Employment Practice involving Mexican-Americans in Texas, New Mexico, Colorado, Arizona, and California, shows that in spite of the constantly increasing demand for manpower for the successful prosecution of the war, the Mexican-American reservoir of available labor has been neither exhausted nor fully utilized at the highest skill of the individual worker.

In the oil industry, basic and essential to the war effort, Mexican-Americans have been refused employment in other than common labor, yardman, and janitor classifications regardless of qualifications or training in higher skills. The practice is so firmly entrenched that it has been reduced to the blueprint stage. Employment charts in general use throughout the oil industry restrict the employment of Mexican-Americans to the three positions mentioned.

The railroads and the brotherhoods and railways unions have likewise generally restricted the utilization of available Mexican labor supply. By Mexican, no distinction is made between Mexican nationals and American citizens of Mexican extraction, who are restricted in general to common labor, trackmen, general maintenance labor, and car droppers, regardless of previous training, time of service, or other qualifications.

The mining industry in the Southwest with very few exceptions employs Mexicans only in common labor and semiskilled jobs. In many instances they are restricted from underground work, where wages are higher and the danger is less. Mexicans can be oiler-helpers, crane operators helpers, and helpers to most skilled jobs and positions and machine operators, but they never can be employed or classed as master craftsmen or machine operators.

In military installations throughout the Southwest, where large numbers of civilians are employed, Mexicans are hired but not always on a level of equality, be they of American citizenship or not. Frequently they are found in jobs that do not utilize their highest skill. They have been promoted slowly and with evident reluctance.

Public utility companies and telephone and telegraph companies throughout the Southwest have failed to utilize the available Mexican labor supply in other than common-labor jobs, with rate exceptions here and there.

The aircraft and shipbuilding industries, be it said in all

99

justice, have given the Mexican worker practically equal opportunities to develop his various skills and to attain promotion in accord with his qualifications. This is true also of munition and arms factories. But since these are essentially war industries that on VE - and VJ-day will not be readily reconverted to civilian goods production, their workers will be the first to seek employment in the newly acquired industrial skills.

Wives, sisters, and other women relatives of men in the armed forces have been refused employment in war and essential industries because of their Mexican origin. One Maria Garcia, of Clifton, Arizona, declared that her son was in the Army; that he had previously worked in the mines and had been the chief support of the family; and that when she learned that women were being employed by the mining company, she applied for a job, but was told that no Mexican women could be hired.

Another complainant, one Cleo M. Garcia, speaking for herself and seven others, said, "We applied at an ordnance plant in north Texas. Here is what was told me: "We cannot hire you because the Latin-American people, men and women, are not capable of doing war work." When I asked him why, and how did he know that we were not capable of doing work if he did not give us a chance to prove we could, and that it is our right as much as anybody else to work in this kind of work, he very rudely disregarded my question and told me that there was a lot of janitor work that had to de done, and that was the only place where they could place us or any other Mexicans. We feel this is an injustice to our boys by holding up production when there's a lot of people that is willing to work to speed victory."

Is the Mexican unfit or incapable of adaptation to other than common or agricultural labor? Mr. Floyd L. Wohlwend, member W. M. C. Management-Labor Committee, and personnel officer in the California Shipbuilding Corporation, stated recently:

"Generally speaking our Mexican workers for the most part have come to us in recent months . . . They just lately began to filter in and our majority of Mexican employees have come in the last 18 months. . . . The Mexican-Americans are not only capable, but the variety of jobs at which they can be utilized is limitless if employers, managers, and general management simply will make a point of using them . . . Production records indicate that they have an equal aptitude with other groups or other individuals . . They are definitely on a par . . there is no difference."

Mr. Robert Metzner, president, Pacific Sound Equipment Co., whose company began to employ Mexican-Americans in 1942, impelled by the stortage of laborers, adds:

"As the result of training, Mexican-Americans qualified for skilled jobs, inspectors, both class A and B, radio repairmen, machinists, turret lathe operators, spot welders and leadmen."

Increasing shortage of labor has forced industry to give the Mexican-American a try, but not without the greatest reluctance and misgiving. Employers agree generally that they produce with the same efficiency as members of any other group. The Fair Employment Practice Committee, set up by Executive Order 9346, has helped to overcome the reluctance of employers to utilize more fully and effectively this remaining pool of available labor. How effective it was in overcoming discriminatory practices in employment and proper utilization has been described in the statement made before this committee in the hearings held during the previous session of Congresss on September 8, 1944, in connection with Senate bill S 2048, indentical to bill S. 101 now before you.

The President's Committee on Fair Employment Practice is a war agency. During its short period of operation it has effectively contributed to the partial integration of Mexican-Americans and the other minority groups in war and essential industries and in the Government employ. Bill S. 101, now being considered by your committee, will assure equal economic opportunities, the right to work and earn a decent living on a part with all other persons regardless of race, creed, color, national origin or ancestry, to all Americans now and in the post-war era. The right to work and to earn a decent living without discrimination is a basic principle of American democracy which will be safeguarded by the establishment of such an agency as bill S. 101 proposes.

Senator CHAVEZ. Does that conclude your statement?

Dr. CASTAÑEDA. Yes, Senator.

Senator CHAVEZ. Doctor, I would like to ask you one or two questions. You have been teaching in the history department of the University of Texas for how many years?

Dr. CASTAÑEDA For 17 years, Senator.

Senator CHAVEZ. Within the State of Texas there are many Mexicans?

Dr. CASTAÑEDA. Yes, that is correct, Senator.

Senator CHAVEZ. Many of those so-called Mexicans are native-born citizens of the State of Texas, and of the United States. Is that correct?

Dr. CASTAÑEDA. That is correct.

Senator CHAVEZ. And a portion of them are immigrant population Mexican nationals?

101

Dr. CASTAÑEDA. Yes, Senator.

Senator CHAVEZ. Have you been able to observe yourself the economic treatment of both classes of those people, both, the so-called Mexican-Texan, and the Mexican national?

Dr. CASTAÑEDA. Yes, Senator. In connection with the work of the committee, and also in the years previous to the establishment of the committee, I have been interested in the condition of the Mexican-American, or the Latin American, in the State of Texas. There are in Texas approximately 1,000,000 persons of Mexican extraction, of which more than 60 percent are American citizens. In employment practices there is no difference made whatsoever between a Mexican national and an American citizen of Mexican extraction. If a worker's name is a Spanish one, he is considered as Mexican and treated as such.

During the days of relief, the various agents who distributed relief, allowed much less to Mexican families on relief than to Anglo-American families, anybody with a Spanish name, be he an American citizen or not, and they did it on the assumption that a Mexican does not have to eat so much, that he is not used to eating butter and bacon and other rich foods, and that if they gave it to them it might make them sick.

Senator CHAVEZ. Well, we have h e a r d that a similar argument was used by some of the State governments in the South. So it is not particularly new. But the reason for my question is because we have heard so much of this good-will business, about how much the people of the United States, and the United States Government, love the people south of the border. Only lately, as you know, we had the big meeting in Mexico City where there developed that charming charter of democracy, the Chapultepec Charter. How much effect do you think that charter, or our lip service, or our so-called feeling of good-will, will have on the average man south of the border when he knows that the conditions that you have just described to the committee exist in Texas?

Dr. CASTAÑEDA. Senator, I would rather leave the answer to the question, which is obvious, to anybody else.

Senator CHAVEZ. But from your experience as a member of the F. E. P. C. agency, you know that those conditions that you have described exist not only in Texas but throughout the entire Southwest, wherever Americans of Mexican or Spanish extraction live?

Dr. CASTAÑEDA. In speaking before Clubs interested in Pan-Americanism, this question has been asked, "Do the people south of the Rio Grande feel kindly toward this country?" And I

102

have had to say that there are many people south of the Rio Grande who seriously doubt the protestations of friendship made, when the ways in which the Mexican-Americans and Mexican nationals are treated in the Southwest are reported in Mexican newspapers.

Senator CHAVEZ. In order to be fair, wouldn't you say, though, that as far as the Government is concerned, including the great State of Texas, they are trying to remedy the situation?

Dr. CASTAÑEDA. Yes; I think there is a sincere effort being made. We have been trying that for many years and at present there are even greater efforts being made through persuasion, but the roots of prejudice are so deep-seated in the Southwest that it is going to take something more than persuasion to bring about a change of conditions.

Senator CHAVEZ. You would, then, say that legislation such as is proposed by senate bill 101, which contains some enforcement powers, would help out the educational features and efforts that are being made by good-hearted people?

Dr. CASTAÑEDA. As an employee of the Fair Employment Practices Committee I could not make such a statement for fear it could be possible to be interpreted in the wrong light.

Senator CHAVEZ. Why should an employee of the Federal Government, just because he happens to be an employee of the Federal Government, not be allowed, in our democracy, to express his opinion?

Dr. CASTAÑEDA. It might be interpreted as an effort to perpetuate the agency that employs him, which is temporary.

Senator CHAVEZ. Well, suppose we were to abolish that agency, and its personnel, would you still be for a Fair Employment Practices Committee?

Dr. CASTAÑEDA. Yes. I would say that we in Texas - and I am speaking now not as an employee of the F. E. P. C. but as one of those who has worked for many years in trying to eradicate discrimination against Mexican-Americans—I would say that we in Texas are convinced that the solution to the problem is legislation, legislation that can be effectively enforced so as to restrain that small minority, but very aggressive minority, that, because of ignorance, perhaps, practice discrimination that brings shame upon our American democracy.

Senator CHAVEZ. And isn't it true that the more ignorant they are, the more is their sense of superiority emphasized?

Dr. CASTAÑEDA. That has always appeared to me to be the case.

103

Senator CHAVEZ. May I also add this, that the sponsors of Senate bill 101 are not interested in the personnel, Doctor, of the F. E. P. C., whatsoever, but they are interested in the legislation.

Dr. CASTAÑEDA. Thank you, Senator.

Senator CHAVEZ. Thank you, Doctor, for your very fine statement.

Mr. Quevedo. Please state your name, Mr. Quevedo, to the reporter.

--------◄◦▌◦►--------

STATEMENT OF EDUARDO QUEVEDO, PRESIDENT, COORDINATING COUNCIL FOR LATIN-AMERICAN YOUTH, LOS ANGELES, CALIFORNIA.

Mr. QUEVEDO. My name is Eduardo Quevedo. I am the president of the Coordinating Council for Latin-American Youth and I reside in Los Angeles, Calif.

Mr. Chairman, for years, a great number of the English-speaking Americans in the United States have believed that the people of Mexico and the Latin-Americans in the Western Hemisphere harbored a feeling of hatred against them. In fact, immediately after the treacherous attack on Pearl Harbor, rumors were spread by our enemies that Mexico was pro-German. This is erroneous.

Very recently the Honorable Adolfo de la Huerta, former President of Mexico, and a great friend of the American people stated to me, and I quote:

"How can anyone conceive the idea that we hate Anglo-Americans when the record shows that when Mexico is at peace an Anglo-American can travel from Juarez, Chihuahua, to Mexico City, at all times treated with courtesy, friendliness, and cordiality. In contrast, when a Mexican or Latin-American enters the United States his attention is immediately drawn to numerous cases of discrimination toward his people. I am sure that the word to use is not hatred. They have resentment, perhaps even fear, because they doubt the sincerity of the good-neighbor policy. When the true good-neighbor policy is demonstrated here in the United States to the 3,000,000 Mexican-Americans with fair treatment and better human understanding, the Mexican and Latin-American countries will believe in the true sincerity of their neighbors to the north."

I believe this gentleman was expressing the sentiment of many others.

In a previous conference with Mr. Nelson D. Rockefeller, who was then Coordinator of Inter-American Affairs, he outlined to me the fine work that his office was doing outside of continental United States. I then felt it my duty, as an American, to impress Mr. Rockefeller with the necessity of doing the same fine work within the United States. Because I am convinced that the 3,000,000 Spanish-speaking Americans constitute the soundingboard for the Western Hemisphere, at this time. I am convinced that the Coordinator took a wise step by establishing some of the activities of his office within our own country, and certainly has been instrumental in bringing about better understanding, and is helping us in the direction of an early assimilation.

The interviews I have just related, and many others too numerous to mention, came about as a result of my active participation in various social and civic organizations - activities that I first became interested in in my early youth and have been carrying on in California for the past 18 years.

I have been an active member for many years of the Federation of Spanish-American Voters, Inc.; president of the Coordinating Council for Latin-American Youth; officer of the Citizens' Committee on Latin-American Youth, appointed by the Los Angeles County Board of Supervisors; Adult Americanization Program of the Roosevelt High School; I was appointed by the former Governor of California, Culver L. Olson, to the Committee Investigating Discriminatory Practices in the Whittier State School; Director of the Los Angeles Mexican Chamber of Commerce; field commissioner of the Boy Scouts of America; and many other national associations interested in better understanding between the Anglo and Latin-American.

In fairness to justice, I feel it my responsibility to bring to the attention of this committee the fact that there are on the west coast industries which have seemingly tried since the beginning of the war, and undoubtedly some of them before our present conflict, to be as fair as possible to the minorities. Among them I can mention the California Shipbuilding Corporation at Terminal Island, Calif., whose officers, in conjunction with Navy officials, went out of their way to help me clear many thousands of Mexican nationals through proper authorized Government channels, and who employ and retain them to this day without any discrimination that I know of.

That holds true, also, for the American Brakeshoe & Foundry Co., and the Owl Drug Co., of California. It is also true that

Lockheed Aircraft, Douglas Aircraft, and others now have what we may call a fair policy, these latter ones as a result of the efforts of the President's Committee on Fair Employment Practice.

However, as an American, I feel it my duty also to report at this time the other side of the picture, and this is not a bright one.

I have information from reliable sources that there are files to show that discrimination is increasing in the area of Southern California.

Indications from F. E. P. C. files show that discrimination is increasing in this area. During the past 4 months the "walk in" or unreferred cases validated by F. E. P. C. have been as follows: November 1944, 12; December 1944, 16; January 1945, 20; and February 1945, 23. The total number of cases validated since the opening of the office, September 16, 1943, in this area, is 488. Private businesses have been the parties charged in 79 percent of the cases; Government agencies in 17 percent of the cases, and labor unions in 4 percent of the cases.

In the category of race, under the reasons for discrimination, there has been a noticeable increase from 59 percent on September 1, 1944, to 62 percent on December 31, 1944. However, the category of creed has decreased from 14 percent to 12 percent; and national origin has decreased from 27 to 22 percent. The persons of the Jewish faith and Mexicans have been reluctant to report cases of discrimination and the indication is that they still are, despite the increasing reports of numerous incidents.

The types of discrimination show alarming increases in two categories. Refusals to hire have increased from 39.2 to 45 percent and discriminatory working conditions, from 25.9 to 33 percent since September 1944. Testimony given by complainants indicate that the subtle statement "No openings today," made to minorities 6 months ago, has been changed now to a bold, "We are not hiring your kind any more; we never wanted you anyway." Other statements are "Let's make it so tough for the _____ that they'll quit;" and threats of bodily harm have been reported. While discriminatory discharges have remained at 18 percent, discriminatory union conditions have decreased from 16.5 to 4 percent since September 1944.

Senator CHAVEZ. Let me get that right. The percentage of 16.5 percent was in what year?

Mr. QUEVEDO. Up to September of 1944 it was 16.5 percent.

Senator CHAVEZ. That is where the unions were doing the discriminating?

Mr. QUEVEDO. That is right.

Senator CHAVEZ. And that has now been reduced to 4 percent?

Mr. QUEVEDO. That is right, sir.

Thirty-six percent of the cases have had to be dismissed on merits mainly because of high absenteeism and tardiness rates, and refusals to accept assigments in outlying plants when their nearby branches were reducing personnel or being closed. When the absenteeism and tardiness rates were investigated a direct relation was found in the housing and transportation problems.

It was found that a disproportionate number of minority group workers are having to travel 30, 50, and 80 miles per day to and from industries because they must live in designated areas which have been prohibited from expansion by restrictions elsewhere. Reports show that only 3,000 Negro families are in public housing projects; 550 families in restricted and vacated areas; and only 500 families in privately constructed war housing units. Negroes have filed 55 percent of the current eligible applications for public war housing while they constitute only about 4 percent of the population. The reports show further that these conditions have caused over-crowding, "hotbeds," and transportation problems which, in many instances, have resulted in high absenteeism and tardiness rates. Of course the industries are interested in the efficient and constant employee.

Other indications may be inferred from a special 2-day survey on January 23-24, 1945, made in Six Los Angeles County U. S. E. S. offices. The report states that "The special 2-day tally should, however, reflect with reasonable accuracy the general proportion of Negroes in the various labor markets at present." Reception contacts were as follows: Negro percentage of total, Los Angeles (Eleventh and Flower Sts.) 14.2; Los Angeles (Casual Labor Office) 79; San Pedro, 25.7; Wilmington, 18.9; Long Beach, 4.8; and Huntington Park, 14.6. It has been impossible to get such figures on other minority groups.

Despite the unemployment figures mentioned above, the following statements are found in current cases and have been made in conferences:

1. We will reconsider the employment of Negroes if a directive is issued by higher authorities.

2. We employ Negroes and Mexicans in our Los Angeles plant, but we don't think it can work out, out here.

3. The confidential information we have indicates that the integration of workers has not been successful.

4. I want to be fair about this but the United States Employment Service seems to send me only Negro workers. My white workers are beginning to talk and ask why we have to hire so many, while none are hired over there.

5. The other Jews here don't complain about discrimination.

6. The Mexicans seem to be better fitted for that type of (dirty) work.

7. One of our oldest employees, in number of years, is a Jew.

I have individual cases, Mr. Chairman, and I would like to call your attention to two or three of them, and If I may, I would like to file this report, showing a number of individual cases, by name, with the committee.

Senator CHAVEZ. Well, you refer to the two or three cases that you want to, and then you may file the remainder of the list with the committee.

Mr. QUEVEDO. Mrs. Mary Delgado, of 2021½ Irving Avenue, San Diego, complained against the Consolidated Aircraft Co. and Mrs. Peggy Clayton, of the personnel department, stated that she was refused employment because she was of Mexican descent.

Senator CHAVEZ. May I say that I recall that name very vividly. That happened about 3 years ago when the war effort first started around the San Diego area. I had a letter from this girl and two other girls, that the three of them were graduates of high schools in the city of San Diego; the three of them wrote passing English, good English; and every one of them stated that the city of San Diego had provided training that would qualify them to go to work in aircraft industry, but that they had been turned down, notwithstanding their qualifications and their training that the citizens had paid for, because they happened to be of Mexican descent.

I wrote to Mr. Fleet, at that time the president of the company, and I am glad to say that I think the matter was rectified.

Mr. QUEVEDO. That matter was corrected, Senator, but many, many others are not yet corrected and won't be until Senate Bill 101 goes through.

Lee J. Montoya, 3431 Smith Street, Los Angeles, complains against the Pacific Fruit Express Co., their car department at Los Angeles that they refused to up-grade seven Mexican nationals whc had seniority rights, but that new comers took preference.

108

Miss Elis M. Tipton, 213 South San Dimas Avenue, San Dimas, Calif., has a complaint against the San Dimas Orange Growers Association and the San Dimas Leon Association, of San Dimas, Calif., of discrimination against Mexican workers; that it has been their policy to do so for the past 20 years; and that those living in close proximity to plants have to travel far to find employment.

The others run along the same line, and I ask your permission to file that at this time with the committee.

Senator CHAVEZ. That may be done.

(The list of discriminatory cases submitted will be found on file with the committee.)

Mr. QUEVEDO. I would like, with your permission, Mr. Chairman, to recall to your attention the quotation that I just mentioned by Adolfo de la Huerta, the former President of Mexico. You will recall that he said "when Mexico is at peace an Anglo-American can travel from one end of the Nation to the other, being treated with courtesy, friendliness, and cordiality." I asked him what he meant or intended to imply when he said "when Mexico is at peace". I remember his answer distinctly. He said, "the reason I put it there is because I want my people to be treated in peacetime in your country as well as they have been treated in wartime."

Then in Los Angeles County itself we have better than 300,000 Spanish-speaking Americans. In the entire State of California there are very close to three-quarters of a million.

Senator CHAVEZ. Are you talking now of citizens of the United States?

Mr. QUEVEDO. No; that is the total population of that particular group. But the best estimates and surveys made show that out of the 310,000 Americans of Mexican extraction residing in the county of Los Angeles, State of California, 65 percent are either American-born or naturalized citizens of the United States.

Senator CHAVEZ. Then they are citizens of the United States?

Mr. QUEVEDO. Correct.

Senator CHAVEZ. Subject to all the duties and obligations that go with citizenship. They go to war, do they not?

Mr. QUEVEDO. Well, Mr. Chairman, with your permission I would say that this statement is heard quite often in Los Angeles and throughout the State. Not only do the American citizens of Mexican extraction go to war but in fact it is common knowledge that the only time in the history of the United States where these

109

people have been treated with equality was immediately after Pearl Harbor when they were called to the colors to wear the uniform.

In discussing some of these cases at public meetings, in committee work, it is interesting to note that the parents, and brothers and sisters of these boys in uniform are not anxious to see the war end, Mr. Senator, we always talk of an early victory and of the peace that will follow, but their reaction is this: "We are not happy about it; when our boys come back we are going to be treated just as bad as we were treated before."

Mothers of soldiers who have died in the front lines of battle today cannot come to visit their folks in the United States, although their sons were good enough to go to war.

So there is a strong sentiment, and I can safely say here in the name of the Coordinating Council for Latin-American Youth, which represents 72 organizations with an approximate membership of 15,000 in the county of Los Angeles, and we have various other organizations, that the entire American population of Mexican extraction in the State of California is 100 percent for the passage of Senate bill No. 101.

Senator CHAVEZ. Now, let's get that a little clear. You represent a certain group of people in California?

Mr. QUEVEDO. That is right.

Senator CHAVEZ. Who happen to be of Spanish or Mexican extraction?

Mr. QUEVEDO. That is right.

Senator CHAVEZ. But they are citizens of the United States and naturally, probably believe in the right of petition, like the rest of us do?

Mr. QUEVEDO. Yes.

Senator CHAVEZ. What is it that you feel that the people that you represent want, or that the Americans of Mexican or Spanish extraction desire from the Government, with reference to this bill; what is it?

Mr. QUEVEDO. That is a fine question, Mr. Chairman.

"We want to assume all our responsibilities and obligations to our Government; we want to do our duty by Government. We do not want any special privileges whatsoever. We do not even want a job, or feel that we are entitled to a job, just because we happen to be of a certain racial extraction. But inasmuch as we accept our duties and responsibilities as Americans, even to the extent of losing our lives as Americans, we do not want to be deprived of a job on account of our ancestry or national origin or race. We desire an equality in opportunity and to have some dignity as citizens."

Senator CHAVEZ. I think that is a fine answer. Thank you, Mr. Quevedo.

Mr. QUEVEDO. Thank you.

Senator CHAVEZ. Does that conclude your statement?

Mr. QUEVEDO. That concludes my remarks; yes.

Senator CHAVEZ. Mr. Paz. Please state your name and your connection for the reporter.

STATEMENT OF FRANK PAZ, PRESIDENT OF THE SPANISH-SPEAKING PEOPLE'S COUNCIL OF CHICAGO.

Mr. PAZ. My name is Frank Paz. I am a resident of Chicago, Ill. and a member of Hull House in Chicago. I am also the president of the Spanish Speaking People's Council of Chicago, interested in the establishment of a permanent F. E. P. C.

Senator CHAVEZ. How much of a population, of Spanish or Mexican extraction, is there in Chicago?

Mr. PAZ. In the Chicago area there are 45,000 Spanish-speaking people, residents of the Chicago area.

Senator CHAVEZ. And is that in Cook County alone or does it extend into Indiana?

Mr. PAZ. I would include in those 45,000 people, part of Indiana as well as the southern part of Wisconsin, including Milwaukee.

Mr. Chairman, I am interested - as well as the other people residing in the Chicago area of Spanish extraction - in the passage of Senate Bill 101, for the simple reason that we are interested fundamentally in the principles of American democracy.

In American democracy there is no room or place for racial discrimination. Our people, as other speakers have already said, do not want any special privileges. All they want is the right to enjoy full citizenship.

111

I will tell you the relation of the people living in the Chicago area with the Southwest. In Chicago, of the 45,000 people that live there, they are primarily occupied in three industries—in the railroad industry, in the steel mills, and in the packing industry. But just as they are occupied primarily in these three industries, they also find employment in very peculiar jobs in these respective industries.

In the railroads, the overwhelming majority of those employed find employment only as section hands. Very few find employment in the higher skilled trades. And it is ironical, when there are thousands and thousands of Mexican-American workers on the railroad today, that one of our railroads in Chicago is bringing in, within 5 weeks from now, 150 workers from Mexico to work as skilled laborers as electricians, as pipe fitters, steam fitters, millwrights, and so forth. Yet they refuse to give opportunity to these people who are residents of the Chicago area and the overwhelming majority of them citizens of this country. These people who are coming here from Mexico are coming on a temporary basis, so that when the contract is finished they will go back to their country. But we, who will remain as part of this country, are not given the opportunity to use our skills to the fullest.

Let me give you a couple of instances of how Mexicans are discriminated against. In one of our steel mills there is a man who has been working there for over 20 years. His name is Ramon Martinez, and his address is 8817 South Buffalo Avenue. At this mill he works in the yard - and most of the Mexicans that are employed in the mills work in the yard - which means that they have to work outdoors during the heat of the summer and the cold of winter and in rainy weather. The other group works in the coke plant where they burn the coke and extract the poisonous gas. Also there is a group employed as chippers, and now and then you may see - but as a rule you do not - people employed in the departments.

This Ramon Martinez was put in charge of a gang of workers in the yard because they were Mexicans and he could speak their language. He was supposed to be a foreman and he discovered that he was making $50 a month less than the wages paid to the average foreman in the same capacity as he was working. He went to the proper authorities in the plant and asked why he was receiving much less money than the others. The answer was that he was not a citizen of the United States. True, at that time he was not. He was interested enough in his country to acquire his citizenship, and after he acquired his citizenship, he went back and said that he was a citizen of the United States and still he was not receiving the normal wages of other foremen.

Excuse number 2 given to Mr. Martinez was that he had not a high school education. Mr. Senator, you as well as everyone else here knows that the average education of a foreman is not necessarily that of a high-school graduate. Nevertheless, this man was interested enough to go to evening school and he received a high-school diploma.

Again he went and asked for the same wages as the other foremen. The answer was that he had to be there a longer period of time than he had been there. That is in the steel industry.

Senator CHAVEZ. Was that case reported to the F.E.P.C., do you know?

Mr. PAZ. We had a meeting with Mr. Williams of the Chicago area, where Mr. Martinez related his case. Whether the F.E.P.C. will follow through on that, or not, I do not know.

Then there is a man by the name of Garcia Herrera, 728 West Fourteenth Place, who works in a packing plant, in the car shops. He has been working there for the last 20 years. That is a mechanics shop and he works there as a helper and has done so for 20 years. He was interested enough to go to evening school and learn welding. As a welder he applied for that position. Up to now that position has been refused to him "because they have no room." Yet ironically enough he has trained many of the younger men, not of Mexican descent, who have come to the car shops to be trained for higher skilled jobs.

These are some of the incidents that have happened.

Today in Chicago we have a crisis in streetcar transportation. There are signs all over the city asking for workers to work in the streetcars. A boy - and I say a boy because he is only 22 or so- by the name of Villar, decorated with the Purple Heart, discharged, honorably discharged, from the United States Army after three years and 3 months of service in the Pacific - he was one of the very first to arrive in the Pacific, Guadalcanal, and other islands - applied for a position with this streetcar company and the answer was, "Our policy up to now has been not to discriminate, but our experience has been that you are from a minority group and we don't know wether that would work so well if you were to work in the street railway industry."

Senator CHAVEZ. Just a minute. Mr. Ross, will you kindly come forward, please? I don't know whether you heard this last incident described or not?

Mr. ROSS. (Chairman, Fair Employment Practice Committee). I heard a good deal of it but I didn't hear where it was.

113

Mr. PAZ.   In Chicago.

Senator CHAVEZ.   Here is a boy who was given the Purple Heart and as I understand it that is only given after you suffer the agonies of the damned in combat against the enemy - who was refused a job by the streetcar company in Chicago because he happened to belong to certain minority racial group. The boy is an American. I wish you would make a note of that and look into it for the committee.

Mr. ROSS.   I will, Senator.

Mr. PAZ.   Therefore, Senator, we are interested in this bill for only one reason, for the equality of opportunity that this bill will make possible for the people to find employment, not to be deprived of work due to their national origin, race, or religion.

I believe that this bill is fundamentally American. I believe in the principles of democracy that give an opportunity for all to achieve their proper place. I believe that this bill will not only tend to improve the conditions and relations on a more sincere level between this country and the 20 other republics of this hemisphere but it also implies that in this country we will find the true path to democracy - and discrimination is un-American, undemocratic, and un-Christian.

Senator CHAVEZ.   Thank you, Mr. Paz.

Mr. PAZ.   Thank you.

Senator CHAVEZ.   Alonso Perales.

STATEMENT OF ALONSO S. PERALES, CHAIRMAN, COMMITTEE OF ONE HUNDRED, DIRECTOR GENERAL, LEAGUE OF LOYAL AMERICANS, SAN ANTONIO, TEXAS.

Mr. PERALES.   My name is Alonso S. Perales; I am chairman of the Committee of One Hundred, and director general of the League of Loyal Americans.

Senator CHAVEZ.   What is your home city?

Mr. PERALES.   San Antonio, Tex., sir.

114

Senator CHAVEZ. What is this League of Loyal Americans, and what is the Committee of One Hundred?

Mr. PERALES. The Committee of One Hundred, sir, is strictly a political organization composed of American citizens of Mexican descent. The League of Loyal Americans is a civic and patriotic organization composed also of Americans of Mexican descent.

Furthermore, sir, I have with me credentials from organizations throughout the State of Texas which I believe warrant me in stating that I represent 1,000,000 Americans of Mexican descent from the State of Texas.

Senator CHAVEZ. That is what we want to know.

Mr. PERALES. Including over one-quarter of a million American soldiers of Mexican descent from Texas now in the battlefields of Europe and other parts of the world.

Senator CHAVEZ. Mr. Perales, you are a native of Texas, are you not?

Mr. PERALES. Yes, sir.

Senator CHAVEZ. You have written some works on Texas, have you not?

Mr. PERALES. Yes, sir.

Senator CHAVEZ. Will you state for the Committee's information the names of some of the works you have written?

Mr. PERALES. Sir, I have devoted over 25 years to this problem of discrimination and better relations with our brethren south of the border. In fact, I have written two books entitled "En Defensa de Mi Raza," which, translated into English means "In Defense of My Race."

I served in the diplomatic service of the United States for a period of 10 years, on 13 different assignments which carried me to Central and South America and the West Indies. I also served in the First World War. Since 1930, however, I have devoted my entire time to the practice of law in San Antonio.

With your permission, sir, I should like to incorporate in the record or offer at this time a little biographical sketch regarding the speaker, which, I think will save a lot of time.

Senator CHAVEZ. Very well; that may be put into the record.

(The biographical sketch referred to is as follows):

PERALES, ALONSO S.: Lawyer, legal adviser to the United States Electoral Mission in Nicaragua, 1932. Born in Alice, Tex., October 17, 1898. Married. Graduated from public schools of Alice, Texas, and preparatory school, Washington, D. C. Attended School of Arts and Sciences, George Washington University; graduated from the School of Economics and Government, National University, A. B.; and from National University Law School, LL. B.; admitted to Texas bar, 1925. Served with the United States Army in Texas during the World War; 2½ years in the Department of Commerce, Washington, D. C. Served in the Diplomatic Service of the United States as assistant to Hon. Sumner Welles, personal representative of the President of the United States in the Dominican Republic, 1922; assistant to the United States delegation, Conference on Central American Affairs, Washington, D. C., 1922-23; assistant to Inter-American High Commission, Washington, D. C., 1923; attorney and interpreter, United States delegation, Plebiscitary Commission (Gen. John J. Pershing, president), Tacna-Arica arbitration, 1925-26; special assistant to United States delegation to Sixth International Conference of American States, Habana, Cuba, 1928, attorney with agency in the United States, General and Special Claims Commission, United States and Mexico, 1928; attorney, United States Electoral Mission in Nicaragua, 1928; special assistant, United States delegation to International Conference of American States on Conciliation and Arbitration, Washington, D. C., 1928-1929; special legal assistant, Commission of Inquiry and Conciliation, Bolivia and Paraguay, Washington, D. C., 1929; assistant to United States delegation, Congress of Rectors, Deans, and Educators, Habana, Cuba, 1930; legal adviser to the United States Electoral Mission in Nicaragua in 1930. At present engaged in the private practice of law in San Antonio, Texas.

Senator CHAVEZ. You may proceed with your statement.

Mr. PERALES. At the outset, Mr. Chairman, in the name of the people that I represent, I wish to thank the committee for this opportunity of appearing before it to express our views on Senate bill 101 and Senate bill 459.

In the first place we are strongly in favor of Senate bill 101 and opposed strongly to Senate bill 459, for the simple reason that Senate bill 459 has no teeth in it, and Senate bill 101 has; and in order to get anywhere, Mr. Senator, we have to have Federal legislation with teeth in it - plenty of teeth.

Also I should like to ask permission, Mr. Chairman, to have incorporated in the record of this hearing my statement made to this committee at the previous hearing in connection with Senate bill 2048, last September.

116

Senator CHAVEZ. That may be done.

(The testimony referred to will be found on file with the committee.)

Mr. PERALES. The President's Committee on Fair Employment Practices, Mr. Chairman, has proved to be, beyond the shadow of a doubt, the most constructive piece of legislation ever enacted by our Federal Government, both in justice to Americans of Mexican descent and to the end of cementing better relations with the 130,000,000 inhabitants of the Western Hemisphere that happen to be of Mexican or Spanish lineage.

To illustrate. Before the President's Committee on Fair Employment Practices came into existence, we had a most deplorable situation in Texas, particularly in San Antonio.

At Kelly Field, for example, where our Federal Government employs 10,000 people, approximately, on three shifts, our men of Mexican descent never could hold a position of a higher category than that of laborer or mechanic's helper.

Our Government, the Federal Government, established at San Antonio what was known as an aircraft school in order to train these young men from high school to become mechanics. Our boys of Mexican descent went directly from high school there, together with the boys of Anglo-Saxon descent; they graduated with good grades, and were assigned by the United States Aircraft School to Kelly Field for employment. And our boys of Mexican descent were employed as laborers or as mechanics' helpers; and the Anglo-American boys in a very short time were promoted to junior mechanics, senior mechanics, and journeymen; whereas our boys remained as laborers and mechanics' helpers forever.

Now, here is an example:

STATEMENT OF ROMAN ALVARADO.

I have been employed at the San Antonio Air Depot, Kelly Field, Texas, since October 5, 1942, as a classified laborer. During this time I have had occasion to observe that the American citizens of Mexican descent do not have the same opportunity to advance that is given to citizens of other extractions. He is always given rough, hard work; and, to make matters worse, they are placed under Negro foremen. There is only one foreman of Mexican descent, while in the section where I am working there are about eight or nine Negro foremen. I am speaking of the second shift which is from 3:15 p. m. to 11:45 p. m., and am referring only to the section where I work.

117

Citizens of other racial lineages, including those of Negro extraction, have opportunity for promotion.

There are about 200 classified laborers employed in the shift I am referring to.

Witness my hand at San Antonio, Texas, this 20th day of May, A. D. 1943.

> Roman M. Alvarado.

The next is a statement by Jose Doroteo Salas, made under oath:

My name is Jose Doroteo Salas. I am 32 years of age and married. I reside at 1702 San Fernando Street, in San Antonio, Texas. I was born in Seguin, Guadalupe County, Texas, and I am a citizen of the United States of America. I am able bodied, and am enjoying good health. I am an air-raid warden.

On February 24, 1943, about 3 p. m., I went into the United States employment Service, 210 West Nueva Street, San Antonio, Texas, for the purpose of applying for a job as a watchman. I was interviewed by an Anglo-American man who appeared to be about 30 years of age. I do not know his name. He asked me what kind of a job I preferred, and I told him that I would like to be a watchman. He replied that he would not consider Spanish people for that kind of job because those jobs were reserved for "white" people only. I told him that I am an American citizen, white, and just as good as any other citizen, whereupon he said: "Well, those are the orders I have." When I asked him who had given him such orders, he refused to answer.

Now, Mr. Chairman, I have read those two statements just as an example of the situation existing on the economic phase of this problem. I have many, many more here, but I am not going to bore the committee with them. I just want the committee to know that the evidence is here, open to the inspection of the committee.

Now the Shell Oil Co., in Houston, in 1942, entered into an agreement with a chapter of the C.I.O. union at Houston whereby Mexicans, regardless of skill, could be employed only as gardeners, yardmen, and laborers.

Senator CHAVEZ. That is kind of a new one for the C.I.O. union to do that.

Mr. PERALES. It actually happened, sir, so that, a Mexican who was an electrician, a mechanic, or a plumber, didn't have a ghost of a chance to get in there unless he wanted to work as a

118

gardener, a yardman, or a laborer. But even in those three categories, Mr. Chairman, their agreement - and it was a written agreement - and I have a copy of it.

Senator CHAVEZ. (interposing). You say you have a copy of that?

Mr. PERALES. I am sure I do. I may have left it in San Antonio, but I can get it.

Senator CHAVEZ. I would like to see it.

Mr. PERALES. Very well; I will furnish you with a copy.

But even in those three categories, Mr. Chairman, the agreement was that the Mexican laborer or yardman or gardener was to receive less pay than the Anglo-American laborer or yardman or gardener.

Senator CHAVEZ. When they were referring to Mexican labor, that Mexican laborer could have been a citizen of the United States who had been in continental United States, and possibly in Texas, longer then the fellow who made the agreement?

Mr. PERALES. Yes, sir; and it was broad enough to cover any worker of Spanish or Mexican descent, regardless of what country he was a citizen of.

Senator CHAVEZ. It might have included the descendants of some of the boys of Mexican extraction who died at the Alamo?

Mr. PERALES. Yes; exactly.

Senator CHAVEZ. Of course, there were some Mexican-Texans who died at the Alamo, too.

Mr. PERALES. Quite a number.

Senator CHAVEZ. With Bowie and with Travis?

Mr. PERALES. Yes.

Senator CHAVEZ. And nevertheless the descendants of some of those boys who fought for Texas' independence were subjected to this type of contract?

Mr. PERALES. Yes, sir.

Now that was in the year 1942. The Fair Employment Practices Committee came into being, as I remember it, around about July or August of 1943, and just as soon as that Committee got into action we made it our business to see that the Committee had plenty of work, and we sent them a lot of complaints, and I am happy to report that the situation was greatly improved, thanks to the President's Committee on Fair Employment Practices.

The Shell Oil Co., for example - and I say this to illustrate the value of the persuasive method - had the matter taken up with them by the Fair Employment Practices Committee as soon as the committee came into being. They talked and talked with them, they negotiated for a year and a half, and they got nowhere until the Fair Employment Practices Committee had to threaten them with a public hearing, and even then they wouldn't give up.

So they had the public hearing in Houston, Tex., on December 28, 1944. Because I am interested in the problem, I made it my business to be there. Well everbody got ready for the big case. The Shell Oil Co.'s battery of lawyers appeared on the scene, and the Fair Employment Practices Committee appeared with a battery of lawyers and others who were just as good and perhaps knew more about the matter than the lawyers. And just as they were going into the actual trial of the case, the Shell Oil Co., asked for a private hearing. They didn't want it public, because, they said: "We believe we can get together, we are beginning to see the light of reason."

So they had the private hearings, much to the disappointment of those of us who had gone all the way from San Antonio to be in on the kill. And after a few days' negotiation the Shell Oil Co. agreed to a directive proposed by the Committee on Fair Employment Practices. The directive was issued by the proper authorities in Washington, and the situation there is remedied: the problem has been solved.

As I say, the situation is greatly remedied, also, thanks to the F. E. P. C., at Kelly Field.

Now at this time, Mr. Chairman, I should like to state that I am not on the pay roll of the Fair Employment Practices Committee; I have no connection whatever with them. I am here stating these facts because it is only fair.

Senator CHAVEZ. (interposing). Well, most of the witnesses who have appeared before this committee are outside of the F.E. P.C.

Mr. PERALES. I see - the same as the speaker?

Senator CHAVEZ. Yes.

Mr. PERALES. In fact, I have come here at my own expense, sir.

Now, Mr. Chairman, I believe that in order to get a good picture of this problem we ought to touch very lightly, briefly, on the various aspects of the discrimination problems, because, sir, it is our honest conviction that this problem is of the utmost importance; and next to the war in which we are now engaged, it is our considered opinion that it is the gravest problem facing our Nation today, and it calls for action by our National Congress now, for tomorrow may be too late.

The discriminatory situation in Texas is truly a disgrace to our Nation. Mexicans - regardless of citizenship - and, for that matter, citizens of Honduras, Venezuela, Colombia, Argentina, and the other republics, have been humiliated merely because they happened to be of Spanish or Mexican descent, time and again.

I have compiled here, Mr. Chairman, a list of 150 towns and cities in Texas where there exist from 1 to 10 public places of business and amusement, where Mexicans are denied service, or entrance. I have here the name of the city or town, the name of the place - that is, the name of the establishment - and the name of the owner. In nearly every town and city of Texas the Mexican children are segregated from the Anglo-Saxon children in the public schools. In nearly every town and city in Texas there are residential districts where Mexicans are not permitted to reside, regardless of their social position. The purpose, Mr. Chairman, has been to keep the Mexican at arm's length and to treat him as an inferior.

Senator CHAVEZ. Possibly you had better give that list to some of the boys who are going to San Francisco. (Laughter.)

Mr. PERALES. I will.

Senator CHAVEZ. That list may be filed with this committee, Mr. Perales.

(The list referred to will be found on file with the committee.)

Mr. PERALES. The same situation exists, Mr. Chairman, in the States of Arizona, Colorado, California, and, I am sorry to say, in a part of New Mexico.

Now soldiers of Mexican descent - members of the United States Navy - their medals, their Purple Heart, their uniform, make no difference. They too are victimized, they are the victims of these Nazi tactics.

THE STATE OF TEXAS. COUNTY OF BEXAR:

Before me, the undersigned authority, on this day personally appeared Jose Alvarez Fuentes, seaman, second class, United States Navy, Pvt. Joe D. Salas, Army Serial No. 38557190, Company B, Sixty-fifth Battalion, M. R. T. C., United States Army, and Pvt. Paul R. Ramos, Army Serial No. 38557007, Company B, Sixty-fifth Battalion, M. R. T. C., United States Army, who being by me duly sworn upon oath did depose and say:

Our names are Jose Alvarez Fuentes, Joe D. Salas, and Paul R. Ramos. We are members of the armed forces of the United States as above indicated. We are permanent residents of the city of San Antonio, Tex., but are temporarily residing elsewhere. We are now on furlough. On Tuesday, March 7, 1944, about 2:30 p. m. when we were on our way home the bus stopped at Fredericksburg, Texas.

Senator CHAVEZ. (interposing.) Where?

Mr. PERALES. Fredericksburg - the h o m e of Admiral Nimitz. (Continuing:)

We were hungry and, therefore, we went into the Downtown Cafe, at 323 East Main Street, Fredericksburg, to order something to eat. We sat on stools at the counter. There were two waitresses in the restaurant, but neither one waited on us. One of them went and told the manager or proprietor that we were there. He came to where we were and Seaman Jose Alvarez Fuentes told him that he wanted a barbecue sandwich. The manager or proprietor said, "I am sorry, but I cannot serve you in front; you will have to go out and around to the rear." Seaman Alvarez Fuentes asked him why and he said: "Those are the orders." Whereupon we left the place. Seaman Juan Garcia, United States Navy, was also with us at the time. He lives in San Antonio, Texas, and he too was on his way home on a furlough.

Then the next one:

THE STATE OF TEXAS, COUNTY OF BEXAR.

Before me, the undersigned authority in and for said county, State of Texas, this day personally came and appeared Alejo Lara to me well known, and who, after being by me duly sworn, did depose and say:

My name is Alejo Lara. I am 45 years of age and a native-born citizen of the United States of America. I reside at Ozona, Crockett County, Texas.

On or about August 16, 1944, Pvt. Tomas Garza, United States Army, who was born and reared in Ozona, Texas, went to the Ozona Drug Store, at Ozona, Texas. I accompanied him. Private Garza sat at the counter and ordered a Coca-Cola. An Anglo-American lady told Private Garza that she was sorry, but that she could not sell refreshments to Mexicans. Then Private Garza asked her why she would not sell to him, that his money was just as good as anybody else's and, furthermore, he was a soldier.

122

The lady replied that all that did not make any difference. A watchman named Fleetcoats happened to be there drinking a refreshment and he got up and told me to tell Private Garza to leave the drug store. I told the watchman for him to tell Private Garza, that perhaps he had more authority then I. Whereupon the watchman said to Garza: "You had better leave here at once." Just then Sheriff Frank James arrived, pistol in hand, and ordered Private Garza to leave the drug store immediately. Then Garza started to leave, but as he did so he told Sheriff James that he was going to report the case to his captain in order that the latter might come and have the place closed.

Sheriff James told Garza to go ahead and tell the capitan. Private Garza went to the telephone office to call his captain and when he arrived he placed the call, but the telephone operator refused to make the connection for him. Private Garza was wearing the United States uniform at the time.

About 4 months ago Pvt. Arturo Ramirez, United States Army, went to the same drug store accompanied by his wife, and ordered some refreshments, but they refused to sell same to them merely because they were of Mexican descent. Private Ramirez was killed in action in France about July 10, 1944.

Imagine the disappointment this soldier of ours must have felt, knowing that his wife had been denied the sale of a refreshment in a drug store in his home State of Texas, and yet there he was giving his life, the last measure of devotion, in order, according to the theory of the Nazi-minded, that that owner of the drug store might be here free, safe, secure, that he might have the privilege of denying such boys as Ramirez a Coca-Cola because they happened to be of Mexican descent.

I have an affidavit here referring to' the same incident, but it adds one important fact, and that is that Sheriff James was the one that ordered the telephone operator not to make the connection for the soldier so that the soldier could not speak with his captain.

I have some more about soldiers here, but I am not going to bore the committee with reading them.

Senator CHAVEZ. I wish you would file them with the committee.

Mr. PERALES. I will, sir.

Senator CHAVEZ. Are they certified; are they taken before notaries public?

Mr. PERALES. Yes, sir.

(The affidavits referred to will be found on file with the committee.)

Senator CHAVEZ. Then you feel that a bill like this bill, S. 101, is a good thing?

Mr. PERALES. It is indispensable, sir.

Now it has been said, Mr. Chairman, that men who, like the speaker, are constantly pointing out these blunders on the part of certain citizenry of ours, are agitators. I have not lost a bit of sleep over the accusation, sir. But for the record I should like to quote very briefly two or three words from each man that I am going to refer to, of other extractions, as to how they feel about this shameful situation.

Before I do that I would just like to quote very briefly here what happened in San Antonio, in regard to the housing situation. This was published in the San Antonio Light:

Anthony van Tuyl, director of the War Housing Center in the Municipal Auditorium, said he had 306 listings of apartments for rent, but that not one of the apartments could be rented to Latin-Americans or Negroes who are supplying thousands of workers for local fields and camps.

Senator CHAVEZ. Who was that person?

Mr. PERALES. Anthony van Tuyl, director of the War Housing Center in the Municipal Auditorium at San Antonio, Tex. He went on to explain, sir, that the owners of these 306 apartments had so requested him that he should not offer them to Latin-Americans or Negroes.

Senator CHAVEZ. They were private homes?

Mr. PERALES. Presumably, sir, and apartment homes.

Senator CHAVEZ. Well, they weren't governmentally owned?

Mr. PERALES. That is right.

Here is the case of a man who sent a long telephone telegram from McCamey, Tex. His name is Casillas. He says that he works in McCamey, but in order to get a haircut he has to travel 45 miles to Fort Stockton, because there is no barber shop in McCamey that would cut his hair. There are no Mexican barber shops there, only American barber shops.

Senator CHAVEZ. And he has to go to Fort Stockton?

Mr. PERALES. Yes.

124

Senator CHAVEZ. I understood that was just as bad.

Mr. PERALES. He probably found a Mexican barber shop there. By the way, Fort Stockton is also on my list of 150 cities and towns in Texas which I filed with the committee. Yes; it *is* just as bad.

At Big Springs the pubic sentiment against the Mexicans apparently went so far as to influence the commanding officer of an Army field there to cause a sign to be erected at the field saying, *"Any soldier who considers himself white shall not go into the Mexican district of Big Springs."*

I have two additional affidavits that I am going to file with the committee with your permission.

One of them refers to a Fourth of July celebration at Lockhart, Tex., where they roped off several blocks for dancing purposes, and some of the citizens of Mexican descent went there, since they had heard so much about the good-neighbor policy, and they thought they would join their Anglo-American neighbors in celebrating the Fourth of July.

Well, somebody got up, who was acting as master of ceremonies, and made the following announcement:

"I have been asked to make this announcement: That all Spanish people gathered here must leave the block." (*This part of the announcement was received with many cheers and hurrahs by the people of Anglo-American extraction*). *"Since this is an American celebration,"* the speaker went on to say, *"it is for the white people only."* (*This other part of the announcement was likewise received with great applause and hurrahs on the part of the Anglo-Americans.*)

That is a good way to promote the good-neighbor policy.

Senator CHAVEZ. Our time is getting short, Mr. Perales. Of course those matters that you are discussing now are most interesting but they do not have to do with the meat of the legislation that we have in mind at the moment.

Mr. PERALES. That is correct, but it shows the broad picture.

Senator CHAVEZ. That is true, but I wish you would devote a little more time to the proposition of Senate bills 101 and 459, and you may file all of that with the committee. But we would like to save a little time because time is getting short, it is getting late, and we want to close this afternoon, and there are still several witnesses to be heard.

Mr. PERALES. Yes, sir. I would like to file that affidavit with the committee and also one covering a similar situation at Poteet, Tex., during an Armistice Day celebration.

Senator CHAVEZ. That may be done.

(The affidavits will be found in the files of the committee.)

Mr. PERALES. Now I am just about to close. But, Mr. Chairman, would you object to my reading one paragraph from a statement made by the Archbishop of San Antonio regarding the situation, both economic and otherwise?

Senator CHAVEZ. No; I wouldn't object to that.

Mr. PERALES. This is an extract from an address delivered by His Excellency, the Most Reverend Robert E. Lucey, Archbishop of San Antonio. The title is, "Are We Good Neighbors?"

"This is the story of a large minority group in the United States, our Latin-American brothers, generous and warm-hearted, simple, charming, and lovable yet segregated, persecuted, and submerged. It is the story of many Anglo-Americans who have shown stupidity, ignorance, and malice in treating their Mexican brethren with injustice, discrimination, and disdain. It is not a lovely story; it is profoundly disturbing because it tells of poverty and tragedy, of disease, delinquency and death.

During the past quarter of a century many good citizens of our country sincerely believed that the race question might well be let alone to work itself out to a happy conclusion by the slow, sure formula of peaceful evolution and patient progress. It was a comfortable philosophy and, if not very hopeful of the minority groups, it largely satisfied the master race.

But the present world-wide and devastating conflict has disturbed peaceful consciences, opened unseeing eyes, and posed stubborn questions that simply will not be downed without direct and adequate answers. Some of these questions sound like this: Why did the Burmese natives refused to fight for England? What truth is there in the Japanese contention that the white races despise the yellow men? Can we keep our self-respect if we demand that the colored American fight for freedom in Africa and deny him freedom at home? Can we make the Western Hemisphere a bulwark of liberty and law while we maim and mangle Mexican youth in the streets of our cities? Can we condemn our Latin-Americans to starvation wages, bad housing, and tuberculosis and then expect them to be strong, robust soldiers of Uncle Sam? Can we tell our Spanish-speaking soldiers that dishonorable discharge from the Army will deprive them of civil rights when they never had any civil rights? In a word, can we, the greatest Nation on earth, assume the moral leadership of the world when race riots and murder, political crimes and economic injustices disgrace the very name of America?"

These sharp questions are getting under the skin of every decent American and all are agreed that something has got to be done about it.

The Honorable Sumner Welles, former Under Secretary of State, writing recently about this situation, said:

"The visit of President Roosevelt to Mexico last April, and the visit paid by President Avila Camacho to this country immediately thereafter, signalized the commencement of a new epoch in Mexican-American understanding."

But no such relationship as that which the vast majority of people of both countries desires to see built up can long continue if unfair, humiliating and wounding discriminations are practiced by communities in either nation against nationals of the neighboring country.

Discriminations of this character inevitably cut deep. They create lasting resentments which no eloquent speeches by Government officials, nor governmental policies, however wise, can ever hope to remove. They exist only in a few places. They are regarded as detestable, and as wholly un-American, by every thinking United States citizen. But so long as they continue anywhere in the United States they are bound to undermine the foundations which the two Governments have laid for those cooperative ties which are so greatly to the interest of both countries, and they will, in the wider sense, impair that inter-american relationship which is today more necessary than ever before. Unless these discriminations are obliterated, and obliterated soon, the term "good neighbor policy" will lose much of its real meaning.

Now, Mr. Chairman, I notice that you asked some of the previous speakers, at least one or two of them, what in their judgment was the reaction of the people from Mexico regarding this problem. Well, sir, I am happy to have here the reaction of the Mexican press, which I think reflects public opinion in Mexico, referring to the Spears bill. We have a bill, sir, pending before the Texas State Legislature now, unfortunately it doesn't include a F.E.P.C.; we tried to get it in there, but whoever was in charge of it in the senate, where the bill originated, omitted the F.E.P.C. provision, and limited it only to the social phase of discrimination - but this is how "Fraternidad," the official organ of the "Comité Mexicano Contra el Racismo" of Mexico - a strong

127

committee fighting racism and fighting discrimination - puts it, in an editorial dated February 1, 1945.

"The antidiscrimination bill presented by Senator J. Franklin Spears before the Senate of the State of Texas is one of the most important bills that will come before the Texas legislators during the session that began more than a month ago.

The interest which the presentation of such a bill involves is not only local, it is not something that concerns only the population of Texas, nor only the Mexicans and Latin-Americans by birth or origin residing in that State. Its importance is of national, North American and of continental scope.

On the other hand, public opinion in our Latin countries would see in the approval of the Spears bill, strong proof that the legislators of Texas know how to interpret the sentiment of the majority of the North American people and understand the spirit of the good neighbor policy, which would contribute, in a larger measure than many other acts of collaboration, to reaffirm the basis of a true and genuine continental friendship.

In Mexico there exists the conviction that the great North American masses do not harbor any racial sentiment and that they repudiate the theory of the superiority of one race over another, which has made so many victims—especially among the Jews—in Europe. Likewise, public opinion in Mexico applauds the efforts of President Roosevelt to broaden the basis of North American democracy which must necessarily include the abolition of discriminatory acts against racial minorities. But Mexico knows that it is not sufficient to live persuaded of these positive realities, but rather prefers deeds that will put an end to the painful situation of many of our compatriots in the southern section of the United States, which has prevented a complete understanding and a frank friendship between the people of Mexico and the people of the United States."

This shows that while the governments of the Americas are united now, the people of the Americas, Mr. Chairman, are not united and never will be until discrimination is ended in the United States once and for all time to come.

Now, a newspaperman, referring to the conference of foreign ministers—Mr. Chairman, you referred to the conference that is to take place in San Francisco in the near future—well, this conference took place in Mexico City. Every effort was made to interest the foreign ministers of these various republics, beginning with our Secretary of State Stettinius, to enter into an agreement, international agreement, designed to abolish discrimination in all its phases in the Western Hemisphere.

128

The following is an extract from an editorial which appeared in "La Prensa", of San Antonio, Tex., on February 21, 1945; and extracted from an article by M. J. Montiel Olvera, one of Mexico's outstanding newspapermen, writing recently from Mexico City, in an article entitled, "The Approaching Conference of Foreign Ministers and Racial Discrimination".

"We do not understand how it is possible for such cordial friendship to exist from country to country, nor for our contribution to the war effort to be overestimated, at the same time that our fellow-citizens in certain sections of the North American Union are segregated as though they were afflicted with leprosy.

We do not understand the attitude of those who deny to the good neighbor admission to a restaurant, a theater, or a church, after said neighbor has offered his blood in the fields of battle against nazi-ism and nipponism.

We do know that on the one hand there is the most cordial attitude on the part of the American Government toward our Government and our people, and on the other hand there is the different, diametrically opposed and positively adverse attitude of the private citizens of that Republic."

While I am at it, and without reading it, I should like to have incorporated the following additional statement, an extract from an editorial in the Mexican newspaper, "Novedades", of January 12, 1945, entitled, "In the Interest of Good Neighborliness."

Senator CHAVEZ. That may be made part of the record.

(The editorial referred to is as follows:)

Extract From an Editorial in "Novedades", of Mexico, D. F., dated January 12, 1945, In the Interest of Good Neighborliness.

"We have never been satisfied with the sporadic recommendations made by various authorities or private institutions in the sense that an effort be made not to humiliate the Mexican and men belonging to that same race. We have very much appreciated such gestures because we understand the magnificent intention which inspires them, but we have not been able to see in them any effective force when it comes to the atmosphere in which there seems to exist the conviction that a hostile spirit to things pertaining to us must be maintained as if it were a matter of a social physionomical characteristic of vital importance. We have contended that it is necessary that these recommendations be taken into consideration as human premises for something else; that is, of something that will have to be heeded as an imposed obligation. In other words, we have striven for the creation of

129

antidiscriminatory legal provisions, with all the characteristics of positive norms, including penalties for those who refuse to observe them. This is what can be done in Texas."

"Withal, this moment we witness the most important phenomena, perhaps, in the history of our relations with the United States. We have been living in a climate of official understanding between the two Governments, with basis which do not fit precisely in the legal texts, but in principles of cooperation, of continental solidarity, or mutual aid and good will. Should the antidiscrimination law encounter unsurmountable legal obstacles, perhaps it could be based upon those principles . . . It will have to be that way, sooner or later, because it is not possible indefinitely to perpetuate errors against which a strong propaganda has been launched."

Mr. PERALES. So much for Mexican public opinion, Mr. Chairman, which I think is something to be taken very much into consideration by our country if we want to continue to have the support and cooperation of those people, those 130,000,000 people south of the border, in time of peace.

Senator CHAVEZ. I think that is extremely important in the development of the theory of the bill and the justification for the bill, but if you don't mind, if you have some other things to insert just give them to the reporter and I would like to have you limit yourself as much as possible to what we have here under consideration.

Mr. PERALES. I have a written statement, a summary of what I have said, Mr. Chairman, as to what the people of Mexico and the other countries think of our way of dealing with the people of Mexican descent here. However, I will not read it but would like to have it inserted in the record.

Senator CHAVEZ. We would be glad to have that inserted in the record.

(The document referred to is as follows:)

Statement of Alonso S. Perales, Lawyer, San Antonio, Tex., Before The Senate Committee on Labor and Education, in the Hearings Held March 13, 1945, on Senate Bills S 101 and S 459, to Prohibit Discrimination Because of Race, Creed, Color, National Origin, or Ancestry.

"We, and you, have heard again and again that progress against discrimination must be gradual and only by voluntary cooperation and education. But we, in Texas, and in the entire Southwest, and on the west coast, have been trying to make pro-

gress against discrimination for 25 years, ever since the end of the last World War, by means of cooperation, and education, with no results. We, American citizens of Mexican extraction, variously designated as Spanish-Americans, Latin-Americans, Mexican-Americans, some 3,000,000 in Texas and the Southwest, find that our efforts to eliminate discrimination by mutual cooperation and education, have accomplished nothing. We are discriminated against more widely today than 25 years ago—socially, politically, economically, and educationally. American citizens of Mexican extraction, whether in uniform or in civilian attire, are not allowed in public places, cannot buy food or clothes except in certain designated areas, cannot secure employment in any industry except as common or semi-skilled labor, cannot receive the same wages as other Americans in the same area, because of the widely held theory that a Mexican does not need as much to live. There are the conditions that exist today after 25 years of patient effort to eradicate discrimination by mutual cooperation and education.

We are convinced that legislation is the only solution to the problem today—legislation with effective powers of enforcement and not merely a pronouncement of pious good intention. Those who claim that education is the solution ignore the fact that legislation has a powerful educative effect. What little progress has been made in securing for the Mexican-Americans equal economic opportunities for employment and promotion in the last 18 months can be traced directly to no other factor than Executive Order 9346, which set up a temporary war agency known as the Fair Employment Practice Committee. This war agency has done more in 18 months toward removing discrimination against Mexican-Americans in war and essential industries than all the educational efforts of various private and governmental agencies in the last 20 years, including the Coordinator's Office for Inter-American Affairs.

We, the American citizens of Mexican extraction in the Southwest, are firmly convinced that it is time for the Government of the United States to go unequivocally on record in support of the doctrine that all Americans have an equal right to jobs. The passage of Senate bill S 101, to establish a permanent Fair Employment Practice Commission, is essential, in our opinion, to the preservation of American democracy. It, and it alone, will guarantee to every American citizen, regardless of race, creed, color, national origin, or ancestry, his rights to equal opportunities for employment, promotion in industry, and to earn a decent living.

If we want to prevent the sad spectacle of human misery and suffering that followed the last World War, if we want to prevent Pachuco riots (California and Colorado), Sleepy Lagoon cases

131

(California), Leveland mock trials *(Texas)*, and economic strife in the post-war era, which is almost at hand, if we want to build for an enduring peace at home and abroad, we need to take steps now to remove all possibilities for a continuation of economic discrimination by the passage of a bill such as that you are considering today. Would to God that it will eradicate all forms of discrimination."

Mr. PERALES. If you will permit me, I would like to quote one little paragraph, as I am not going to leave this letter because I treasure it highly; it will show how our Mexican-American soldiers feel about this matter—the ones who are in the trenches right now, fighting for democracy.

This young man, Mr. Chairman, prepared for the Diplomatic Service of the United States. He graduated from the University of Texas; took the examination for the Foreign Service offered by the United States Department of State, and was awaiting his assignment when he was drafted into the United States Army. He served as a buck private for over a year and took part in the invasion of Normandy. By the way, he is now a first lieutenant. Here is what he has to say:

"When I think of the men left dead on the beaches, I wonder if the people at home understand their tremendous sacrifice. I wonder particularly if those who are charged with the responsibility of framing the peace to come, fully realize the cost of victory. I pray that when the fighting is all done, our boys can go back with the utmost assurance that they can live and work in peace and that America still remains the symbol of liberty, justice, and freedom. I have sworn that if ever the combatants of this war are cheated of the things they risked their lives for, and for which thousands of their comrades gave their lives, I shall take the stump loud and strong and shall not cease in my condemnation of such fraud." *

With these words, Mr. Chairman, I say again: thank you for having invited us, and we sincerely hope that your committee will approve Senate bill S 101 because it has teeth in it, and it will undoubtedly make the Mexican-American feel more secure.

Senator CHAVEZ. Well, if we ever get through with the hearings we will report the bill out. (Laughter.)

Mr. PERALES. It will strengthen his faith in our American form of government and our institutions.

Senator CHAVEZ. Thank you.

---

*This young man is Mr. Oswaldo V. Ramírez, of Mission, Texas.

THE COMMITTEE OF ONE HUNDRED is one of the most active and hardworking organizations in Bexar County, Texas, and has done much for the progress and welfare of the inhabitants of Mexican descent of this community. Because of its outstanding civic work it has the support of nearly every Mexican-American and Mexican organization in the United States. Its directors are:

Charles Albidress, Sr., Florencio R. Flores, Esteban E. Barrera, Ernesto Vidales, J. J. Miranda, Victoriano Váldez, Susano Diaz, Luis H. Castillo, Daniel A. Lopez, Pedro Hernandez B., Gregorio R. Salinas, Alberto Lozano, Pete Ramirez, Dan Medina, Marcos Zertuche, Leonardo Laborde, William (Bill) Maldonado, Moises Maldonado, Ernesto Garza, Max Martinez, Joe Villarreal, Charles Albidress, Jr., Jesus M. Canales, Laureano Flores, Bennie J. Cantu, Vicente Mireles, Manuel A. Urbina, Antonio Valencia, Luis Gamez, Alberto U. Treviño, Dr. Carlos E. Castañeda and Alonso S. Perales.

———————

STATEMENT BY THE MOST REVEREND ROBERT E. LUCEY, ARCHBISHOP OF SAN ANTONIO

The number of cases of discrimination investigated and adjusted by the FEPC during the war period and immediately afterward, shows the necessity of continuing study and interpretation in this field of human relationships.

Now that the strains of war are over, and business men are returning to the competition of normal times, there is no longer any pressure to adhere to justice in their relationships with workers who belong to minority groups. As long as there are some who will not administer justice in their dealings with others, there is need of legal compulsion, backed by educational interpretation, to bring security to those who need it most.

Robert E. Lucey
Archbishop of San Antonio

San Antonio, Texas
March, 1945

THE GOOD NEIGHBOR POLICY AND THE PRESENT ADMINISTRATION

Address Delivered by Senator Dennis Chavez, New Mexico, in Los Angeles, California, October 19, 1944.

The story of the Good Neighbor Policy toward Latin America was one of erratic and desultory effort until the advent of the present national administration. To be sure, the history of this policy goes well back into the 19th century, but the ebb and flow of North American interest, and the intervening incidents of a decidedly unpleasant nature served only to strengthen our neighbors in their historical belief in the insincerity of our operations, and has engendered in them a material fear of the Colossus of the North. The Good Neighbor Policy began to assume significant proportions with the entry of the present administration, following those initial steps which had been taken so conservatively and even gingerly by previous administrations. Under the auspices of a well conceived plan carried into effect by an informed personnel, and guided by sincere and understanding leaders within the State Department and other agencies of our Federal Government, the movement initiated in the year 1933 has blossomed into one of promising proportions and of encouraging import.

In spite of the tremendous task of bringing about those myriad changes in the international thinking of the average citizen, both in our own country and in the republics of Latin America, the progress made during the past twelve years is too notable to be depreciated in superficial phrases of isolated condemnation. You are all more or less familiar with the importance of the inter-American movement, as evidenced by the attention being paid to it by every pertinent agency of our Governmental structure, headed by our able Secretary of State, Cordel Hull. The marked success of the recent Pan American Conference stands as substantial proof of the contemporary brilliance of the inter-American ideal, capped by the striking cooperation of our neighboring republics with relation to the crisis in world affairs which faced the United Nations a few years ago and which today has not by any means diminished. With the exception of a single republic, our efforts to mould the Western Hemisphere into a solid block of democratic resistance has met with a success far beyond the expectations of the most pessimistic among us.

This is the over-all picture of the Good Neighbor Policy, and, considering the situation in its better and more encouraging aspects, the various elements of success add up to a most suprising total of achievement.

Under the banner of Pan Americanism we can, in the words of that outstanding American, the Mexican Minister of Foreign Affairs, Dr. Ezequiel Padilla, "build a fortress of dignity . . . In its natural resources it will find all the requirements for its needs . . . Each man will have a purpose in living, a hope for which to fight, and a faith for which to die, if need be."

We are very definitely on the road to that Pan Americanism of which men like Simon Bolivar dreamed, but just because we find ourselves on a relatively comfortable highway, this is no reason to settle in the easy seats of satisfaction and expect to travel, from now on, without encountering sharp curves and deteriorated sections of the road. These sharp curves have been and are a part of the road, although they are one by one being straightened. Deteriorated sections are more than prominent, and it is of these that I should like to speak now.

We know, better than any group within our national boundaries, of the economic discrimination practiced against the American citizen of Spanish or Mexican extraction. It is indeed as present as the air we breath, but certainly not as healthy, either spiritually or materially. Official sanction, either local, state, or national, has never been given to this type of discrimination, but it does exist in our economic system and because this is true we long ago determined that something should be done about it.

Let me explore the effects of these practices upon the Good Neighbor Policy. For many years the republics of Latin America have been cognizant of the treatment given their nationals in our industrial and business structures, and this has worked toward the nurturing of an attitude of suspicion and mistrust towards us. To add insult to injury, they became aware of the fact that American citizens, whose great-grandfathers before them were American citizens, but who happen to be of Spanish or Mexican extraction, must also suffer submission to economic discrimination in the United States.

The record of these American citizens shows a consistently loyal attitude toward our great country, so much so that the archives of the War Department record the fact that they have participated with distinction in the wars of the United States, and have made outstanding contributions to the martial record of the Republic for almost one hundred years. This group does not ask, and has never asked for equality of economic opportunity to be handed to them on a silver platter. In the first place, this right belongs to them, to the same extent that it belongs to any American citizen, on purely *Constitutional* grounds. In the second place, they have purchased the right of political and economic freedom with their tears, their sweat, and their blood, all of these shed on the civilian front throughout the years, and upon the field of honor whenever they were called upon to do battle under the Stars and Stripes.

A recognition of these ulcerous conditions was a part of the reason for the establishment by directive of the President's Committee on Fair Employment Practice on June 25, 1941. The activities of this Committee in adjusting cases of economic discrimination called to its attention have gone far towards indicating to our Latin American allies that our government is determined to bring about an arrangement whereby equality of economic opportunity will be the right of every citizen of the United States of North America. The establishment of the President's Committee referred to took the problem out of the sphere of theory and good wishes and placed it in that of application and practice. Contrary to the ideas of most North Americans, Latin Americans are realists, and rightfully decry the strange discrepancy that exists between our practices and our preachments, between our actions in the every-day affairs of our economic life and the idealization of those principles and supposed traditions which we so loudly proclaim to be the body and soul of the great American way of life. They very reasonably cannot comprehend our flowery oratory on the ideals of Washington, Jefferson, and Lincoln, so long held before the world as the very foundations of the American political, social, and economic edifice, and in the next experience to hear these beautifully-sounding instruments of patriotism smothered by the strident notes of hypocrisy as manifested in our actions, when American citizens are denied the very rights and privileges which we so enthusiastically pretend to endorse.

The obstancies of the Spanish Americans of the Southwest, and other areas of the United States where this minority group is concentrated, is not one, but rather a series of complicated problems. These problems have been demanding solution for many, many years, and they call for realistic, courageous treatment. The three million people of Spanish and Mexican extraction in Texas, Colorado, New Mexico, Arizona, and California face today, and have faced in the past, intensive and extensive economic discrimination. Although the war has served to take up a great deal of unemployment within this group, still it is bound to return to plague the American and inter-American scene unless action is taken to obviate such a disaster. As a group, the minorities mentioned are economically destitute, educationally deprived, socially disorganized, and are beset by severe housing, health, sanitation and nutritional deficiencies.

Too many of the so-called great minds in our midst, talk sheer nonsense about the un-Americanism of racial intolerance. It is so nonsensical to say that prejudice is born of ignorance, for the most vicious varities of prejudice issue from the supposed intellectual classes, nursed and fed from the public purse in our municipal and state institutions of education. These intellectuals who walk about bending under the weight of so much learning are just the ones who inveigh against the importation of evil forces, and include prejudice and intolerance in their list of foreign-made goods. I have heard it said a hundred times, and from a hundred different kinds of lips, that "it is unfair, indecent, and *un-American*" to deprive a man of his job because of his racial, religious, or political origins or persuasion. On the contrary, my fellow Americans, racial and religious prejudice are common among us; they are even characteristic of us. *They most certainly are unfair and indecent,* but they are *not* un-American. They are un-American when weighed in the scale of their constitutionality; but they are *not* un-American when examined in the light of everyday American practice. In this latter respect, intolerance, prejudice, bigotry and discrimination are as American as a hot-dog.

The above conditions are precisely why, I, in collaboration with other Senators, introduced Bill 2048 in the Senate of the United States to prohibit discrimination in employment because of race, creed, color, national origin, or ancestry, and I am most happy to say that this legislation has already been reported out of the Committee on Education and Labor, and will soon be considered by the Senate. However, this is only a first step. Do not expect miracles to happen with regard to this legislation, for there exists powerful, unsympathetic, even though sincere opposition to it. We are in for a fight; but when has an American run away from a good fight? There are those who either misunderstand, or deliberately misinterpret this legislation to mean that we are trying to make people love each other; in other words, that we are sponsoring legislation to force American citizens to accept every other American citizen as a social equal. I happen to lean towards the opinion that all men are created equal, but all I am interested in is equality of opportunity, so that any American, regardless of his complexion, can go out into the byways of our economic countrysides and find honest and gainful employment for the material support of his loved ones and for the maintenance of those extra institutions within his spiritual and artistic life which make of man's existence something beyond mere vegetation.

Can there possibly be any man who holds to the slightest pride in a sense of justice and Christianity who can say that this is Utopian, impractical, idealistic, or unreasonable! I have no doubt whatsoever concerning the attitude the Founding Fathers would have entertained towards Senate Bill 2048! I am just that positive in my belief in their sincerity of purpose, in their greatness of spirit, in their lofty sense of justice, and in their embracing political, social, and intellectual integrity!

No man in his right senses would ask for legislation prohibiting social discrimination. No one is stupid enough to think that Christian principles of human conduct can be legislated into existence, these high ideals are seemingly far beyond the reach of our poor spirits to embrace. But we *can* raise our voices in support of the provisions of our Declaration of Independence, of our Constitution, and our Bill of Rights, and work towards the actuality of their operation. Let us put an end to that type of Fourth-of-July oratory where would-be-Patrick-Henrys drape t h e i r tailored shoulders with the glorious flag of our Republic and sing to the high heavens of Columbia, the land of the free, the home of the brave, and the melting pot where all races of mankind meet in harmony and beauty! I say, let us put a stop to this sort of rhetoric, and take such steps as will bring about the just and benevolent working of those more than magnificent human documents which have made my America and yours the envy of the world. In these ways we can help somewhat to bring about a still better America, an America united within itself by the bonds of righteousness and justice, and joined to the nations of the world by those golden links of mutual respect and consideration which have made of this world during happier epochs of peace a better place in which to labor at an honest bench.

To you Americans, whatever your racial origins may be, I say: Strive with all your might, with all your soul, to attain a high sense of social, economic and political justice! Do this with relation to your own groups and to every other group with whom you come into contact! Keep abreast of developments in our country! Indoctrinate your sons and daughters with the highest principles of material and spiritual living! Make it your business to know the laws of your community, of your state, and of your country! Abide by these laws! If you are out of sympathy with some of them, again strive towards their abolition or rectification, but always through legal and decent methods! Following these procedures, you will bring upon yourselves and your children the respect and admiration of your fellow Americans; you will be better Americans for it; and you will be marching shoulder to shoulder with your brothers under the Flag toward the vivid goals of a greater Hemisphere, a greater America!

PART III

CONCRETE CASES IN TEXAS.

AFFIDAVITS

THE STATE OF TEXAS, COUNTY OF BEXAR

My name is Perfecto Solis, Jr. I am a native of Laredo, Texas. At present, I am attending the Law School at St. Mary's University in San Antonio, Bexar County, Texas. I was in the United States Army during World War II. I served in the European Theater, and I was in combat for a period of nine months. I was severely wounded and was evacuated to the United States for hospitalization. I am now receiving compensation in the amount of 100% for total permanent disability. I am married to the former Hope Sachtleven. She is a native of Hackensack, New Jersey. She is a registered nurse. I met her in the Army and married her after I returned to the United States from the European Theater.

One of my wife's patients recommended the Burkshire Addition, located at 4220 Zarzamora Street, as a good place where we could purchase a home. Subsequently, we saw it advertised in a newspaper as being an addition for veterans. On Saturday, April 10, A. D. 1948, my wife and I went to see the homes in that addition and, after seeing the model homes, spoke to one of the salesmen. At first, the salesman told us he could not obtain a home for us for a period of from three to six months. Subsequently, he stated however, that he remembered of a home which had not been purchased because the loan had not been approved and that he believed he could obtain this place for us within a period of three weeks. He then took us in his car to visit the homes, and we decided to attempt to negotiate the deal. We then returned to his office, which is located on the addition itself, and he started filling out the papers in connection with the purchase. When he asked me my name, and I told him that it was Solis, he stated that he was sorry but that he could not sell it to us because of a restrictive clause against the purchase or use by Latin-Americans. My wife, who comes from the East, was not able to understand this restriction, but I told the salesman that I was not surprised that these restrictive clauses against Latin-Americans in general, and veterans in particular, seem to be quite common around here. We then left the office.

Perfecto Solis, Jr.

Subscribed and Sworn to before me on this 29th day of April, A. D. 1948.

Given under my hand and seal of office.

Peggy Humphrey

Notary Public in and for Bexar County, Texas.

THE STATE OF TEXAS, COUNTY OF BEXAR

My name is Pedro R. Hinojosa. I am 45 years of age, married and reside at 1728 Arbor Place, in San Antonio, Texas.

I have a son in the United States Army in Japan.

On December, 1947, I arrived in Sterling City, Sterling County, Texas, about 2:00 A. M., in my 1932 Chevrolet automobile, accompanied by my wife and eight children. We were coming from O' Donnell, Texas and were enroute to San Antonio, Texas. I stopped at a combination gasoline station and cafe and had my tank filled with gas and I also purchased four quarts of oil. I told the gasoline attendant to prepare some hamburgers for me and that I would take them with me. In the meantime I drove my car out of the station so as not to be in the way. Then I went into the restaurant to get the hamburgers and to drink a cup of coffee. As soon as I sat down at the counter the attendant (the same man that had filled my tank with gas) said to me: "Get up. We do not serve Mexicans here." Whereupon I got up, went outside, got into my car and drove off. I said nothing to him and did not provoke him in any way.

I had travelled about 10 miles approximately when he overtook me in a truck (he was accompanied by another man). He passed me and then drove his truck in front of mine so as to stop me. I stopped and he came to me and handed me the hamburgers. I paid him for them. Then he told me to drive back to Sterling City and that he would drive behind me. When I arrived at Sterling City he told me to get into the truck with him and I did. He then drove to the home of the Justice of the Peace A. L. Dearens and there the said Justice of the Peace fined me $19.60 on the ground that I did not have a tail light on my automobile. The man had a pistol in his right hand when he approached my car to hand me the hamburgers. He did not tell me that he was an officer, or by what authority or for what reason he was arresting me. Once in the house of the Justice of the Peace he filled in a

140

blank and the gasoline station attendant signed it. The Judge then told me that he was fining me $19.60 because I did not have a tail light on my car.

Further affiant sayeth not.   Pedro R. Hinojosa

Sworn to and subscribed before me, this the 2nd day of January, A. D. 1948.

Alonso S. Perales,
Notary Public in and for Bexar County, Tex.

STATE OF MICHIGAN
COUNTY OF SAGINAW

Mr. & Mrs. Mateo Castillo who now reside at 3117 Lowell St. of the City of Saginaw in the County of Saginaw and State of Michigan being duly sworn, deposes and says, that they went to buy a home at 1002 & 1004 Madison St., in the City of Saginaw, and they at the time gave a deposit of $47.00 to hold the premises in order. And that after that they were to give the down payment on the following week which that date would be the 16th day of October, 1947, so they went to the same address to proceed with the transaction, and they were informed that they would not accept any further dealings, because they were "Mexicans".

Further this deponent sayeth not.

Mateo Castillo

Subscribed and sworn to before me, this 18th day of October, 1947.

Alex D. Garza. Notary Public in and for the County of Saginaw, State of Mich. My commission expires June 15, 1950.

(SEAL OF THE OFFICE)

THE STATE OF TEXAS, COUNTY OF BEXAR

My name is Jose Garcia. I reside at Rio Hondo, Texas. My address is Box 334. I am a veteran of World War II. I served in the European Theatre as a member of the Third Army, and I was wounded in Germany. I was wounded in both legs and I am now partially disabled veteran drawing compensation as such. I am a native-born citizen of the United States.

On the 16th day of October, A. D. 1947, I was driving some seasonable workers on my truck to West Texas. It was about ten-thirty at night and I was very hungry, so I stopped at a place called "The Limit Cafe" in the town of Hamlin City in Fisher County. When I entered the restaurant, I was greeted rather abruptly by a heavy-set individual, who asked me what I wanted. Even before

141

I could answer, he added, "We don't serve Mexicans here." I asked him why and began talking with him when he cut me off by saying, "I am not the owner talk to him if you want to." He pointed out a man sitting in the back, whose name, I later learned, was Loy Fry, who, also, cut me off before I said a single word. He said, "I am the owner of this place and I won't serve any Mexicans, regardless of who you are." I then told him that the money I had was not Mexican money and that I was not a Mexican citizen, but he told me it didn't make any difference to him; that everybody belonging to what he called the Mexican Race was the same as far as he was concerned.

Not wishing to become involved in any difficulty, I left the place. I want to state that I had not been drinking: that I was neatly dressed and that I did not cause any disturbance whatsoever when I entered the place. I sought out some authority in the City and the only one that I could find was the City Marshal who expressed his regret at the incident but stated that there was nothing that he could do about it. I pointed out to the Marshal how disappointed it was to me, after having served in the Army and having been wounded in the service of my country, to come back and find conditions such as existed in his town. He stated he was sorry too because that region depended upon Mexican labor for its agricultural wealth and that now they were having difficulty obtaining Mexican labor, especially since the Mexican Government had cut off the laborers coming from across the border. I told him that as far as I was concerned, he and Mr. Fry could both start picking the cotton and we would be glad to remain away from his community. I then left Hamlin City after buying some barbecue at a grocery store, which I ate on the outskirts of the town.

(Signed)   Jose Garcia

SUBSCRIBED AND SWORN TO BEFORE ME at Rio Hondo, Texas, on this the 18th day of October, A. D. 1947.

(Signed)   Seledonio G. Sauceda. Notary Public in and for Cameron County, Texas.

THE STATE OF TEXAS, COUNTY OF BEXAR

My name is Leopoldo C. Mancilla. I reside at 318 W. Johnson St., San Antonio, Texas.

I served two years and eleven months in the United States Army during World War II, eighteen months of which I spent overseas. I was wounded in action twice.

142

In the month of April, 1947, in San Antonio, Texas, I called at the Field Office of Mr. Frank Robertson, Builder, on West French Street. At said addition there was a big sign, reading: "Homes for Veterans Only". There were several homes completed there and a man in the office showed them to me and told me to choose the one I wanted. Then he gave me a slip of paper for an appointment with Mr. Frank Robertson, Builder, in the Majestic Bldg. I went to Mr. Robertson, introduced myself and showed him my G. I. Loan Certificate of approval and my Army discharge. He said that addition was restricted and that the homes there were not for sale to Latin-Americans.

Further affiant sayeth not.   Leopoldo C. Mancilla
Sworn to and subscribed before me, this 24th day of September, A. D. 1947.

Alonso S. Perales
Notary Public in and for Bexar County, Texas.

THE STATE OF TEXAS, COUNTY OF BEXAR

My name is Maria de los Santos. My husband's name is Estanislao de los Santos. We reside at 302 Matagorda Street, in San Antonio, Texas. We have two children. We are all native born Americans. My husband served in the United States Army about three years and six months during the World War II.

About a month ago I called at the office of Phipps & Cobb, realtors, 1225 S. Gevers, San Antonio, Texas, in response to a newspaper advertisement in which they offered to sell houses to veterans. When I arrived at the office a man about 75 years of age, who appeared to be one of the members of the firm, told me that he was sorry, but that it was a restricted area and they did not want any Mexican people there. I told him that my husband was a veteran of World War II and that he had the same rights as any other veteran, and he said that he was sorry, but that the homes were not for Latin-Americans.

Further affiant sayeth not.   Mrs. Maria de los Santos
Sworn to and subscribed before me, this the 8th day of August, A. D. 1947.

Alonso S. Perales
Notary Public in and for Bexar County, Texas.

THE STATE OF TEXAS, COUNTY OF BEXAR

My name is David R. Garcia. I am a native born citizen of the United States of America. I am 26 years of age, married and reside at 911 Veracruz St., in San Antonio, Texas. I am a veteran of World

143

War II. I served in the United States Army three years and two months. I am a Commercial Artist and am employed by the Glazer Wholesale Drug Company, in San Antonio, Texas.

On July 21, 1947 (this morning to be exact) I saw a big sign on a homes division in the western section of the City of San Antonio, reading: "HOMES FOR VETERANS, 100% G. I. LOANS". There were about twenty or thirty homes built there. The sign further said that other information should be obtained from the Field Office situated in the Division itself. I went to the Field Office and they gave me the prices of the various homes. Then they told me to come to the office of Lee and Orts, Contractors, 814 Gunter Building, San Antonio, Texas. I went to see Lee and Orts, Contractors. I spoke with Mr. H. P. Orts. He asked me how much money I made monthly and I replied that I made $261.00. He said that I was eligible for the loan, but that there was a restriction against Mexicans. I told him that I was not a Mexican; that I am an American. He then told me that I was not considered a Latin American of the Caucasian Race and that because of that he could not sell me a home there. I told him that I thought that was a very undemocratic move and that as far as I was concerned I considered myself an American as well as the rest of them and that I deserved my rights as such. _Then he said he was sorry, but that there was nothing he could do; that the restriction was there and that the Guaranty Title Company would not approve the title to the property. Thereupon I left.

Further affiant sayeth not.   David R. Garcia.

Sworn to and subscribed before me, this the 21st day of July, A. D. 1947.

Alonso S. Perales
Notary Public in and for Bexar County, Texas.

THE STATE OF TEXAS, COUNTY OF BEXAR

My name is Walter A. Gipprich. I live at 315 Fair Avenue in the City of San Antonio, Bexar County, Texas. I am married to the former Esther Leyva and we have two children, one of whom is 14 months of age and the other is three weeks old.

On or about the 13th day of July A. D. 1947 I rented an apartment located at the above address. At that time my wife was in the hospital. On the 18 day of July A. D. 1947 my wife returned from the hospital but she is still in a very weak condition and is barely able to get out of bed. Today, the 21st day of July A. D. 1947 I was approached by my landlady whose name is Mrs. Ulrich, who told me that the neighbors were complaining because my wife is of Mexican descent but that she was not personally against anyone regardless of nationality. She felt that it was to the best interest of all concerned for us to move out at once. I was rather shocked

144

by what took place and did not know what to answer, since I was originally from Baltimore, Maryland where this type of prejudice is unknown because the citizens of my state believe in practicing as well as professing Americanism.

I cannot see how we can possibly move from that apartment in view of the difficulties encountered in obtaining quarters even when one does not have any children and particularly in light of my wife's delicate condition. It is my intention to remain where I am and leave it up to the fairmindedness and decency of the citizenry in general.

I feel that my case will afford an excellent opportunity for San Antonians who so proudly proclaim the Alamo as a symbol of freedom and liberty to rally to my support and help to eliminate bigotry and prejudice.

Walter A. Gipprich

SUBSCRIBED and Sworn to before me the undersigned authority at San Antonio, Bexar County, Texas on this the 21st day of July A. D. 1947.

GIVEN UNDER MY HAND and Seal of Office.

Victor Keller.   Notary Public, Bexar County, Texas

THE STATE OF TEXAS, COUNTY OF BEXAR

My name is Raul C. Garcia. I am 24 years of age, a native born citizen of the United States of America, and reside 2720 Saunders Avenue, in San Antonio, Texas.

On June 27, 1947, about 4:00 P. M., Roberto Abitia, Jose B. Gonzalez, my brother Luis C. Garcia and I were coming from Trinidad, Colorado, where we had attended a convention of young people of the Assemblies of God, and we stopped at the Old's Cafe in Lamesa, Texas. I entered the restaurant first. My brother and the other two young men had gone to a garage next door to wash their hands. Incidentally, the manager of the garage refused to permit the three young men to wash their hands there. They went and washed their hands elsewhere. Then they came into the restaurant. By that time I had sat at a table and had ordered some orange juice and the waitress had brought it to me. Evidently, she did not take me for a Latin American, as when the other three young men came in the waitress asked us if we were Spanish. I asked her why, as we wanted to be served anyway. Then she said that she had orders not to serve Spanish or Mexican people. Whereupon I asked her what kind of a democracy we had here, and I told her that it looked to me like we had a lot of communists in Texas that are stirring up strife. We then left the place.

Roberto Abitia and I served in the U. S. Army during World War II. Further affiant sayeth not.   Raul C. Garcia

Sworn and subscribed to before me this 2nd day of July, A. D. 1947.

Alonso S. Perales
Notary Public in and for Bexar County, Texas.

THE STATE OF TEXAS, COUNTY OF BEXAR

My name is Oralia Garza Rios. I am 19 years of age, married, a native born citizen of the United States of America, and reside at 303 South Pinto Street, Apartment No. 1, in San Antonio, Texas.

On June 11, 1947, I telephoned Lee & Orts, Contractors, Gunter Building, San Antonio, Texas, and I asked them about some homes advertised for sale at University Park Subdivision, in San Antonio, Texas, supposed to be homes for veterans. One Mr. P. J. Manly answered the telephone. He gave me every detail about the homes and then he asked me if I was "white", and I answered in the affirmative. I then asked him if there were any racial or social restrictions on these homes, and he told me that the homes were to be sold only to "white" people and not to Latin Americans. I also called up E. J. Burke & Sons regarding homes for veterans and they said the same thing.

My husband, Mr. Rudolph Rios, served in the United States Navy, three years and eight months, during World War II. He was aboard the U.S. Battleship NEVADA. We wanted to purchase one of the homes for veterans above referred to.

Further affiant sayeth not.   Oralia Garza Rios

Sworn and subscribed to before me this 12th day of June, A. D. 1947.

Alonso S. Perales
Notary Public in and for Bexar County, Texas.

THE STATE OF TEXAS, COUNTY OF BEXAR

My name is Lydia Garza Colin. I am 27 years of age and reside in Yorktown, Texas.

The following places refuse to serve persons of Mexican descent in Yorktown, Texas, regardless of economic or social position.

Sinclair Inn; proprietress Mrs. Bennett.
Leatherwood's Cafe; proprietor Mr. Leatherwood.

L. and L. Cafe.
Jerry's Place.
Billing's Barber Shop.
City Barber Shop; proprietor Mr. Ledwig
Yorktown Beauty Shop.
Lively Beauty Shop; proprietress Mrs. Lively.
Elizabeth's Place; proprietress Mrs. Plasckycz.

American soldiers of Mexican extraction, in uniform, have been denied service also, and the same is true of Mexican-American veterans who fought for our country overseas in World War II.
Further affiant sayeth not.   Lydia G. Colin.
Sworn and subscribed to before me this 16th day of May, A. D. 1947.

Alonso S. Perales
Notary Public in and for Bexar County, Texas.

THE STATE OF TEXAS, COUNTY OF BEXAR

Our names are Manuela Suarez, Josefina Leal, Consuelo Guzman, Pedro Buitron and Hector Martell. We live in Poteet, Texas, and are 8th grade students in the Poteet Elementary School.

On March 6, 1947, Mrs. Leola Kloss, our teacher in said grade, separated all the students of Mexican descent from those of Anglo-American extraction, placing the former on one side of the room and the latter on the other. There are 32 students in the eighth grade, 11 of which are of Mexican lineage. We have always gotten along very well with the Anglo-American students.

When Miss Manuela Suarez asked Mrs. Leola Kloss why she was separating us she replied that she wanted to know whether we could get along better this way and also whether we could make better grades when separated from the others.

The children of Mexican descent are segregated from the Anglo-American children up to and including the fifth grade. They are housed in separate buildings.

Further affiants sayeth not. Mamie Suarez, Consuelo Guzman, Josephine Leal, Pedro Buitron, Hector Martell.

Sworn to and subscribed before me, this the 7th day of March, A. D. 1947.

Alonso S. Perales
Notary Public in and for Bexar County, Texas.

THE STATE OF TEXAS, COUNTY OF BEXAR

My name is Miguel Garcia Migar. I am 45 years of age and a Magician by profession. I make my living as a Magician.

On Monday, March 3, 1947, I went to Poteet, Texas, to perform that evening at the JUAREZ THEATER. About 6:00 P. M. I went to the only hotel in town to register. A lady, who I understand is the proprietress and whose name is Mrs. Hays, received me and when I asked her if there was a room for me she said "Yes". As soon as she realized that I was of Mexican descent she said: "Excuse me, but I do not rent rooms to Spanish people".

About 7:00 that same evening my daughter, Miss Angela Migar, went to register at said hotel, and Mrs. Hays asked her where she was from and what she was doing in Poteet. My daughter replied that she was from Mexico City and that she was in Poteet on a pleasure trip. Mrs. Hays replied that she was very sorry, but that she did not rent rooms to Spanish people. My daughter was well dressed.

Further affiant sayeth not.   Miguel Garcia Migar

Sworn to and subscribed before me, this the 4th day of March, A. D. 1947.

D. I. Davis
Notary Public in and for Bexar County, Texas.

THE STATE OF TEXAS, COUNTY OF BEXAR

My name is Julian Suarez. I am 54 years of age, married and I reside in Poteet, Atascosa County, Texas. I am a Veteran of World War I and I belong to Post 192 of the American Legion in Poteet, Texas. I am the owner of the Juarez Theater in Poteet and I also own and operate a grocery store there.

The statement made on this date, in a separate affidavit, by Miguel Garcia Migar to the effect that he was refused a room at the only hotel in Poteet, Texas, which is owned and operated by a Mrs. Hays is true and correct. It is not the first time that persons of Mexican descent have been refused rooms there. To my knowledge rooms have been refused to Mexican people there for the past two years.

Mr. King Hays, a son of the said Mrs. Hays, owns and operates a Barber Shop in Poteet, and he has always refused to serve persons of Mexican extraction. He has even denied service to wounded Veterans of World War II. Two of these Veterans have been Mr. Fito Herrera and Mr. Roman Rendon, of Poteet, Texas.

In the public schools our children of Mexican descent are segregated from the Anglo-American children up to and including the fourth grade. Up to two years ago they were segregated only up to and including the second grade. In the first grade our Mexican children are attending in two shifts; some go in the morning and some in the afternoon, for lack of space. There is room for them in the first grade in the Anglo-American school, authorities will not accept our children there.

Further affiant sayeth not.   Julian Suarez

Sworn to and subscribed before me, this the 4th day of March, A. D. 1947.

Alonso S. Perales
Notary Public in and for Bexar County, Texas.

148

THE STATE OF TEXAS, COUNTY OF BEXAR

My name is Carlos Tovar. My wife's name is Bernardina Tovar. We reside at 1920 Culebra Avenue, in San Antonio, Texas. We are both native born citizens of the United States of America. I have two brothers who served in the United States Army in World War II; one is Ernesto Tovar, who served in the infantry overseas three years; the other is David Tovar, who served overseas as a parachutist for about twenty months. The latter was wounded in action. They are both living in San Antonio, Texas.

On November 8, 1946, we purchased the following property for $900.00 from Mr. Henry A. Gaudren and wife, Mrs. Mary M. Gaudren.

The East 13 feet of Lot No. 6 and all of Lot No. 7, Block 6, New City Block 6589, in the corporate limits of the City of San Antonio, Bexar County, Texas, known as Plainview Addition, according to plat thereof recorded in Volume 614, page 128, of the Deed and Plat Records of Bexar County, Texas.

About four months ago we built a house on said lot, but did not move into it until February 3, 1947 for the reason that the house had not yet been made ready for occupancy. We had been living in our said home about one week when Mr. W. B. McNeil, Real Estate man of San Antonio, Texas, filed suit against us in the 37th District Court of Bexar County, Texas, on the ground that we had no right to occupy said premises because we are of Mexican descent, and that was a restricted addition. Other Anglo-Americans from San Antonio joined him in his petition. They contended that we could own the property, but could not live in it for the simple reason that we are persons of Mexican blood. We are poor people and cannot afford to pay what it cost to defend a suit like this. Therefore, we reached a compromise agreement with the plaintiffs to the effect that we are to remain on the premises for a period of ninety days so as to enable us to dispose of the property.

Further affiant sayeth not.   *Carlos C. Tovar*

Sworn to and subscribed before me, this the 1st day of March, A. D. 1947.

Alonso S. Perales
Notary Public in and for Bexar County, Texas.

LAY COUNCIL FOR THE SPANISH SPEAKING
Archdiocese of San Antonio
Room 218, Bedell Bldg.
San Antonio, 5, Texas

Mr. Henry B. Gonzalez, Pres.   Miss Mary Estelle Daunoy, Secy.
Dr. John L. McMahon, Vice-Pres.   Mr. Luis E. Gamez, Treas.
February 28, 1947

To whom it may concern:

In view of the facts presented in the accompanying affidavit,

149

we the members of the Lay Council for the Spanish Speaking of the Archdiocese of San Antonio, hereby vigorously protest the act of discrimination of the manager of the P. K. Cafe at 165 W. San Antonio Street in New Braunfels. We declare that this action is not only un-American but it is un-Christian. We heartily agree that a business firm may refuse service to people on the grounds that they are unclean or disorderly but when American citizens of whatever descent who are neat and clean and conduct themselves in a manner that is above reproach are refused service because their parents or grand-parents were born in another country, we feel that it is high time to cry out against it.

The persons involved in this case happen to be outstanding representatives of the group of people known as Latin Americans. One of them, for example, is a senior student at Our Lady of the Lake College. Another, possesses two Master's Degrees, one granted by the University of Texas and the other by St. Mary's University of San Antonio. The third is president of a women's church group in San Antonio. The brother of Miss Castillo died in the service of his country. He was a member of the Army Air Forces during the last war. Mrs. Gomez's son is still in the U. S. Navy, having served in combat during the war. The brother and seventeen close relatives of Miss Elizondo served in the armed forces of this country during World War II. All three women have records of unquestioned calibre of patriotism to the country of their birth, the United States of America. They were deeply hurt by this discrimination and we feel that they deserve at least an apology.

The action of this person discriminating against these three women is contrary to the principles on which our country was founded. Such acts of discrimination cause all good Americans to hang their heads in shame. As loyal Americans we feel it our bounden duty to see that discrimination such as this is given all possible attention to the end that this disgraceful blight on our way of life be eliminated once and for all.

(Signed)

Mr. Henry B. Gonzalez, Executive Secretary
Junior Deputy Organization

Dr. John L. McMahon, President
Our Lady of the Lake College

Miss Frances Smith, Dean of Girls
Thomas Jefferson High School

Mr. Andrew Rivera, Vice-President
National Bank of Commerce

Reverend Paul J. Ehlinger, Director
Catholic Welfare Bureau

Mr. Alonso S. Perales, Attorney

Miss Alice Des Marais, Director
Social Service Department, Santa Rosa Hospital

Miss Mary Piña, School teacher
Bowie School

Mrs. Terrell Bartlett, President
Archdiocesan Council of Catholic Women

Miss Christine Carvajal, School teacher
Ruiz School

Reverend John M. Hayes, Professor of Religion
Incarnate Word College

Mr. Juan L. Hidalgo, Men's Field Worker
Bishops' Committee for the Spanish Speaking

Mr. Richard S. O'Connor, Director
Graduate School of Social Service
Our Lady of the Lake College

Miss Emma Solis, Director
Spanish Department, St. Mary's Hall

Dr. Austin J. App, Professor of English
Incarnate Word College

Miss Henrietta Castillo, Womens' Field Worker
Bishops' Committee for the Spanish Speaking

Dr. Jasper Cross, Professor of History
Our Lady of the Lake College

Dr. Alice M. Christensen, Professor of Sociology
Our Lady of the Lake College

Brother Theodore J. Brenner, Director
Spanish Department, St. Mary's University

Reverend John J. Birch, Executive Secretary
Bishops' Committee for the Spanish Speaking

cc: The New Braunfels Chamber of Commerce

cc: The New Braunfels Ministerial Association

cc: Right Rev. John J. Robling, Pastor St. Peter
      and St. Paul Church, New Braunfels, Texas

cc: Reverend William Janning, M.S.F., Pastor of Our
      Lady of Perpetual Help Church, New Braunfels, Texas

151

cc: The Texas Good Neighbor Commission, Austin, Texas

cc: Dr. George I. Sanchez, University of Texas
Austin, Texas

cc: Dr. Carlos E. Castañeda, University of
Texas, Austin Texas

cc: New Braunfels Herald

cc: Alamo Register

cc: La Prensa

cc: La Voz

cc: Southern Messenger

cc: San Antonio Ministerial Alliance

cc: San Antonio Chamber of Commerce

cc: Mexican Chamber of Commerce

cc: New Braunfels Business and Professional Women's Club

THE STATE OF TEXAS, COUNTY OF BEXAR

"Friday, February 14, at 3:00 P. M., Mrs. Anita Gomez President of the Mother's Club of San Alphonsus Center, Lucy Elizondo, student of Our Lady of the Lake College and I, Henrietta Castillo, Field Worker of the Bishops' Committee for the Spanish Speaking, after buying $60 worth of materials at the New Braunfels Textile Mills went to the P. K. Cafe, 165 W. San Antonio Street at New Braunfels to dine. As we entered we sat at the first table in the cafe. The waitress came over to our table and told us if we wished to be served to go around the back. Mrs. Gomez got up immediately and walked out. Miss Elizondo walked out too. I got up, picked up my coat, walked to the back where the waitress was standing and asked her why we should go to the back when there was so much room in front. She told me that those were her orders and that I could talk to the manager. I asked her who the manager was and she pointed out a lady who was sewing the hem to a dress at the counter near the door and the cash register. I walked up to her and told her the waitress had refused to serve us in front where we were sitting. She said: "We'll serve you people but you have to go to the back, behind the screen." When I asked why, she said: 'The lady with you is obviously a Mexican and that is where we serve them.' By that time Miss Elizondo had walked back into the cafe and I said: 'We are Mexicans, too.' The manager answered: 'Well, that's where we serve you people.'

152

"Even though we were hungry, we came straight to San Antonio for fear of running into more of such discrimination".
Further affiant sayeth not.   (Signed) Henrietta A. Castillo
Sworn to and subscribed before me, this the 21st day of February, A. D. 1947.
(Signed) D. F. Davis, Notary Public, Bexar County, Texas.

CATHOLIC WAR VETERANS
STATE DEPARTMENT OF TEXAS— REV.
J. R. CASSIDY, O. M. I., CHAPLAIN
P. O. Box 416
WESLACO, TEXAS. Feb. 24, 1947

Alonso S. Perales,
Attorney At Law,
714 Gunter Building
San Antonio, Texas.

Dear Mr. Perales:

During the past weeks much discrimination has shown itself here in the Rio Grande Valley. Cases have come to the public attention in Edinburg, McAllen and Harlingen, and our Organization, the Catholic War Veterans, Inc., which has some eight hundred members here in the Rio Grande Valley wish to counteract this attitude as much as possible for our members are all American Citizens of Mexican extraction with an honorable discharge.

Respectfully yours
Rev. James R. Cassidy, O. M. I.

THE STATE OF TEXAS, COUNTY OF BEXAR

My name is Ramon Treviño. I am a native born citizen of the United States and reside at Charlotte, Texas. I served three years, one month and ten days in the United States Army, fourteen months of which I spent serving overseas. I am 23 years of age.

On Saturday, Dec. 14, 1946, about 9:00 P. M., the following friends and I went into the "OASIS" Beer Parlor and Recreation Hall, in Jourdanton, Texas: Jose Lopez, Jr., Reymundo Cruz, Celestino Cordova, Jr., and Leonardo Ortiz. We drank a bottle of beer each at the bar. Then we sat down at a table and drank another bottle each. Then I called Jim Ormond, the bartender and owner of the place, and I asked him what were the requirements in order for one to become a member of the Club which they have there in the second section of the building. First they have the beer parlor and then in another section toward the rear they have a Club in which they have billiard tables and a dance hall. He told me that each member of the Club had to pay $200.00. Then I asked him what benefits a member could enjoy by belonging. I told him that I was willing to pay the $200.00, whereupon he said

153

that he was just joking when he said $200.00, that what was required was that the member be "white", he said: "what you really need to be is a white boy". Then Jose Lopez Jr., asked him if an American soldier in uniform, of Mexican descent wanted to belong to the Club, whether he would be admitted, and he replied in the negative. Then Lopez said to him: "That means, then, that as long as he is of Mexican descent he can not belong to the Club", and he replied: "That's right". Then I asked him why they did not accept persons of Mexican descent as members, and he said: "This is why" and he struck me on the left side of my head with a wooden club similar to those used by policemen. Jose Lopez, Jr., remained inside. The rest of us left the place. Lopez asked him whether persons of Mexican descent could continue to come into the beer parlor section to drink beer, and he said "Yes, but only in front".

(At this point Mr. Jose Lopez, Jr., who is present, states that he has read the foregoing statement made by Mr. Ramon Treviño, and that the same is true and correct.)

Further affiants sayeth not.   Ramon Treviño, Jose Lopez, Jr.

Sworn to and subscribed before me, this the 16th day of December, A. D. 1946.

Alonso S. Perales
Notary Public, Bexar County, Texas

THE STATE OF TEXAS, COUNTY OF BEXAR

My name is Roberto Canales. I am a native born citizen of the United States, 23 years of age and reside at 115 Alazan Street, in San Antonio, Texas. I am a veteran of World War II.

On Tuesday, December 10, about 5:30 P. M., my brother Andres Canales and I went into the Hanger VII Grill, at Uvalde, Texas, and we sat at a table. A man who appeared to be the owner came to us and asked us where we were from and whether we were Mexicans. We told him that we were from San Antonio, Texas, and that we were of Mexican descent. He then said that he was from San Antonio, Texas, also and had been reared among Mexicans, but that the Anglo-American people of Uvalde did not approve of his serving Mexicans in his restaurant. I told him that I was a veteran of World War II and that I had served overseas fighting for my country, and that it was rather disappointing to see now that it did not help me any when it comes to escaping humiliations just because I happen to be of Mexican extraction. He replied that he, too, had been a soldier, but that he could not do anything about it.

I served three and one half years in the United States Army, one year of which I spent overseas.

Further affiant sayeth not.   Roberto Canales

154

Sworn and subscribed before me, this the 11th day of December, A. D. 1946.

Alonso S. Perales

Notary Public, Bexar County, Texas

THE STATE OF TEXAS, COUNTY OF BEXAR

Our names are *Joseph Robles Ramon* and *Alfonso Galindo Robles*. We live in San Antonio, Bexar County, Texas. We are twenty four years and twenty one years of age respectively.

On Saturday, October 5th, about 8:30 P. M., we stopped at the Helotes Dance Hall and Tavern. I, Joseph Robles Ramon, went into the tavern and Alfonso Galindo Robles remained in our truck outside. I told the bartender to sell me a sandwich and a bottle of beer to take to my mother who lives on a ranch about four miles from said tavern. We were on our way to said ranch. He said that he had orders not to serve Mexicans. I talked with him in a nice manner and tried to make him see that it was wrong to deny us service just because we are of Mexican descent. I, Joseph Robles Ramon, told him that I had served in the United States Marine Corps, had fought overseas and had been badly wounded, and that I had done all of this for the sake of democracy and freedom. I added that I am totally disabled as a result of the wounds inflicted upon me in the fields of battle. He said that did not make any difference, that I still was a mexican and he could not serve me.

I was so angry because of his refusal to serve me merely on account of my being of Mexican descent that I went outside, got into my truck and ran the truck against the building. I then got off the truck and went into the tavern. The man who had refused to sell me the sandwich jumped upon me as soon as I went into the tavern and we fought each other. Someone there, the bartender I believe, struck me with a blunt instrument in the head and cut my head. He also struck me in the nose. My cousin, Alfonso Galindo Robles, came in and assisted me.

Neither of us had a drink of any kind. We were coming from work and were on the way to the ranch to see our mother and aunt.

Further affiants sayeth not.

Joseph Robles Ramon, Alfonso Galindo Robles.

Sworn to and subscribed before me, this the 8th day of October, A. D. 1946.

Alonso S. Perales

Notary Public, Bexar County, Texas

155

THE STATE OF TEXAS, COUNTY OF BEXAR

*My name is Macario Garcia. I am 26 years of age, single, and
I reside at 1908 Franklin Avenue, in Houston, Texas.*

*I served in the United States Army two years, ten months
and twenty eight days, eleven months and six days of which I
served overseas. On August 23, 1945 President Harry S. Truman
bestowed upon me the Congressional Medal of Honor.*

*On October 10, 1945, about 11:15 P. M., I went into the Oasis
Cafe in Richmond, Fort Bend County, Texas, and I sat at the
counter and ordered a cup of coffee. One of the waitresses asked
me what I wanted and I told her that I wanted a cup of coffee.
She then said to me: "I cannot serve you", and she walked away.
I remained sitting at the counter. In about a minute she returned
to where I was and I asked her why she could not serve me, and
she replied that because Mexicans were not served at that place.
She walked away again. Then her husband, came to me and asked
me what seemed to be the trouble. I replied: "Nothing that I know
of. I asked the lady why she could not serve me a cup of coffee".
He then said to me: "Well, she told you why, so there is the door",
and he pointed to the door, meaning for me to get out. I stood up.
There was a sugar bowl on the counter and what he had told
me made me so angry that I pushed the sugar bowl off the counter.
It fell behind the counter. Then he came from behind the counter
to where I was and started to seize me by the left arm to put me
out. I shoved him off with my left hand and told him not to
touch me, and to stay away from me, that I was telling him that
for his own benefit. When he tried to get closer to me I picked
up an empty water glass and threw it at him, hitting him on the
chest. The glass fell and broke. Then he said: "You think you
are smart, eh? I'll fix you up", and he went behind the counter.
When he was standing behind the counter I threw another empty
water glass. He ducked and the glass went and broke a glass
of wine. The reason I threw the second glass at him was that
I thought he was going to get something to hit me with. A customer
who was there then came behind and made a pass at me with a
baseball bat. I dodged the blow and he struck the wall. I asked
him if he too wanted to fight me and he did not say anything, but
he turned the bat lose and it fell to the floor. There were two
sailors in the place and they came and stood between me and the
cafe manager. I forgot to say that before the two sailors interceded,
the Cafe Manager had thrown an empty water glass at me. I dodged it and it went and broke a window glass.*

*When the sailors got between us we stopped throwing things
at each other. That is all there was to it. I walked out of the place
and left. No woman present was thrown anything at or struck by
anybody. Of this I am sure. Charges of aggravated assault have*

156

been filed against me at Richmond, Texas, alleging that I struck a woman in the place, but said charges are unfounded, as I did nothing of the kind.

I was wearing the uniform of the United States Army at the time.

I was born in Villa de Castaño, Coahuila, Mexico, and I was a citizen of Mexico when I joined the United States Army.

Further affiant sayeth not.   Macario Garcia.

Sworn and subscribed to before me this 5th day of October, A. D. 1946.

Alonso S. Perales

Notary Public, Bexar County, Texas

THE STATE OF TEXAS, COUNTY OF BEXAR

My name is Maria Saucedo Flores. I am married. My husband's name is Rafael Saucedo Flores. We reside at 4202 W. Martin St., in San Antonio, Texas.

On September 3rd 1946, about 10:00 A. M., I took our 7-year old daughter, Maria Marta, to the Lakeview Baptist School, situated on the corner of 21st and W. Martin Streets, for the purpose of registering her as a student at said School. The Superintendent, an Anglo-American, said to me: "I am sorry, but I cannot take your little girl because I am not taking Latin American children. I will have to ask permission from the local Board". I asked him if the reason he could not accept my little girl was just because she was a Latin American and he replied: "Yes, she is a Latin American and we are not taking Latin American children."

Further affiant sayeth not.   Maria Saucedo Flores

Sworn and subscribed to before me this 4th day of September, A. D. 1946.

Alonso S. Perales

Notary Public, Bexar County, Texas

SEPTEMBER 1946

BOBBY DAVILA.—On September 2nd another boy, Lorenzo Tellez and I went to Metzger's to drink some malt. An American boy served us carbonated water. We asked him why he had served carbonated water and he replied that we did not have to go in there in the first place. He brought us the malts and we ate them, paid our checks and left. We were mad, because he served us carbonated water and because of the way he had talked to us. I told Lorenzo Tellez that I wanted to see that boy that night when he came out. At 7:45 P. M. we went to a garage on Poplar and Laredo Streets. From the garage we went to Metzger's on N. Flores Street to see about the boy that had waited on us there that afternoon about 5:45 P. M. We left the garage at about 9:45 P. M. We

157

got there before they closed Metzger's so we waited until they closed and for the boy to come out. The boy was talking to some big boys about the trouble we had with him and the big boys came over to us and asked what we wanted. We said we did not want anything from them. One of the big boys said I hear you want to fight the Soda Fountain boys. I said yes that's right. This big boy had a pipe (steel pipe) about two and one half feet long. This big boy said: "well, start fighting". We fought. We saw some cars coming and we thought it was the police and we also saw one of the American boys' father coming on foot so we all ran. We hid in a big truck in this garage on Poplar and Laredo Streets. About 5 minutes later about 15 or 16 of these Anglo-American boys passed by the garage in a car. They did not see us so they went on by and a few minutes later we all went home. When we ran from Metzgers these boys had said they would be ready for us the next night.

The second time, about 9:30 P. M., about 13 Mexican boys met about as many Anglo-American boys at Metzgers. Every one had a stick, a rock or an iron or something to fight with. One of the Anglo-American boys had a gun. I went over to the boy with the gun and told him to put away the gun and I would fight him. _He was holding the gun by his side pointed at the ground and Davila tried to grab it and he told him to keep back and he fired the gun on the ground by Davila's right foot. At this time two cars drove up and the boys that were with Davila started to run. When Davila was running we heard another shot, but we didn't know that anyone was hit. Very shortly thereafter we learned that Jesse Garcia had been shot in the back of the head. Davila identified Kelly Adams as the boy that had the gun and had shot in the ground by his foot.

(This case was tried before the Honorable Charles W. Anderson, County Judge of Bexar County, Texas, who declined to render a verdict, stating that he was not satisfied with the evidence presented to him, that he wanted his Juvenile Officers to investigate the case further, and that he preferred to have the case tried before a jury.

Accordingly, the case was tried in the Juvenile Court before an Anglo-American jury, who acquitted the defendant Kelly Adams.)

THE STATE OF TEXAS, COUNTY OF BEXAR

My name is Frank E. Riley. I am 30 years of age and married. I am a member of the United States Air Force, and am stationed at San Antonio Military Basic Training Center, San Antonio, Texas. I have served 15 months in the U. S. Air Force and three years and seven months in the U. S. Navy. I was born in Guatemala, Central America.

About 15 days ago my wife and I went into the Ray Theater, at Hondo, Texas, and sat down. My wife was born in Guatemala, Central America, also. We had occupied our seats about three minutes when one of the ushers came and told us that because we were Latin Americans we would have to leave the theater, as Latin Americans were not admitted to said theater. I asked for an explanation and the usher said that I had better leave if I did not want to get into a difficulty. My wife and I thereupon got up and left. While going thru the vestibule or lobby of the theater I again demanded an explanation and the usher then said that he was not in a position to give me an explanation, as he had orders from the manager to do this. I was wearing the United States Army uniform at the time. I explained to the usher that my wife and I were Latin Americans from Guatemala, Central America, and he said that did not make any difference because we were still Latin Americans. This happened in the afternoon. That same day I went to the Hondo Chamber of Commerce. I spoke with the Manager and he explained to me that it was customary in Hondo not to admit Latin Americans to theaters, drug stores, restaurants and other public places. The name of the Manager is Allan Webster.

I then went and reported the incident to my Commanding Officer at the Military Basic Training Center, San Antonio, Texas.

My father, the late Harry Joseph Riley, a native of Hartsville, Mo., was Consul General of the United States of America in Central America for twenty seven years.

Further Affiant sayeth not.   *Frank E. Riley.*

Sworn and subscribed to before me this 20th day of August, A. D. 1946.

Alonso S. Perales
Notary Public, Bexar County, Texas

THE STATE OF TEXAS, COUNTY OF BEXAR

My name is Daniel Flores Gonzalez. I am 24 years of age and reside in Brackettville, Texas. I served in the United States Army about 38 months, 26 of which I spent overseas. I took part in four battles. I have two brothers in the United States Army. One of them served about 5 years and the other about 3 years. They served overseas also, and recently they reenlisted for three years.

On Saturday, August 17th, about 7:00 A. M., I was on my way to Brackettville, and while passing thru Hondo, Texas, I stopped at the Manhattan Cafe. I was accompanied by two ladies of Mexican descent. We sat at the counters intending to ask for something to eat. A boy who was employed at said Cafe came and told us that he was very sorry, but that Mexicans were not served there. I as-

ked him why and he said that those were the orders of the manager. We thereupon left the place.

Further affiant sayeth not.   Daniel Flores Gonzalez

Sworn to and subscribed before me this 20th day of August, A. D. 1946.

Alonso S. Perales
Notary Public, Bexar County, Texas

THE STATE OF TEXAS, COUNTY OF BEXAR

Our names are Dolores G. de Garcia and Lupe C. Banasau. We are both married and reside at 103 El Fledo Courts and 1616 Center St., respectively, in San Antonio, Texas.

On Sunday, July 28th 1946, about 9:20 P. M., we stopped at the Manhattan Cafe, in Hondo, Texas, and as soon as we went in a waitress came and told us that she was sorry, but that we could not be served because we were Mexicans. She added that those were the orders given to her by the Manager. We thereupon left. We were accompanied by Mr. Juan Garcia, husband of the said Dolores G. de Garcia, and by a young lady named Maria Magdalena Olvera. Miss Olvera resides in Brackettville, Texas.

Mr. Juan Garcia is a veteran of World War No. 1 and served as Commander of the American Legion at Brackettville, Texas, from 1944 to 1945.

Mr. Richard Banasau, husband of the said Lupe C. Banasau, is now a member of the United States Army. He fought in the Phillippines during World War No. 2. The said Lupe C. Banasau also has a son, Ernest Banasau, who served overseas in World War No. 2.

Further affiants sayeth not. Dolores Garcia de Garcia, Lupe C. Banasau.

Sworn to and subscribed before me, this the 7th day of August, A. D. 1946.

Alonso S. Perales
Notary Public, Bexar County, Texas

THE STATE OF TEXAS, COUNTY OF BEXAR

My name is Jesus Garcia. I reside at 428 Burleson St., in San Antonio, Texas. I am 41 years of age and married. I am a citizen of the United States of America.

On Sunday, June 30, 1946, about 3:00 P. M., seven of us went into the Captain Davis Cafe, in Rockport, Texas, and sat at a table. A waitress brought some water, but before she placed the two glasses of water on the table the lady Cashier called her and told her not to serve us on this side (meaning the side where, according to them, only Anglo-Americans are served) because we were Latin Americans. The waitress came and told us what the Cashier had

160

told her. The two Anglo-Americans told the waitress that if we Latin Americans were not served, they would not eat there either. We all left the place.

The names of the seven men are: Oscar Mayen, Joe Sanchez, Henry _____, Pedro Solis, Jesus Garcia, Louis Leonard and Bob Clay, all residents of San Antonio, Texas, except Pedro Solis, who resides in Rockport, Texas.

Further affiant sayeth not.   Jesus Garcia

Sworn to and subscribed before me, this the 2nd day of July, A. D. 1946.

Alonso S. Perales
Notary Public, Bexar County, Texas

THE STATE OF TEXAS, COUNTY OF BEXAR

My name is Ignacio Riojas. I reside at 614 East Mistletoe St., in San Antonio, Texas. I am 35 years of age. I am an overseas veteran of World War No. 2. I am a native born American citizen. I served 32 months overseas, eleven of which I spent fighting for my country.

I was with Messrs. Samuel Anaya, Jose Flores and Richard B. Cordova, Jr., also veterans of World War No. 2, when they went to a beer parlor situated at 1715 Broadway, in San Antonio, Texas, the evening of May 25, 1946. The bartender told us that they did not sell beer to Spanish people. I have carefully read the affidavit executed by Mr. Samuel Anaya under date of May 27, 1946, regarding this incident, and wish to state that everything stated therein is true and correct.

Further affiant sayeth not.   Ignacio Riojas

Sworn to and subscribed before me, this the 11th day of June, A. D. 1946.

Alonso S. Perales
Notary Public, Bexar County, Texas

THE STATE OF TEXAS, COUNTY OF BEXAR

My name is Ricardo Cordova. I reside at 417 Furnish Ave., in San Antonio, Texas. I am 25 years of age. I am an overseas veteran of World War No. 2. I am a native born American citizen. I fought at Bataan and Corregidor and was a prisoner of the Japanese for three and one half years. I was wounded in action.

I was with Messrs. Samuel Anaya, Jose Flores and Ignacio Riojas, also veterans of World War No. 2, when they went to a beer parlor situated at 1715 Broadway, in San Antonio, Texas, the evening of May 25, 1946. The bartender told us that they did not sell beer to Spanish people. I have carefully read the affidavit executed by Mr. Samuel Anaya under date of May 27, 1946, regarding this incident, and wish to state that everything stated therein is true and correct.

Further affiant sayeth not. Richard B. Cordova, Jr.

Sworn to and subscribed before me, this the 1st day of June, A. D. 1946.

Alonso S. Perales.
Notary Public in and for Bexar County, Texas.

THE STATE OF TEXAS, COUNTY OF BEXAR

My name is Samuel Anaya. I reside at 217 Rose Lane, San Antonio, Texas. I am 38 years of age and married. I am an overseas veteran of World War No. 2. I was born in Durango, Durango, Mexico.

On Saturday evening, May 25, 1946, Jose Flores, Ignacio Riojas, and I, went to a beer parlor situated at 1715 Broadway, in San Antonio, Texas. Before I forget it, I should like to state that another veteran of World War No. 2 by the name of Cordova accompanied us also. Mr. Flores and Mr. Riojas are likewise veterans of World War No. 2 and served overseas; so did Cordova. We stood at the counter of said beer parlor and asked for four beers. The bartender told us that they did not sell beer to Spanish people because the State Liquor Control Board did not allow them to do so. Cordova asked him: Isn't this money good (and Cordova threw the money on the counter), and the bartender replied in the affirmative, but that he did not sell to Spanish people. There was a woman behind the counter also and she nodded approval of what the bartender said as regards their not selling to Spanish people.

Cordova told him that he (Cordova) had fought for this country in World War No. 2, to which the bartender replied: "You were fighting for yourself". The bartender then said: "You all get out (meaning the four of us) before you get in trouble".

We then went to Police Headquarters and asked for the Liquor Control Officer. We asked said Officer if it was true that the Liquor Control Board had instructed said beer parlor not to sell beer to Spanish people. He said that no such instructions had been given, and he and the Police Sergeant went to speak to said bartender about the matter. They returned and said that the bartender denied that he had said that the Liquor Control Board did not allow them to sell to Spanish people.

Further affiant sayeth not. Samuel Anaya

Sworn to and subscribed before me, this the 27th day of May, A. D. 1946.

Alonso S. Perales,
Notary Public in and for Bexar County, Texas,

162

THE STATE OF TEXAS, COUNTY OF BEXAR

My name is Juan S. Gonzalez. I am a native born citizen of the United States and reside at 541 West Mitchell St., in San Antonio, Texas. I am a veteran of World War II. I served about four years in the United States Army, thirty two months of which I served overseas. I took part in three major engagements in the southwest Pacific.

On Friday, May 3, 1946, about 7:30 P. M., Mr. Gilberto G. Gonzalez and I went into the Spanish Village Cafe, at 327 Blum St., in San Antonio, Texas, and as we were going in, a lady, who appeared to be the manager or proprietress, told us that she did not have any room for us. Whereupon Mr. Gilberto G. Gonzalez asked her what she meant by that, whether she meant that she did not serve Mexicans there, and she replied that was exactly what she wanted to tell us. Mr. Gonzalez told her: "I think you are getting a little too big", and she answered: "I want to be that way". We then left the place.

There were only two or three people being served in the Cafe at the time, and there were plenty of tables available.

Mr. Gonzalez and I were well dressed and we deported ourselves like gentlemen when we went into said Cafe.

Mr. Gonzalez is also a veteran of World War II and he likewise served overseas. He lives in San Antonio and both he and I are employed by the Texas Employment Commission, in San Antonio, Texas.

Further affiant sayeth not.   Juan S. Gonzalez

Sworn to and subscribed before me, this the 8th day of May, A. D. 1946.

Alonso S. Perales.

Notary Public in and for Bexar County, Texas.

THE STATE OF TEXAS, COUNTY OF BEXAR

My name is Horacio Guerra. I am 26 years of age and reside at 609 S. San Jacinto St., in San Antonio, Texas. I am an American citizen and a veteran of World War No. 2. I served in the United States Army overseas for a period of eighteen months. I was born in Monterrey, N. L., Mexico.

I am now engaged in the produce business on my own account. On May 1st 1946, I was coming from El Paso, Texas, and I stopped at the Dinette Restaurant in Uvalde, Texas, and sat at the counter. A waitress came to me and said: "she does not serve Mexicans", meaning the proprietress. Whereupon I walked out and went and spoke with the County Judge of Uvalde County, who told me he could not do a thing about it.

Further affiant sayeth not.   Horacio Guerra.
Sworn to and subscribed before me, this the 3rd day of May,
A. D. 1946.

Alonso S. Perales.
Notary Public in and for Bexar County, Texas.

THE STATE OF TEXAS, COUNTY OF BEXAR

Before me the undersigned authority a Notary Public in and
for Bexar County, Texas, on this day personally appeared, Jose I.
Perez, and makes the following statement: I am 56 years of age.
I have worked for the U. S. Government more than 21 years. February 1st 1944, I was a Jr. Leather and Canvas Worker at $1860.00
per year and was transferred to Aircraft Mechanic at $2200.oo per
year, at Kelly Field, Texas. On December 16th, 1945, I was transferred from Aircraft Mechanic to Jr. Flight Clothing Repairer, Grade
8, Over Maximum at $1.06 per hour, at Kelly Field, Texas. I have
gotten all my experience by actual work and I know all the work,
and feel that I am entitled to a Senior position and pay. I also
look after the interest of my Government, and while it is true that
I have not a good education, actual experience for so many years
has educated me in the line of work I am doing, and also in the
line of fabrics. It plainly shows that the grade given me now is
coming down and not going up as I am justly entitled to.

Jose I. Perez

Sworn to and subscribed before me this the 18th day of April,
A. D. 1946.

D. F. DAVIS, Notary Public Bexar County, Texas. My Commission expires June 1st 1947.

THE STATE OF TEXAS, COUNTY OF BEXAR

Our names are Juanita R. Flores, Victoria G. Lozano and Beatriz V. Cano and our addresses are 110 Englishway, 1420 W. Salinas St., and 514 N. San Jacinto St., San Antonio, Texas, respectively.
We all belong to the MARGIL SCHOOL PARENTS AND TEA-
CHERS ASSOCIATION, in San Antonio, Texas.

On April 9, 1946, about 6:00 P. M., we went into the Hangar
VII Grill, 223 N. Getty St., in Uvalde, Texas, and we sat at a table
and waited about 15 minutes and no one would serve us even a
glass of water. Finally Mr. W. W. Moore, owner of said Grill, came
to us and remarked: "Are you ladies strangers in town?" We replied
in the affirmative and told him that we were from San Antonio,
Texas, and that we had gone to Uvalde for the purpose of attending
the 5th District P.T.A. Conference. Then he said: "I knew you
were strangers because Uvalde is not like San Antonio. We do not
give service to Mexican people. If I were to serve Mexicans, my
Anglo-American customers would walk out. I knew you ladies repre-

164

sented some sort of organization, and I wish you would take this matter up with your organization. It is not I that object to Mexicans being served in my place, but the local people". Whereupon he called a waitress and ordered her to serve us anything we wanted.

The said Juanita R. Flores added: *My husband is in the United States Navy.*

The said Victoria G. Lozano stated: *My brother was killed in action while serving in the United States Army overseas.*

The said Beatriz V. Cano declared: *My husband is in the Merchant Marine.*

Further affiants sayeth not. Juanita R. Flores. Beatriz V. Cano. Victoria G. Lozano.

Sworn to and subscribed before me, this the 13th day of April, A. D. 1946.

Alonso S. Perales.
Notary Public in and for Bexar County, Texas.

THE STATE OF TEXAS, COUNTY OF BEXAR

My name is Manuel Delgado. I am 22 years of age and a native born citizen of the United States of America. I served in World War No. 2 thirty three months, twenty seven of which were served by me overseas. I have three battle stars.

On Saturday, March 2, 1946, about 9:00 P.M., I was beaten up by Sheriff W. E. Pond, of Zavalla County, Texas, and by another officer who was with him at the time. He was accompanied by two peace officers when he approached me in front of a billiard hall belonging to Mrs. Mariana Garcia, in Crystal City, Zavalla County, Texas. The said W. E. Pond pushed me when he first approached me. I said to him: "Don't push me". He then seized me by the shirt that he tore it up and he took me to his automobile. When he was putting me in his car one of the officers with him kicked me. I asked them if that was the way they treated their prisioners and they began beating me up again. I remember very distinctly that the said W. E. Pond was one of them. He beat me about my face, lips, and he damaged one of my teeth. I tried to explain to them and they continued to beat me up. They would not let me explain anything to them.

At the time the Sheriff approached me for the first time I was outside the billiard hall speaking with a man named Jesus Olivares.

On March 4, 1946 I was fined $63.00 and the said Sheriff gave me a receipt for said amount.

I am certain that I did not insult the Sheriff or any of the other peace officers and did not offend in any manner whatsoever. I merely tried to ask them why they were arresting me and later

165

I tried to explain matters to them, but they refused to listen to me and instead proceeded to beat me up as aforesaid.

Further affiant sayeth not.   Manuel Delgado

Sworn to and subscribed before me, this the 5th day of March, A. D. 1946.

Alonso S. Perales.
Notary Public in and for Bexar County, Texas.

THE STATE OF TEXAS, COUNTY OF BEXAR

Our names are Felipe Guajardo, Antonio Hinojosa and Pascual Ortega and we reside in San Antonio, Bexar County, Texas. I, Felipe Guajardo, am a citizen of Mexico, and we, Antonio Hinojosa and Pascual Ortega, were born in the United States. We are employed by the Merchants Fruit Co., at 123 Produce Row, in San Antonio, Texas, as truck drivers.

On February 18, 1946, about 11:00 P. M., we were driving from Laredo, Texas to San Antonio, Texas, and we stopped at the Monte Carlo Inn in Devine, Texas, and we sat at the counter and ordered three cups of coffee. We drank our coffee, paid for it and left the place. We did not offend anyone in any manner. In fact, we did not talk to anyone except the waiter who served us the coffee and that was just to order the coffee and pay for it. When we were in the restaurant we noticed that there were about eight Anglo-Americans drinking beer at one of the tables. As we went out of the restaurant one of the Anglo-Americans held Antonio Hinojosa by the left arm and another one struck him in the back of his head and in the face with a blackjack. When the said Antonio Hinojosa fell to the ground one of the Anglo-Americans took $55.00 from the right pocket of his trousers.

Felipe Guajardo was likewise seized by the left arm by one of the Anglo-Americans and struck on the chin and fell to the ground. After he was on the ground he was struck twice on the chin by one of the Anglo-Americans who used his feet to do so. As Pascual Ortega was leaving the restaurant he was struck in the back of his right ear by one of the Anglo-Americans. Pascual Ortega was robbed of $5.00 and a cigarette lighter which he had in his shirt pocket. Ortega ran and when he did so the Anglo Americans pursued him. Felipe Guajardo got up from the ground just then, got into his truck and left to ask for help. About four blocks from the restaurant he met a watchman and told him what had happened. The watchman called the constable. The constable then accompanied Felipe Guajardo to the restaurant and when they went in two of the Anglo-Americans jumped on the said Felipe Guajardo, but did not actually strike him because the Constable prevented them from doing so. Felipe Guajardo identified two of the men immediately, and told the Constable that was the same

166

group of men who were in the restaurant when he and his two friends had first come in and who had assaulted them. The constable took down the names of the said Anglo-Americans.

On Saturday, February 23, 1946, we filed charges against four of the men before the Justice of the Peace at Devine, Medina County, Texas.

Further affiants sayeth not.

Felipe Guajardo, Antonio Hinojosa, Pascual Ortega.

Sworn to and subscribed before me, this the 28th day of February, A. D. 1946.

Alonso S. Perales.
Notary Public in and for Bexar County, Texas.

Law Office of FLY and VANCE

Hondo, Texas, March 19, 1946

Mr. Arthur V. Wright,
Suite 714 Gunter Bldg.,
San Antonio 5, Texas.

Mr. Peña del Barrio,
123 Produce Row,
San Antonio, Texas.

Gentlemen:

The four boys charged by indictment with an aggravated assault came to the County Court here with their parents and entered a plea of guilty before the County Judge and he fined each $25.00 and costs.

Sorry it was so small a fine.

Yours truly,
Frank X. Vance.
County Attorney.

THE STATE OF TEXAS, COUNTY OF BEXAR

Our names are Guillermo Martinez and Benigno Montes. We reside at 1023 South Alamo St., in San Antonio, Texas, but our legal residence is in Del Rio, Texas. We are native born citizens of the United States. We are barbers by trade and are employed by Mr. Mack Robinson, at Camp Bullis, Texas.

On Tuesday, Feb. 5, 1946, about 11:30 A.M., we went into the mess hall for soldiers and civilians, in front of the Dispensary, at Camp Bullis, Texas, and we sat at a table with some Anglo-Americans. The Mess Sergeant in charge of the mess hall came and told us to move to another table separate and apart from the Anglo-Americans. Other persons who were likewise segregated by the Mess Sergeant on the same day are: Justino de la Vega, Marcos Benitez, Benito Perez, Veteran of World War II, Guillermo Ro-

167

driguez, Lorenzo Cabrera, Rosendo S. Piña, Jr., Veteran of World War II, and Johnny Espinoza, Veteran of World War II. I, Guillermo Martinez, am a Veteran of World War II also.

With the exception of us two of the persons segregated were civil service employees who are working at Camp Bullis.

When several Anglo-Americans started to sit with us at the same table, the Mess Sergeant came and told them to move to tables designated for "Whites".

The next day the Mess Sergeant placed signs at the different tables, some reading: "For Whites", others: "For Spanish", and others: "For colored".

Further affiants sayeth not. Guillermo Martinez, Benigno Montes.

Sworn to and subscribed before me, this the 9th day of February, A. D. 1946.

Alonso S. Perales.
Notary Public in and for Bexar County, Texas.

DANCE

BIG   DANCE
MACDONA SHOOTING CLUB
December 9th -- Starting 9-1-Oct.
FOR AMERICAN PEOPLE ONLY
NO LATIN AMERICAN
EVERYONE COME OUT AND HAVE A GOOD TIME
PLENTY OF REFRESHMENTS
GOOD MUSIC   LOTS OF ROOM
MUSIC BY   WILLETTS ORCHESTRA

The above is a copy of a notice printed on a cardboard 22 inches long by 14 inches wide and circulated in San Antonio, Texas. These cardboards were placed in some business establishments and also on some automobiles. The undersigned has one of the cardboards in his possession.

(Alonso S. Perales)

714 Gunter Bldg.
San Antonio, Texas.
1946.

Mr. Alonso S. Perales,
San Antonio, Texas

We, the undersigned, are appealing to you for a view of our standing point of our Civil rights as American citizens of the United States of America, for which we stand for, and have worn, and are wearing, the uniform that we are so proud of and are fully aware and willing to pay with the supreme sacrifice to defend our country for the liberties of those who depend on us, that is why we are

168

appealing to you to know if there are any rights for any of us to be deliberately discriminated and refused to be served in a public place for the simple reason that we are of Latin-American descent.

An incident that occurred to us on the 20th day of November 1941, in the City of San Angelo, Texas, in the business place by the name of Dew Drop Inn, located at 36 North Chadbourne Street. We appealed to the Mayor of said City and its District Attorney also, but we were informed that there's nothing that could be done about it, stating that if any owner of a public business place refused to serve any people of American-Latin descent he was in his rights to do so and no one could prevent him from doing so, regardless if he wore a uniform or not.

I am sure there is no doubt in your mind as to how we felt about it, that's why we hope that some way is found to stop such incidents as the above mentioned, not for us but for someone else of our nationality. We do hope that you will see into this matter, and we trust in God that you grant our request. Trusting to hear from you at the earliest convenience.

We remain loyal and at your service.

Sgt. Baldemar V. Torres. Co. A 53rd Signal Battalion. Pvt. Frank Aguilar (Address same as above). Mr. Joe Reyes, Route 3, Box 1. San Angelo, Texas.

D. LM7 DL PD 4 EXTRA — ALBUQUERQUE
NMEX 25 VIA DALLAS TEX 26
FAIR EMPLOYMENT PRACTICE
San Antonio, Texas

WE DEMAND INVESTIGATION DISCRIMINATION AGAINST SPANISH AMERICANS IN HILTON HOTEL ALBUQUERQUE NEW MEXICO. THIS HOTEL PUBLICLY JUSTIFIES ITS SUBSTANDARD WAGE SCALE ON THE CONTENTION THAT SPANISH SPEAKING AMERICANS ARE NOT WORTH MORE. HOTEL ALSO ATTEMPTING TO INDUCE PEOPLE TO WORK WITH GUARANTEE THAT PAYROLL WILL BE CLEARED OF ALL SPANISH AMERICANS. THIS IS AN URGENT REQUEST AS HALF THE POPULATION OF THE STATE IS SPANISH AMERICAN. IMMEDIATE REPLY REQUESTED.

EARL McDONALD SECRETARY NEW MEXICO FEDERATION OF LABOR AFL E. C. BACA ORGANIZER AF OF L. JOE RIVERA SECRETARY OF LUMBER AND SAWMILL WORKERS COUNCIL AF OF L.

THE STATE OF TEXAS, COUNTY OF BEXAR

My name is Alberto Gomez. I am 14 years of age and reside at 819 Fenfield Avenue, in South San Antonio, Texas. I am in the 6th grade in the South San Antonio Junior High School.

On November 7, 1945, about 3:45 P. M. I went to the_____
Barber Shop in South San Antonio, Texas, and asked one of
the barbers there to cut my hair. He told me that he could not
give me a hair cut, and I asked him why. He replied: "Because
you are a Mexican". I said: "OK", and I walked out.
Further affiant sayeth not.   Albert Gomez
Sworn to and subscribed before me, this 8th day of November,
A. D. 1945.
                                        Alonso S. Perales.
                    Notary Public in and for Bexar County, Texas.

THE STATE OF TEXAS, COUNTY OF BEXAR

My name is Jose Herrera. I live in Adkins, Bexar County, Texas. I am 24 years of age. I served 14 months in the United States
Army in World War No. 2. I was born and reared in Texas.
On October 27, 1945, about 3:00 P. M., I went into a beer
parlor called "4-Points", on the Seguin Highway, about 15 miles
from San Antonio, Texas, but in Bexar County. As soon as I went
in the owner of the beer parlor told me that Mexicans were not
allowed there. I asked him for his name and he said: "I will not
give it to you and you get out immediately." Whereupon I got out.
My information is to the effect that the owner of said beer
parlor is German. I do not know his name.
There is a sign affixed to the glass part of the door reading:
"No Mexicans Allowed".
Further affiant sayeth not.   Jose Herrera
Sworn to and subscribed before me, this 27th day of October,
A. D. 1945.
                                        Alonso S. Perales.
                    Notary Public in and for Bexar County, Texas.

THE STATE OF TEXAS, COUNTY OF BEXAR

Before me, the undersigned authority in and for said County,
State of Texas, this day personally came and appeared Gabriel
Gonzalez and wife, Refugia Rodriguez de Gonzalez, and Agustin
Gonzalez and wife, Berta Barrientes de Gonzalez, to me well
known, and who, after being by me duly sworn, did depose and say:
Our names are as above stated. We live in Hondo, Texas.
On October 14, 1945, about 7:30 P. M., we went into the
PARK THEATER in Hondo, Texas, and sat down. Then one of
the ushers came and told us to move away from there to a section
intended for Mexicans, which is on the extreme right side of the
theater and right in front of the screen. He stated that the seats
we were occupying were for white people only. We told him that
we did not want to move from there because we had paid our
money for these seats just the same as other people, and besides
that we had sat there on previous occasions and no one had objected.

170

He said that we would have to move, otherwise he would call the Sheriff. We told him to go ahead and call the Sheriff. He did, and Sheriff Jack Fossman, Sheriff of Medina County, came in accompanied by Deputy Sheriff Reinhard Weber, and told us to move or else leave the theater and have our money refunded. Mrs. Refugio Rodriguez de Gonzalez told Sheriff Fossman that in San Antonio, Texas, there were large and beautiful theaters and they did not segregate the Mexican people there, and Sheriff Fossman replied that it did not make any difference, that that was San Antonio and this was Hondo. Whereupon we left the theater. We did not ask for a refund of our money for the reason that our feelings were deeply hurt and we did not care to talk to him or see them any longer.

We were all born and reared in Texas and are long time residents of Hondo, Texas.

Further affiants sayeth not. Agustin Gonzalez, Berta B. Gonzalez, Gabriel Gonzalez, Refugia R. de Gonzalez.

Sworn to and subscribed before me, this 15th day of October, A. D. 1945.

Alonso S. Perales.
Notary Public in and for Bexar County, Texas.

THE STATE OF TEXAS, COUNTY OF BEXAR

My name is David Ponce Rodriguez. I am 29 years of age and reside 733 E. Magnolia St., in San Antonio, Texas, I am a native born citizen of the United States of America. I served in the United States Army four years and eight months, 30 months of which was overseas service.

On October 10th 1945, about 4:00 P. M., I went into an Anglo-American barber shop in San Marcos, Texas, for the purpose of having my shoes shined by a colored boy that has a shoe shine stand in the barber shop. An Anglo-American barber told me that the colored boy could not shine my shoes there because that place was for white people only. I told him that I was going to complain to the Sheriff of Hays County and he said: "Go ahead". I went and talked to the Sheriff, but he said he could not do anything about it. Then I went and talked with the Military Police in San Marcos and they said they could not do anything about it for the reason that I was now a civilian and was wearing civilian clothes.

I received an honorable discharge from the United States Army on October 6, 1945, after participating in several battles in the European Theater.

Further affiant sayeth not.   David P. Rodriguez

Sworn to and subscribed before me, this the 11th day of October, A. D. 1945.

Alonso S. Perales
Notary Public in and for Bexar County, Texas

171

THE STATE OF TEXAS, COUNTY OF BEXAR

My name is Longino Mendez Reyes. I am 41 years of age and reside in Hondo, Texas. I am employed at the Air Field Navigation School at Hondo, Texas.

On October 3, 1945, my wife, Mrs. Paula P. de Reyes, and I went to the _____ operated by Mr. Garrison, in Hondo, Texas, intending to order some root beer. As soon as we went in a lady asked Mr. Garrison whether it would be all right to serve us and Mr. Garrison then came and told us that he could not serve us because it was against the rules of the house. Whereupon we left the place.

I served in the United States Army one year and three months during World War No. 2, and received an honorable discharge.

Further affiant sayeth not.   Longino M. Reyes

Sworn to and subscribed before me, this the 6th day of October, A. D. 1945.

Alonso S. Perales
Notary Public in and for Bexar County, Texas

THE STATE OF TEXAS, COUNTY OF BEXAR

My name is Pedro Muzquiz. I am 37 years of age, a citizen of the United States and a resident of Moore, Texas. I am a merchant.

The evening of September 18, 1945, Mr. Henry Crane, Mr. Theodore Juarchek and I went into the MONTE CARLO INN, in Devine, Texas, and we ordered three beers. A man named Davidson, who I understand is the owner of the establishment, brought a beer for Mr. Crane and one for Mr. Juarchek, but he did not bring one for me. When Mr. Juarchek asked him for the third beer (the one for me) he replied that he did not have any more beer. We noticed, however, that he continued to serve beer to the other customers there. I asked Davidson if the reason he did not serve me beer was that I was a Mexican, he replied that he did not have any more beer. Then Mr. Crane and Mr. Juarchek interceded in my behalf and tried to persuade him to sell me a beer, but he refused. Mr. Crane even told Davidson that he should treat me right because I was a good citizen and had a brother in the United States Army overseas. We got disgusted and left the place. Later Mr. Crane went into the place again and asked for a beer for himself and Davidson served it to him. Davidson then told Mr. Crane that he did not serve beer to Mexicans in this establishment.

Further affiant sayeth not.   Pedro Muzquiz

Sworn to and subscribed before me, this the 19th day of September, A. D. 1945.

Alonso S. Perales
Notary Public in and for Bexar County, Texas

EX-SOLDIER STILL UNCONSCIOUS WEEK AFTER ASSAULT; NONE OF ASSAILANTS APPREHENDED.

By GRADY HILL

Pvt. Ben Garcia Aguirre- now just a 20-year-old ex-GI Joe of Latin-American extraction following an honorable discharge from the Army remained unconscious in a basement room in a local hospital late last night.

And a number of Anglo-American youths- Aguirre's two companions asserted that the number was "about 15"- remained at large- a full week after police, answering a call, found Aguirre, beaten unconscious, in the street at 1021 S. Chadbourne St. He could not tell them who his assailants were.

Both eyes blackened and bloody, and with a cut inches long X-ed above his left ear, little 115-pound Ben Aguirre still could not talk last night.

His lips moved without speaking, as his eyes opened without seeing.

His quiet-spoken father, Manuel J. Aguirre of 5 W. Ave. L, said, not with bitterness: "No, I don't know who beat my boy. It is bad".

And in broken sentences: "Ben had a medical discharge. He never was under the care of a doctor before, but he was not a strong boy. He never drinks. He never had a fight before in his life, that I know of. He was a good boy".

And Pete Gonzalez, 16, who was fleeter of foot than Aguirre and escaped the gang which downed his slighter companion, talked a bit, too. However, he indicated that he didn't want to. He had previous experiences with groups of "white boys" who came over into South Angelo.

He agreed last night that "both sides had better stop having these fights". And he insisted that "You won't find us starting any trouble- and we sure didn't start it last Saturday night".

Rudolph Salazar, 19, the third Latin-American in the group attacked, was not interviewed last night. He had got away last Saturday night without injury when the three were first accosted on W. Washington Drive.

Gonzalez said that he "hit at" some five or six Anglo-American boys who seized him on Washington Drive, and broke away. "They tried to hold me, and when I broke away they threw rocks at me," he said. "Ben and I were going down Chadbourne, trying to get away, when they drove up in a pick-up and piled out.

"I broke away from them again and ran down Highland and then down Irving. I didn't know about Ben until the next morning. I thought he had got away, too," the youth declared.

173

Gonzalez said that they first noticed the other group at a service station south of the railroad tracks, as he, Aguirre and Salazar were returning from a Latin-American resort across town in Sharp End where "some television thing with recordings" was being exhibited.

"There are three Mexicans!" the trio heard the larger group shout. But they weren't accosted until they got to Washington Drive.

Chief of Police Clarence Lowe reported Friday that he hadn't been informed of the gang attack until the preceding day. It was confirmed last night that two policemen, answering a station call, had waited beside Aguirre until an ambulance arrived.

The two, J. E. Fread and Bill Owens, turned in a report to Walter Green, then desk sergeant. Last night, Desk Sergeant Frank Wood said the yellow sheet report was on file at the police station.

HE DIDN'T KNOW HOW IT HAD MISSED BEING BROUGHT TO LOWE'S ATTENTION.

It was learned, too, that Dr. J. S. Hixson, president of the Shannon Memorial Hospital, had seen that the casualty report was given to the police.

Giving information last night to others on which afforded possible leads to two of the assailants Gonzalez explained that he didn't discuss those factors with the police "because they didn't ask me just about that".

Chief of Police Lowe, who had joined Sheriff J. F. Bryson Friday in an ultimatum to the teenage gangs to "break it up," reiterated early Saturday his determination to bring a halt to the interracial "gang fights."

He recalled a previous fight in which the Latin-Americans failed to identify several teenage suspects.

Lowe could not be reached Saturday afternoon or early Saturday night for further comment.

Meanwhile, the father of the injured boy said that he had not had time to think about his hospital bill. He had been at the bedside steadily all week.

No organizations had offered to help.

"No, nobody. But of course they couldn't have known about this until yesterday," he sought to explain.

San Angelo, Texas, Sept. 9, 1945.

622 Arbor Pl.
San Antonio, Texas.
Aug. 23, 1945.

Mr. A. Perales,
Gunter Bldg.,
San Antonio, Texas.

Dear Sir:

I hope that the facts in this letter will interest you as much they do me.

The main reason of this letter is to tell you about an incident which happened during a trip I made to Temple, Texas, about two weeks ago.

We happened to stop at Lockhart, Texas to drink some coffee my wife her two sisters and brother. I was really enjoying my coffee when suddendly one of the girls waitress said "do not speak Spanish in this place or I'll be fired".

Tell me are we losing our freedom of speech here in U. S. A.?

Another thing they told us is that we weren't allowed to eat there.

Right now I am wondering how many of us (Mexicans) have gone to this "cheap cafe" as I would say it, and not be served.

Won't you please do something about this or it will go on and on forever.

As a matter of fact, the name of the cafe is "West Side Cafe" on Main Avenue.

I am just a poor decent man, but I still don't like the way they treated us on such small town, I am a veteran of War II, and I should like to see all of us treated like human beings.

I hope to see you personally sometime.

Yours truly,
Mr. Jose G. Cruz.

THE STATE OF TEXAS, COUNTY OF BEXAR

My name is Jose Z. Herrera. I live at Jourdanton, Atascosa County, Texas, where I have resided with my parents for the past eight (8) years. My occupation is farming, and I entered the service of the United States on November 30th 1942, serving up to the present date in Co. L. 333, Infantry Division 84, as Private First Class.

On or about May 5th, 1945, I went to the CITY BARBER SHOP, owned and operated by one KING HAYES, in the town of POTEET, Atascosa County, Texas, seeking to have my hair cut, and Mr. Hayes refused to serve me, and stated to me that he could not give me the service that I wanted, and that I should go to the barber shop called "the Mexican Barber Shop" and when I

175

told him that I had the right to demand service and went and sat on the barber chair, then he went out and talked to Deputy Sheriff Tom Lott, and the Deputy Sheriff sent a boy by the name of Eduardo Treviño to tell me to get out of the shop if I did not want to have any trouble.

Further deponent sayeth not.   Jose Z. Herrera

SWORN AND SUBSCRIBED before me on this the 21st day of May, A. D. 1945.

Jacob I. Rodriguez
Notary Public, Bexar County, Texas

THE STATE OF TEXAS, COUNTY OF BEXAR

My name is Adolfo Salomon. I reside at 1811 Colima St., in San Antonio, Texas. On Sunday, April 15, 1945, my daughters went to the bus station at Seguin, Texas, about 11:00 P. M., to board a bus for San Antonio, Texas. While they were waiting in the white people's waiting room, the ticket clerk told a porter to tell my daughters to go into the waiting room designated for "Colored People". My daughters refused to go into the Colored People's Waiting Room, and then later an officer came and told them to go into the said Colored People's Waiting Room. It was cold and raining outside, so my daughters decided to go into said room, but they did so under protest and because the officer compelled them to do so. The names of my daughters are: Miss Victoria Salomon and Mrs. Juanita Salomon. With them were the following other ladies: Mrs. Margarita Sifuentes, Mrs. Maria Ochoa, Mrs. Lupe Guillen and Miss Rosa Guillen.

The husbands of the following four ladies are in the United States Army: Margarita Sifuentes, Juanita Salomon, Maria Ochoa and Lupe Guillen. The husbands of Margarita Sifuentes and Maria Ochoa are serving overseas.

Further affiant sayeth not.   Adolfo Salomon

Sworn to and subscribed before me, this the 19th day of April, A. D. 1945.

Alonso S. Perales
Notary Public in and for Bexar County, Texas

THE STATE OF TEXAS, COUNTY OF BEXAR

My name is Ofelia B. Martinez. I reside at 114 Rosita Place, in San Antonio, Texas. My husband's name is Fred Martinez. On April 17, 1945, my husband and I make a $500.00 initial payment upon a house that we intended to buy at 1243 Highland Blvd., in San Antonio, Texas. Mr. J. W. Carraway was going to sell it to us for $8000.00 cash. We wanted this home for us and for our daughter, Mrs. Alfonso Cadena, whose husband, Pvt. Alfonso Cadena, is serving in the United States Army overseas. They have one 5 year old daughter.

On April 19, 1945, Mr. and Mrs. J. W. Carraway told us that they were very sorry, but that they could not sell us the property for the reason that they had received several telephone calls warning them not to sell the property to Spanish people. The telephone calls came to them from Anglo-American neighbors of theirs, they said. Mr. and Mrs. Carraway returned the $500.00 to us.

My husband and I and my daughter and her husband are all native born American citizens.

Further affiant sayeth not.   Ophelia B. Martinez

Sworn to and subscribed before me, this the 19th day of April, A. D. 1945.

Alonso S. Perales

Notary Public in and for Bexar County, Texas

(Translation of Telegram received from Dr. Enrique Gonzalez Martinez, President of the Mexican Committee against Racism, of Mexico City).

Mexico City,
March 26, 1945.

ALONSO S. PERALES
SUITE 714 GUNTER BLDG.
SAN ANTONIO, TEXAS.

The reproachable discriminatory act perpetrated in a restaurant in Pecos, Texas, against Senator Eugenio Prado, President of the Permanent Commission of the Congress of Mexico and persons accompanying him is additional proof that only through sanctions imposed upon those who practice discrimination against Mexicans will it be possible to end a situation which offends all Mexicans and which hinders President Roosevelt's Good Neighbor Policy stop We have sent telegrams to Governor Stevenson and Senators Fred Mauritz and Franklin Spears protesting against discriminatory act Stop We are sure that we can count upon good friends of Mexico like you to bring about approval of Spears Bill now under consideration in Texas Senate which will end once for all acts of this nature. Stop. Kindest regards.

ENRIQUE GONZALEZ MARTINEZ
PRESIDENT MEXICAN COMMITTEE
AGAINST RACISM

THE STATE OF TEXAS, COUNTY OF BEXAR

My name is Abel F. Gonzalez. I am a Private First Class in the United States Army. My Army Serial Number is 18105383. I have just returned from the Aleutian Islands where I had been stationed since April 15, 1943. I am now on a furlough. I was born and reared in Gonzalez, Gonzalez County, Texas. I am 21 years of age.

On Thursday, March 15, 1945, about 9:30 A. M., I went into the Smith & Bowen Barber Shop, in Gonzalez, Texas, to have my shoes shined. A negro who shines shoes there told me that he was sorry, but that he could not shine my shoes.

Other American soldiers of Mexican descent have likewise been refused service at said shoe shine stand and the negro shoe shine man has told them that he himself has no objection, but that his Anglo-American boss told him he must not shine the shoes of Mexicans in his barber shop.

There is not a single Anglo-American Barber Shop in Gonzalez, Texas, that will cut the hair of American soldiers of Mexican descent.

Further affiant sayeth not.   Abel F. Gonzalez

Subscribed and sworn to before me this the 16th day of March, A. D. 1945.

Alonso S. Perales
Notary Public in and for Bexar County, Texas

THE STATE OF TEXAS, COUNTY OF BEXAR

Our names are Emilio Uriegas and Sixto Obregon. We are 19 years of age and we were born and reared in Texas. We live at 814 S. Brazos Street and 517 South Leona Street, respectively, in San Antonio, Texas.

On Friday, March 2nd 1945, about 2:00 P. M., we went into the West Side Cafe, in Lockhart, Texas, and we were about to sit down at a table when a waitress came and told us that she was very sorry, but that she could not serve us because the West Side Cafe was for white people only. One of the boys who was with us asked her what we were, and she then turned around and left. We left the place. When we went to the said Cafe we were accompanied by John Estrada, Eusebio Chavez and Ramon Uriegas, all of San Antonio, Texas.

Further affiants sayeth not.   Emilio Uriegas - Sixto Obregon.

Subscribed and sworn to before me this the 5th day of March, A. D., 1945.

Alonso S. Perales
Notary Public in and for Bexar County, Texas

THE STATE OF TEXAS, COUNTY OF BEXAR

My name is Reginaldo Romo. I am 39 years of age and reside at Uvalde, Texas. I am a native born citizen of the United States and have lived in Uvalde fourteen years.

On Wednesday, February 21st 1945, Messrs. Julian Quiroga, Apolonio Canales and I were in a saloon, in Uvalde, Texas, drinking and shooting dice. The saloon was closed, but we were inside drinking and shooting dice, as aforesaid. Just then a peace

178

officer August Zimmerman, who we understand is employed by the City of Uvalde, came in and came to where I was and struck me in the head with his gun. He did not utter a word when he came in, but came straight to where I was and struck me in the head with his gun. After he struck me, he told me to stay away from him or else he would kill me.

I know for a fact that he has beaten up in like manner the following man: Jose Arredondo. He not only struck him in the head with his gun, but shot at him twice. Another man who has been beaten up by the said August Zimmerman.

Further affiant sayeth not.   Reginaldo Romo
Sworn to and subscribed before me, this the 23rd day of February, A. D. 1945.

Alonso S. Perales
Notary Public in and for Bexar County, Texas

THE STATE OF TEXAS, COUNTY OF BEXAR

My name is Felipe Rodriguez. I am 43 years of age and married, and reside at 121 Duval Street, in San Antonio, Texas.

On February 19, 1945, about 4:45 P. M., my wife, Mrs. Maria G. de Rodriguez, and I went into a small cafe situated on the corner of Travis Street and Avenue E, in San Antonio, Texas, and as we went in a lady who appeared to be the Manager of the place, asked us what we wanted, and I told her that we wanted some soft drinks. She then said: You go into the kitchen and I will serve you. My wife and I went out of the place, rather than suffer the humiliation of being served in the kitchen. We were neatly dressed.

Further affiant sayeth not.   *Felipe Rodriguez*
Sworn to and subscribed before me, this the 20th day of February, A. D. 1945.

Alonso S. Perales,
Notary Public in and for Bexar County, Texas.

THE STATE OF TEXAS, COUNTY OF BEXAR

Our names are Ernestina Villarreal and Josefina Garcia. We reside at 307 Hawthorne Street and 300 Howthorne Street, respectively. We are native born citizens of the United States of America. We are both married.

On the 1st day of February, 1945, we went to a restaurant known as _____, situated on the corner of East Commerce and Blum Streets. We sat at a table. Then an Anglo-American or German-American man came to where we were and said: "We cannot serve you at this table." I, Ernestina Villarreal, asked him why, and he replied: "The service is for whites only". Then I asked him what he thought we were, and he said: "I am

179

sorry; we cannot serve you." I told him: "We are just as much Americans as you are", and he again said: "I am sorry". Then we left the place.

I, Ernestina Villarreal, wish to add that my husband, Mr. Cosme Villarreal, has been serving in the United States Navy for two and one-half years.

Further affiants sayeth not. Ernestina Villarreal - Josefina Garcia.

Sworn to and subscribed before me, this the 2nd day of February, A. D. 1945.

Alonso S. Perales,
Notary Public in and for Bexar County, Texas.

THE STATE OF TEXAS, COUNTY OF BEXAR

My name is Rosendo Salinas. I am 39 years of age and married. I reside at Robstown, Texas, where I am in business. I was born in Seguin, Texas, and am an American citizen.

On November 14, 1944, Mr. Alfonso Gutierrez, Mr. Alfredo Gutierrez and Mr. Jose Gonzalez were denied service at the Liddel Cafe, in O'Donnell, Texas. They were told: "We don't serve Mexicans". Alfonso and Alfredo Gutierrez are brothers and reside in Kerrville, Texas. Jose Gonzalez lives in Melvin, Texas. I saw all these men go into the Liddel Cafe and I noticed that they came right out a minute or so after they had gone in. I asked them what had happened and they told me that they had been denied service because they were Mexicans..

The Roy Cafe, at Lamesa, Texas, has a sign on a screen door reading: "No Mexicans". I saw this sign on November 7, 1944.

The Owl Cafe has no sign on the door, but Mexicans are denied service just the same. This Cafe is at Lamesa also.

At the QUICK LUNCH in Big Spring, Texas, there is a sign on one of the screen windows which reads: "Mexicans served on the window only". I saw this sign on November 14, 1944.

TING'S CAFE, at Big Spring has a sign on the door reading: "No Mexicans". I saw this sign on November 14, 1944.

In Lubbock, Texas, the WHITE HOUSE CAFE has a sign on the door reading: "We reserve the right to sell to whites only". I saw this sign on November 10, 1944.

While in O'Donnell I took a shirt to a laundry to have it laundered and an Anglo-American lady told me that they did not do any work for Mexicans.

Further affiant sayeth not.   Rosendo Salinas

Sworn to and subscribed before me, this the 21st day of November, A. D. 1944.

Alonso S. Perales,
Notary Public in and for Bexar County, Texas

180

STATEMENT OF MISS AURORA ALCORTA

Route 1, Box 194
Von Ormy, Texas

My name is Aurora Alcorta. I am 16 years of age and single. I reside at Von Ormy, Texas, and attend the Poteet High School. I am in the 10th grade. My father's name is Guadalupe Alcorta and my mother is Mrs. Angelita Alcorta.

On Oct. 5, 1944, about 8:00 A. M., affiant and the girls named below were riding on the bus on the way to school: Misses Olivia Hernandez, Sylvia Hernandez, Frances Lopez, Asela Aguilar, Maria Lopez, Virginia Lopez, Cristina Alcorta, Virginia Alcorta, and Mr. Manuel Lopez. I was seated with Mr. Manuel Lopez. An Anglo-American boy named Harold was pushing another Anglo-American boy over me or against me. I then told him please do not push the boy against me, and he said: "A darn Mexican like you is not going to make me stop it." He thereupon struck me on my right eye with his closed fist. Then I said to him: "OK, white trash".

After the incident with me, the said Harold boy picked up a fight with Frances Lopez. Then the bus driver stopped the bus and then stopped the fight. As soon as the bus stopped the fight ceased. When we got to Poteet I went and complained to Miss E. O. Mangum. She said she could not do anything to Harold because we Mexicans were to blame. Then Mr. Brown, School Superintendent, called us into the Mathematic Room and asked how the fight had started. Then he started reprimanding us, but he reprimanded me the most. He said that I was very lowdown because I had used bad language on the bus.

The following day, in the morning, when we boarded the bus on the way to school the bus driver, Mr. Cowley, said that the "whites" were to ride on one side of the bus and "Mexicans" on the other. The next day Frances Lopez, Aurora Alcorta, Asela Aguilar and Virginia Alcorta, went and spoke with Superintendent Brown and told him about the segregation on the bus. He asked us: "Do you girls really mind where you sit". Virginia Alcorta said to him: "We do not mind where we sit, but we do not want to be treated that way". Then he said: "Well, girls, we'll arrange that." That was the day we complained and the bus driver is still segregating us. Every time he sees an Anglo-American sitting with a Mexican he tells the whites: "I don't want to tell the whites again where to sit."

The afternoon of the 16th Manuel Lopez sat with two Anglo-Americans on our side of the bus. Then the bus driver got up and said: "Hey, Manuel, there is a seat for you back there, (meaning the rear of our side of the bus), whereupon Manuel got up and went to sit in the rear of the bus as requested.

Further affiant sayeth not.   *Aurora Alcorta*
Sworn to and subscribed before me, this the 17th day of
October, A. D. 1944.

Alonso S. Perales,
Notary Public in and for Bexar County, Texas.

We, the undersigned, were riding on the same bus and witnessed what happened. What Miss Aurora Alcorta says is true.

Olivia Hernandez   *Virginia Alcorta*
Christine Alcorta   *Sylvia M. Hernandez*

THE STATE OF TEXAS, COUNTY OF BEXAR

My name is Oscar Molina. I am 47 years of age. I reside at
309 San Luis Street, in San Antonio, Texas. I am employed by the
Ferd Staffel Co., 321 E. Commerce St., in San Antonio, Texas.

On Saturday, September 2, 1944, about 12:30 P. M., I went
to the Spanish Village Restaurant, situated at 237 Blum Street,
in San Antonio, Texas. I was accompanied by Mrs. Francisca Arriaga
and Miss Alicia Yzaguirre, both of whom are also employed by
the Ferd Staffel Co. I had been to said restaurant about three times
previous to this one and I had always been served. To-day, however, after we had been served, one of the waitresses, who happened
to be a Mexican girl, came and told us that the owner of the
Spanish Village Restaurant did not want her to serve us Mexicans
and that she was going to be reprimanded for having served us.
Before she told us this the waitress had told us that we would have
to leave the table ten minutes before one o'clock, as that table had
been reserved. Then she returned and said: "I am very sorry to
have to tell you that the lady owner of this restaurant does not
want us to serve persons of Mexican descent, and she is going to
reprimand me for having done so." Whereupon we left the place.

I should add that all three of us were well dressed and we
deported ourselves with propriety. Mrs. Arriaga and I are Mexican
citizens and Miss Izaguirre is an American citizen.

Further affiant sayeth not   *Oscar Molina*
Sworn to and subscribed before me, this the 2nd day of
September, A. D. 1944.

Alonso S. Perales,
Notary Public in and for Bexar County, Texas.

THE STATE OF TEXAS, COUNTY OF BEXAR

My name is Ben Martinez. I am a Corporal in the United
States Army. My Organization is Company I, 162nd Infantry, 41st
Division. I am a legal resident of Rotan, Fisher County, Texas,
where I was born and reared. I am now on a furlough after having
served in Southwest Pacific for a period of two years. Altogether
I have been in the United States Army two and one-half years. I
am 25 years of age.

I have three other brothers in the United States Army. Their names are : Emilio Martinez, Jose Martinez, Alejandro Martinez.

On July 3rd 1944, I went to the City Barber Shop, at Rotan, Texas, and sat down on the Barber's Chair to get a hair cut. The Barber told me: "We don't cut you people's hair", meaning that he did not cut the hair of Mexicans. I am an American citizen of Mexican descent and I was wearing the United States Army uniform at the time.

My brother, Alejandro Martinez, was likewise refused service in the same Barber Shop last year, and he, too, was wearing the United States uniform at the time.

Further affiant sayeth not.   Ben Martinez

Sworn to and subscribed before me, this the 26th day of July, A. D. 1944.

Alonso S. Perales,
Notary Public in and for Bexar County, Texas.

THE STATE OF TEXAS, COUNTY OF BEXAR

My name is Emeterio Pastrán. I am a legal resident of San Antonio, Bexar County, Texas, but am temporarily residing at Eagle Pass, Texas, where I am employed by the United States Government at Eagle Pass Army Air Field.

On Sunday, June 11, 1944, about 10:15 P. M., Mr. Bruno Salazar, of Eagle Pass, Texas, went into the "Dinette Cafe", at Uvalde, Texas, for the purpose of dining there, and as soon as we went in a lady, who appeared to be the owner or manager, told us that we would have to go somewhere else. When we first went into the Cafe a waitress saw us and went and told the other lady, who, as I said, appeared to be the owner or manager, and the latter came and told us to go somewhere else. She appeared to be in an angry mood as she advanced toward us.

An Anglo-American man who was travelling with us in Mr. Martin Delgado's car, on our way to the Eagle Pass Army Air Field, went into said Cafe at the same time we did, and he was served, but we were not.

Further affiant sayeth not.   Emeterio Pastrán.

Sworn to and subscribed before me, this the 28th day of June, A. D. 1944.

Alonso S. Perales,
Notary Public in and for Bexar County, Texas.

THE STATE OF TEXAS, COUNTY OF BEXAR

Our names are Enrique Flores and Hilda Gonzalez de Flores. We reside in Port Lavaca, Texas. We own and operate a restau-

rant there. We were born and reared in Texas, and we are American citizens. We have about fifteen nephews in the United States Army, most of whom are serving overseas.

On Sunday, April 2, 1944, about noon, we stopped at the WHITE SPOT CAFE, at Nixon, Texas, on our way to San Antonio, Texas, and as soon as we went into the Cafe a waitress told us to go out and around into the kitchen if we wanted service, as we could not be served in the front part of the Cafe. There were five of us in the party and we were all clean and well dressed. The names of the other three members of our party are: Mrs. Juanita Dominguez, 33 years of age, who is our sister; Miss Juanita Garcia, 17 years of age; and our son Manuel Flores, who is 12 years of age.

There are several public places of business in Port Lavaca, Bay City, New Gulf and Palacios where persons of Mexican descent are not served.

In Port Lavaca our school children are segregated up to and including the fourth grade. The school bus driver separates the Mexican children from the Anglo-American children on the buses.

Further deponents sayeth not. Henry Flores - Gilda G. Flores

Sworn to and subscribed before me this 3rd day of April, A. D. 1944.

Alonso S. Perales,

Notary Public in and for Bexar County, Texas.

THE STATE OF TEXAS, COUNTY OF BEXAR

Our names are Jose Alvarez Fuentes, Joe D. Salas and Paul R. Ramos. We are members of the Armed Forces of the United States as above indicated. We are permanent residents of the City of San Antonio, Texas, but are temporarily residing elsewhere. We are now on furlough. On Tuesday, March 7, 1944, about 2:30 P.M., when we were on our way home the bus stopped at Fredericksburg, Texas. We were hungry and, therefore, we went into the "Downtown Cafe", at 323 East Main Street, Fredericksburg, to order something to eat. We sat on stools at the counter. There were two waitresses in the restaurant, but neither one waited on us. One of them went and told the Manager or Proprietor that we were there. He came to where we were and Seaman Jose Alvarez told him that we wanted a barbecue sandwich. The Manager said: "I am sorry, but I cannot serve you in front; you will have to go out and around to the rear." Seaman Alvarez Fuentes asked him why and he said: "Those are the orders." Whereupon we left the place. Seaman Juan Garcia, United States Navy, was also with us at the time. He lives

184

in San Antonio, Texas, and he too was on his way home on a furlough.

Further deponents sayeth not.

Jose Alvarez Fuentes

Joe D. Salas

Paul R. Ramos

Subscribed and sworn to before me this 11th day of March, A. D. 1944.

Alonso S. Perales,

Notary Public in and for Bexar County, Texas.

THE STATE OF TEXAS, COUNTY OF BEXAR

My name is Leonardo Rodriguez. I was born in Hoye, Texas, and am now residing in Boerne, Kendall County, Texas. I am 21 years of age and single, I attended the public schools at Boerne for about eight years. I finished the seventh grade.

On Sunday, March 5, 1944, about 8:00 P. M., I went to the CASCADE THEATER in Boerne. Mexicans are segregated from the Anglo-Americans downstairs. There is a special section downstairs where Mexicans may sit. That section was occupied. Therefore, I went upstairs. There were no seats available upstairs either and for this reason I remained standing. I had been standing there for about ten minutes when Mr. Miller, the Manager of the Cascade Theater, approached me and requested me to go downstairs. I told him that the only way we could see the show was to remain where we were; whereupon he stated that if I did not like his telling me to go down, that he could refund me my money. I told him to bring me the money. Then he went and got the money and brought it to me, but he also brought with him a stick about two and one-half feet long, one inch thick and two inches wide. He handed me the money and he punched my ribs with the stick and told me to get out. I told him that it was not necessary for him to get angry about it, and as I turned around to get out he struck me in the head with the stick and fell me to the floor and while I was lying down he struck me in the back with the stick. When he struck me in the head he broke my glasses. As soon as I got up he struck me on my left cheek with the same stick. He also struck me on my right hand and in the mouth. I told him that was no place to fight and for him to come outside. He came outside of the theater, but he brought a pistol with him. I was unarmed.

185

I reported the case to Sheriff Sidney F. Edge, of Kendall County, but he said there was nothing he could do about it.

Further deponent sayeth not.   Leonardo Rodriguez

Sworn to and subscribed before me this 7th day of March, A. D. 1944.

Alonso S. Perales,
Notary Public in and for Bexar County, Texas,
My Commission expires on May 31, 1945.

THE STATE OF TEXAS, COUNTY OF BEXAR

Our names are Beatriz Balboa de Espino and Zenobia Silva de Aguirre, ages 33 years and 23 years, respectively, and married. We reside at 523 Santa Clara Street, in San Antonio, Texas.

About 2:00 P. M., to-day we called at the Office of R. L. White Co. 314 Nolan Street, San Antonio, Texas, and made application to rent a house situated on Elm Street. We had seen a "For Rent" sign on said house which stated that any one interested should apply at the Office of R. L. White Co. When we told the young lady at the office of the R. L. White Co., that we wanted to rent the house on Elm Street she replied: "We don't rent to Spanish people. We rent only to whites". Mrs. Beatriz Balboa de Espino asked her: "What is the matter with Spanish people?" and she replied: "We have our choice to rent it to whomever we want to." Whereupon Mrs. Beatriz Balboa de Espino retorted: "But they can go to war all right, can't they?", whereupon the young lady said: "Well, get out, get out, I don't want to be bothered."

Speaking for herself the said Beatriz Balboa de Espino further says: I have two brothers in the United States Army; one is stationed in England and the other is in Wisconsin.

Speaking for herself the said Zenobia Silva de Aguirre further says: My husband, Daniel Aguirre, is in the United States Army and is stationed in India. I also have a brother-in-law (the husband of a sister of mine) serving in the United States Army overseas. I wanted to rent the house on Elm Street in order that my family and myself might occupy it as a homestead.

Further deponents sayeth not.   Beatriz Balboa de Espino
                                        Zenobia Silva de Aguirre

Sworn to and subscribed before me this 26th day of January, A. D. 1944.

Alonso S. Perales,
Notary Public in and for Bexar County, Texas.

THE STATE OF TEXAS, COUNTY OF BEXAR

"My name is Dionicio Mendez Ortiz; I was born in Lockhart, Caldwell County, Texas; I am 19 years of age; I enlisted in the Army of the United States on April 1943; I attended the public

186

schools at Lockhart and went as high as the fourth grade; I have lived practically all of my life at Lockhart.

"On Wednesday, December 1st 1943, at about 2:30 P. M., I approached a barber shop located at 111 San Antonio Street in Lockhart and saw a colored boy shining shoes; I was accompanied by Eron Mendez, who was also born and reared at Lockhart, and I entered the barber shop for the purpose of getting my shoes shined; I was wearing the uniform of a Private in the United States Army, Medical Corps; the colored boy told me that he could not shine my shoes, I asked him why, and he said he could not tell me and for me to talk to the boss. The owner was cutting the hair to a customer and I asked him why I could not get my shoes shined in his barber shop. He stated that he could not permit me to have my shoes shined, but he would not give me any specific reason; then, he grabbed a hold of my coat by the chest with one hand and he doubled up his fist with the other and began pushing me backwards, so I decided to leave the place.

I then went to the Court House to complain to the Sheriff, because I had been directed to do so by the local Draft Board. Inasmuch as the Sheriff was not in at the time, I told my cousin Eron Mendez, to go with me to a nearby restaurant to drink a cup of coffee. When we entered the South Cafe, which is located in the Court House Square, we sat by the counter and waited a little while to be served. As one of the waitresses passed in front of us, I told her, "We want two cups of coffee, please", she said that she could not serve us there; then, we left the restaurant and went to the Court House to find the Sheriff, who had already arrived. It appears that the Sheriff had already been advised as to the purpose of my visit, because when I entered his office he told me, "you were not born in that restaurant," I told him that I just wanted a cup of coffee and he then got up and slapped me and told me to get out.

"I was deeply wounded because of the fact that I had been twice humiliated while wearing a soldier's uniform."

Dionicio Mendez Ortiz (signed)

Subscribed and sworn to before me this 3rd day of December, A. D. 1943.

M. C. Gonzales, (Signed)
Notary Public in and for Bexar County, Texas.
My commission expires 6-1-45.

Affiant resides at 1323 Burleson St., San Antonio, Texas

The statements above made by Dionicio Mendez Ortiz occurred in my presence and are correctly stated.

Eron Mendez (Signed)
Lockhart, Texas
Route 3, Box 22

187

From:
Fausto S. Toscano,
105 Mirasol St.,   San Antonio, Texas
San Antonio, Texas   October the 27th 1943.

To:

Dr. Carlos E. Castañeda,
Acting Regional Director,
President's Committee on Fair Employment Practice
1001 Mercantile Bldg.
Dallas, Texas

Dear Sir:

On Monday October the 26th 1943, I was sent to Austin, Texas, to look for a home to rent, as part of our Normoyle Ordnance Depot was moved to Camp Mabry at Austin.

Upon arrival at Austin, I went to several Real Estate offices to secure information about renting a home. At Harrison & Wilson Real Estate Firm, on 7th street, I was given a certain home to go and see and if place was suitable to me I could rent it.

On returning to their office and offering to pay the stipulated rent. I was told that I coudn't rent the said place because, "I was a Mexican".

This for your information, and if further information is needed, I will be glad to submit it.

Respectfully yours,
Fausto S. Toscano

CC Ordnance Depot, Camp Normoyle,
CC Alonso S. Perales, San Antonio, Texas

P. S. The address in question—where house was situated is:
906 Morgan Street (East), Austin, Texas.

THE STATE OF TEXAS, COUNTY OF BEXAR

My name is Leonardo Gonzalez, I reside at 206 Zavalla Street, in San Antonio, Texas. I am 34 years of age and married. I am a rockmason by trade.

On Saturday, October 9, 1943, about 10 P. M., my wife, Mrs. Cecilia Gonzalez, my daughter Virginia Gonzalez (8 years of age), Mr. Isidro Silva and his wife, Mrs. Anita Torres de Silva, and I went to a restaurant situated at 303 _____, and we sat at a table and asked to be served some dinner. The waiter told us that they could not serve us because we were Mexicans. We left the place immediately.

Then we went to another restaurant named the IVEY GREEN CAFE in New Braunfels, Texas. There we asked to be served some dinner and the waitress told us that they could not serve us

because we were Mexicans. We left the place immediately.
Further deponent sayeth not.   Leonardo Gonzalez
    Subscribed and sworn to before me this 11th day of October,
A. D. 1943

Alonso S. Perales,
Notary Public in and for Bexar County, Texas.

THE STATE OF TEXAS, COUNTY OF BEXAR

STATEMENT OF GERONIMO VILLELA

On Saturday, October 2nd 1943, Mauro Campusano and I went to the Ivey Green Cafe, in New Braunfels, Texas, about 10:30 P. M., and ordered a beer apiece. Mrs. Fifer, wife of the proprietor Mr. Fred Fifer, handed us the beers and told us that we could not drink it inside the establishment and that we would have to drink it outside.

Both Mr. Campusano and I were wearing clean clothing and we were not intoxicated when we asked for the beers.
       Geronimo Villela - Maurilio Campusano
New Braunfels, Texas,
Oct. 6, 1943.

THE STATE OF TEXAS, COUNTY OF BEXAR

My name is Olivia Garza de Dominguez. I am 36 years of age and married. My husband is Antonio Dominguez and we reside at 425 Mohawk Street, in Corpus Christi, Texas.

On April 12, 1943, we purchased the following property:

"The North one half (N. ½) of Lot No. Three (3) in Block No. Twenty Two (22) in Meadow Park Addition to Corpus Christi, as shown by the official map or plat of said addition, of record in Volume 4, page 52, of the Map Records of Nueces County, Texas, to which reference is here made."

We purchased same from Mrs. Clara N. Johnson, a widow. About April 20, 1943 we moved into said property for the purpose of occupying it as our homestead. On August 16, 1943, about 10:30 P. M., a group of Anglo-American men and women came to our home and one of them knocked on our door. A brother of mine, Agustin Garza, answered the call. He asked them what they wanted, and one of the men replied that what they wanted was for us to vacate the house; that they did not want any Mexicans to live there, and that they wanted to know just when we expected to leave the premises. My brother replied that we did not intend to move, whereupon the spokesman for the group stated that we would have to move out or else he would come to put us out. My brother told him that he could not do that, unless he wanted

189

to buy the property from us. Then the spokesman asked how much we wanted for the place and my brother told him that we wanted $5000.00, whereupon the spokesman said that it was not worth that much, and that, furthermore, he had not come to purchase the property but to tell us to move out. The spokesman then repeated that they did not want Mexican people to live there. My brother told him that he was just as much of an American as he was (the spokesman), whereupon the spokesman said: "Don't talk to me that way", and he opened the door of our home in an effort to get in. My husband then called the police and two policemen came. By that time the group had left. One of the police officers said that he and the other officer had met the group before they (the officers) had come to our house and had talked with them, and for us not to fear anything; that the group was not going to do anything to us. We have not been bothered since.

Further deponent sayeth not.   Olivia Garza de Dominguez

Subscribed and sworn to before me this 29th day of September, A. D. 1943.

Alonso S. Perales,
Notary Public in and for Bexar County, Texas.

THE STATE OF TEXAS, COUNTY OF BEXAR

My name is Willie Benavides. I am 37 years of age and married. I am a farmer. I have my farm in Bexar County. My mail address is 718 Granado St., San Antonio, Texas.

On Sunday, September 12, 1943, about 6:00 P. M., I went to a beer garden called Shady Oak, situated on the 66 Highway, in Bexar County, Texas. I was accompanied by Messrs. Wenceslao Guerra, Alberto Rodriguez, Faustino Villagrande and Francisco Gonzalez.

We ordered some beer. We drank about three beers apiece. After we had been there about a half hour I started to dance. I danced one piece and when I was dancing the second piece a man, who appeared to be the Manager or Proprietor of the establishment and whose name I do not know, came to where I was and said to me: "We do not allow any Mexicans in this place". I told him that I was just as good an American citizen as anyone else, and I asked him if he knew what he was talking about. He did not answer, but he went behind the counter and brought either a gun or a stick (I do not know exactly which) and without saying anything he struck me in the head with it. I fell to the floor in the first blow, and while I was on the floor I sized the stick or gun with my hand to prevent him from hitting me any more. Altogether he hit me in the head twice. I bled profusely. I then went out, got into my car and came home to have my wounds treated.

190

I did not curse said man or abuse him in anyway and all I did was to tell him that I considered myself just as good an American citizen as any, and then I asked him whether he knew what he was talking about.

Further deponent sayeth not.   Willie Benavides
Sworn to and subcribed before me this 13th day of September, A. D. 1943.

Alonso S. Perales,
Notary Public in and for Bexar County, Texas.

THE STATE OF TEXAS, COUNTY OF BEXAR

My name is Ramon Tellez. I am 34 years of age and married. I reside in Devine, Medina County, Texas.

On Saturday, August 14, 1943, about 12:30 P. M., my brother-in-law, Mr. Jesus Benavides, and I went to Gene's Grill, at Devine, Texas, with the intention of having a refreshment. When we went in we sat at a table. An Anglo-American man was sitting at one end of said table. Just then the owner of the establishment, Mrs. Thelma Bohl, came to where we were and said to us: 'What are you boys doing sitting over here?' Can't you boys see that a white man is drinking at this table? Don't you know the difference between a white man and you all?'

I told her that I did not see any difference, whereupon she said: "Well, I do, because this is my place". I told her that I was sorry, and we left the place.

She did not ask us what we wanted, but immediately proceeded to express herself as above stated.

Further deponent sayeth not.   Ramon M. Tellez
Sworn to and subscribed before me this 16th day of August, A. D. 1943.

Alonso S. Perales,
Notary Public in and for Bexar County, Texas.

THE STATE OF TEXAS, COUNTY OF BEXAR

My name is Gerónimo Navarro. I reside at Natalia, Texas. I am 34 years of age and married. On July 24, 1943, about 10:30 A. M., I went into the Dick's Cafe, owned by Mr. W. R. Lay, at Natalia, Texas, and ordered a hamburger. I was accompanied by Mr. Pablo Rodriguez and Mr. Gilberto Morales, of Natalia, Texas; also Mr. Emilio Peña. We were all served what we ordered, buth when we finished and were paying him at the cash register he said that he did not want us to come there any more because he did not want the business of the Mexican people.

Jose Torres, Domingo Herrera and Cipriano Cruz, all of Natalia, Texas, have been refused service there.

One day of the week before last three truck loads of young men stopped there on their way to Laredo, and the said W. R. Lay, proprietor of the said Dick's Cafe, refused to serve them. These boys had been sent by the Draft Boards to the Fort Sam Houston Reception Center; some had been accepted for military service and some had been rejected, and they were all returning to Laredo, Texas.

Further deponent sayeth not.   Gerónimo Navarro.

Sworn to and subscribed before me this 24th day of July, A. D. 1943.

Alonso S. Perales,
Notary Public in and for Bexar County, Texas.

The contents of the above affidavit are true and correct. I was with Mr. Gerónimo Navarro when Mr. W. R. Lay told us that he did not want the business of the Mexican people and for us to stay away from his place.   Pablo Rodriguez

THE STATE OF TEXAS, COUNTY OF BEXAR

My name is Ruben M. Castillo. I am 45 years of age and married and reside at 426 Morales Street, in San Antonio, Texas. I own and operate a grocery and meat market business at 426 Morales Street.

On Sunday, July 18, 1943, my brother, Mr. Ruben B. Castillo, and I stopped at a tavern named "Cox Place", if I remember correctly, situated in Natalia, Texas, being the first tavern on the right side of the highway going toward Laredo, Texas. My brother went into said place and ordered a bottle of beer apiece. The waitress told us in very low voice and in a very nice way that she was sorry, but that she could not serve us beer. She said she could serve us food and soft drinks, but not beer. We noticed that quite a number of Anglo-American people were drinking beer there at the time.

Further deponent sayeth not.   R. M. Castillo.

Sworn to and subscribed before me this 22nd day of July, A. D. 1943.

Alonso S. Perales,
Notary Public in and for Bexar County, Texas.

THE STATE OF TEXAS, COUNTY OF BEXAR

My name is Alberto Macias Garcia. I am 32 years of age and married. I reside at 1610 Guadalupe Street, in San Antonio, Texas. I am a sheet metal worker by trade.

On Friday, July 9, 1943, while in the employ of the Brown & Root, Inc., W. S. Bellows, Columbia Construction Co., I was assigned to duty at Beeville, Texas. Until that date and for a period

of fifteen months I had been on duty, for the same Company, at Kingsville, Texas. Accompanied by Mr. John L. Hawkins, Foreman, Mr. Joe Frost, Mr. Fred Kutemann and another gentleman whose name I do not recall, I went to a place known as the Gaun Rooming House, at Beeville, and applied for a room. So did the gentlemen who accompanied me. The proprietress of the house stated that the men who accompanied me could room there, but I could not for the reason that she did not rent rooms to Mexicans. This made me so angry that I resigned my job with said Construction Company and came home.

We had gone to Beeville to work on a defense job -- an air base ordered by the United States Government.

Further deponent sayeth not.   Alberto Macias Garcia.

Subscribed and sworn to before me this 14th day of July, A. D. 1943.

Alonso S. Perales,
Notary Public in and for Bexar County, Texas.

THE STATE OF TEXAS, COUNTY OF BEXAR

My name is Leo B. Martinez. I am married and reside at 127 Kline Street, in San Antonio, Texas. I am employed as Labor Foreman in the Utilities Department at Kelly Field, Texas. I am a United States Government employee.

On Friday evening, June 23, 1943, a party took place at the Alamo Country Club, in Bexar County, Texas. It consisted of a dinner, dance and refreshments. It was attended mainly by men employed by the United States Government as foremen in the various departments at Kelly Field, and I understand the party was financed by the United States Government. Apparently it was sponsored by the Utilities Club of which I am a member, but to my knowledge it was not financed by our Club. I joined the Club about six weeks ago and I paid a One Dollar membership dues.

I attended said party accompanied by my wife. We arrived there about 9:30 P. M. We had been there about one hour when a man named Albert C. Evans, who is a foreman in the Sheet Metal Department, at Kelly Field, came to me and said: "You had better get out before I put you out." I told him that I had a right to be there inasmuch as I am a member of the Utilities Club. He said that it did not make any difference to him and that I would have to get out, or else he would put me out.

About five minutes later he met me again and said to me: "Listen, you get out or I will put you out, you son-of-a- . . ." I replied that I did not understand why he felt that way toward me since I did not even know him, and he said that what he had against me was that I was a Mexican and that he did not want to see any Mexican in front of him. Every time he addressed me he

193

did so in the presence of my wife.

Further deponent sayeth not.   Leo B. Martinez

Subscribed and sworn to before me this 28th day of June,
A. D. 1943.

Alonso S. Perales,

Notary Public in and for Bexar County, Texas.

THE STATE OF TEXAS, COUNTY OF BEXAR

My name is Ernesto Perez. I am 40 years of age and married
and reside at 304 Tulipan Place, in San Antonio, Texas.

On Monday, June 21st 1943, about 9:00 P. M., I went to the
Ray Theater at Hondo, Texas, and purchased a ticket. When I
started to sit about the center of the theater the usher told me that
I could not sit there because that was for white people only, and
that the section reserved for Mexicans was on the right. I told him
that I was classified as white by the United States Government
in Washington, whereupon he stated that those were the orders
he had from the Manager. I asked to see the Manager and he
took me to a man who represented himself to be the Manager
and who confirmed what the usher had told me, and he added that
I would either have to sit where the Mexicans were supposed to
sit or get out. When I told him that I was white he said: "No, you
are not white; you are a Mexican". I then told him that I was
going to get a lawyer to represent me on the matter of whether or
not I should be humiliated like that, and he sarcastically remarked:
"Go ahead and bring your lawyer".

Mexicans are segregated also at the Park Theater at Hondo.

Further deponent sayeth not.   Ernesto Perez

Subscribed and sworn to before me this 24th day of June,
A. D. 1943.

Alonso S. Perales,

Notary Public in and for Bexar County, Texas.

THE STATE OF TEXAS, COUNTY OF BEXAR

My name is Pedro Muñoz. I am 41 years of age and married,
and reside at 1818 Monterrey Street, in San Antonio, Texas. I am
an automobile mechanic.

On Sunday, June 13, 1943, I went into the Three Star Tavern,
situated at the corner of New Braunfels and Lamar Streets, which
is a beer parlor and pool hall combined owned by Mr. Charles
Schaefer, and I was told by one of the employees that I could not
play pool there. I was wearing the United States Army uniform
at the time. A few minutes later Enrique de la Rosa and Jose Vidal,
civilians, came in and started to play pool with another, but the
same employee told them that they were not permitted to play
pool there. We noticed that Anglo-Americans, both soldiers and

194

civilians, were playing pool there; therefore, we believe the reason we were not permitted to play was because we are of Mexican descent.

I was recalled into the United States Army as a Private First Class on December 8, 1943, and was honorably discharged, on account of being over the age limit and about to engage in national defense work as a civilian, on May 28, 1943. I also served in the United States Army (36th Division, Texas National Guard) from November, 1940 to November, 1941.

Further deponent sayeth not.   Pedro R. Muñoz.

Sworn and subscribed before me this 17th day of June, A. D. 1943.

Alonso S. Perales,
Notary Public in and for Bexar County, Texas.

THE STATE OF TEXAS, COUNTY OF BEXAR

My name is Manuel Flores. I am 24 years of age, a native born citizen of the United States of America, married and reside at 2015 West Salinas Street, San Antonio, Texas.

About the 20th day of February, 1943, I went to a restaurant at Luling, Texas, and asked for a sodawater, and the waitress told me that I would have to go into the kitchen to drink it.

On May 24th 1943 I went to a restaurant at Happy (between Amarillo and Lubbock, Texas) and I was told by a man, who appeared to be the owner, that Mexicans were not served there.

On April 29, 1943 I went into a barber shop at Borger, Texas, and I was told that they did not cut the hair of Mexicans there. The name of the barber shop is the "Deluxe Barbershop".

I am presently employed by the Phillips Petroleum Company, at Borger, Texas.

Further deponent sayeth not.   Manuel Flores

Sworn and subscribed before me this 25th day of May, A. D. 1943.

Alonso S. Perales,
Notary Public in and for Bexar County, Texas.

THE STATE OF TEXAS, COUNTY OF BEXAR

My name is Gregorio A. Gaitan. I am 30 years of age and married. I am Production Manager for the Texas Infants Dress Company, in San Antonio, Texas, and reside at 1610 West Martin Street.

On Saturday, April 17, 1943, at about 9:30 P. M., while I was at the Silver Blue Cafe, 111½ West Houston Street, San Antonio, Texas, the lady owner of the establishment refused service to two couples and two soldiers of Mexican descent, telling them that

195

she did not want Mexicans in there, and later the lady told me the same thing.

The two soldiers mentioned were wearing the uniform of the United States Army.

Further deponent sayeth not.   *Gregory A. Gaytan*

Sworn to and subscribed before me this 20th day of April, A. D. 1943.

Alonso S. Perales,
Notary Public in and for Bexar County, Texas.

THE STATE OF TEXAS, COUNTY OF BEXAR

My name is Octaviano S. Gonzalez. I am a Doctor in Chiropractic, and reside at 1011 Guadalupe Street, in San Antonio, Texas.

On Saturday, March 27th 1943, about 9:50 P. M., Pvt. Emilio A. Valle, a member of the United States Army, Pvt. Eduardo M. Contreras, also a member of the United States Army, and I, went into a business place known as the Silver Blue Bar & Cafe, situated at 111½ W. Houston Street, in San Antonio, Texas, and sat in a booth. Pvts. Contreras and Valle ordered a beer apiece. I did not order anything for myself. A waitress brought us the two beers. Pvt. Valle paid for same and gave the waitress a tip. As Pvt. Contreras started to pour some beer into his glass the proprietress of the place, whose name I do not know, came to where we were and demanded that we give up the booth because she said she had five men ready to take it. She asked me if I was taking anything and when I replied that I was not she said that I did not have any business there. Then she added: "You are a Mexican (referring to me), why don't you take your friends to some place where they take care of Mexicans. That is your race of people. We do not want you here and we do not want your trade. This place is for white people, especially for men in uniform." Then she addressed Pvt. Eduardo Contreras, whom she thought was not a Mexican, and asked him if he associated "with this kind of people" (and she pointed at me and Pvt. Valle), and Pvt. Contreras answered that he did, whereupon she said: "You must be one of them". Pvt Contreras answered: "You are right, I am a Mexican." Then she said: "I don't want you here, and you get out before I have to throw you out." One of the soldiers demanded his money back. She took one of the bottles that had not been touched and she gave him ten cents back. We left the place.

Both Pvt. Contreras and Pvt. Valle were wearing the United States uniform at the time. Neither one of them was intoxicated when we came into the place, and they had just ordered their first bottle of beer when the proprietress requested us to leave.

Pvt. Contreras and Pvt. Valle are members of Battery "B",

196

358th Field Artillery, Fort Sam Houston, Texas.
Further deponent sayeth not.   Octaviano S. Gonzalez
Sworn to and subscribed before me this 29th day of March,
A. D. 1943.
                                        Alonso S. Perales,
                    Notary Public in and for Bexar County, Texas.

THE STATE OF TEXAS, COUNTY OF BEXAR

My name is Jose Doroteo Salas. I am 32 years of age and married. I reside at 1702 San Fernando Street, in San Antonio, Texas. I was born in Seguin, Guadalupe County, Texas, and I am a citizen of the United States of America. I am able bodied and am enjoying good health. I am an air raid warden.

On February 24, 1943, about 3 P. M., I went into the United States Employment Service, 210 West Nueva Street, San Antonio, Texas, for the purpose of applying for a job as a watchman. I was interviewed by an Anglo-American man who appeared to be about 30 years of age. I do not know his name. He asked me what kind of a job I preferred, and I told him that I would like to be a watchman. He replied that he would not consider Spanish people for that kind of job because those jobs were reserved for "white" people only. I told him that I am an American citizen, white and just as good as any other citizen, whereupon he said: "Well, those are the orders I have." When I asked him who had given him such orders, he refused to answer.

Further deponent sayeth not.   Jose Doroteo Salas

Sworn to and subscribed before me this 27th day of February,
A. D. 1943.
                                        Alonso S. Perales,
                    Notary Public in and for Bexar County, Texas.

THE STATE OF TEXAS, COUNTY OF BEXAR

My name is Dolores Vargas. I am 58 years of age and married. I am a native born citizen of the United States of America and reside at Spur, Dickens County, Texas. I am a farmer. I have resided in Dickens County for about seventeen years.

There is a moving picture theater at Spur, Texas, named "The Palace Theater", where Mexicans are segregated from the Anglo-American patrons and are placed with the Negro patrons. The Anglo-Americans are seated downstairs and the Mexicans and the Negroes are seated in the balcony. Persons of Mexican descent purchase their tickets and try to sit downstairs together with the Anglo-Americans, but the employees of the said Theater do not permit them to do so and instead they tell them that they will have to sit in the balcony with the Negroes or else go out.

*The City Drug Store and the Red Front Drug Store, at Spur,
Texas, refuse to serve Mexicans at the fountain. They will sell
them ice cream cones, but they are told to go and eat them outside.
Further deponent sayeth not.*   *Dolores Vargas*

*Sworn to and subscribed before me this 23rd day of Feb-
ruary, A. D. 1943.*

Alonso S. Perales,
Notary Public in and for Bexar County, Texas.

THE STATE OF TEXAS, COUNTY OF BEXAR

*My name is Telésforo Oviedo. I reside at 712 South Laredo
Street, in San Antonio, Texas. I am 37 years of age. In October
1942 I had occasion to visit O'Donnell, Lynn County, Texas; Lamesa,
Dawson County, Texas, and Big Spring, Howard County, Texas,
and in each one of these towns I saw signs in certain restaurants,
drug stores and theaters reading as follows: "No Mexicans Allowed".*

*In the said month of October, 1942 Espiridion Paez, of Mathis,
Texas, and I went into Bill's Cafe, at Lamesa, Texas and ordered
some coffee, and we were told that we could be waited on in the
kitchen, but not in the dining room. Then we went to the Blue
Bonnett Cafe, at Lamesa, Texas, and we ordered some coffee and
we were told that no Mexicans were served there. At the Blue
Bonnett Cafe I asked the waitress why we were not served, and she
said that just because we were Mexicans.*

Further deponent sayeth not.   *Telésforo Oviedo*

*Subscribed and sworn to before me this 23 day of January,
A. D. 1943.*

Alonso S. Perales,
Notary Public in and for Bexar County, Texas.

THE STATE OF TEXAS, COUNTY OF BEXAR

*My name is Antonio Hernandez. I am 28 years of age and re-
side at 702 Columbus Street, in Our Lady of the Lake Addition,
in San Antonio, Bexar County, Texas. I was born in San Antonio,
Texas and am a citizen of the United States of America.*

*On Saturday, December 26th 1942, about 4:00 P. M., I went
into a Barber Shop which I understand is owned and operated by
one Gus Siebenniecker. The Barber Shop is situated in front of
the Edgewood School on the Cupples Road, in Bexar County, Texas.
I asked the said Gus Siebenniecker how many patrons he had
ahead of me and he said there were three. I sat down and waited.
When he had finished cutting the hair of all three patrons he came
close to me and asked me where I was born and I replied that in
Texas. Then he asked me if I was of Mexican lineage and I replied
in the affirmative, whereupon he told me that he was sorry, but
he could not cut the hair of Mexicans. I told him that I was just*

as much of an American as he was, and he stated that he was sorry, but he could not cut the hair of Mexicans.

Further deponent sayeth not. Antonio Hernandez

Subscribed and sworn to before me this 28th day of December, A. D. 1942.

Alonso S. Perales,
Notary Public in and for Bexar County, Texas.

THE STATE OF TEXAS, COUNTY OF BEXAR

My name is Martina G. de Flores. I reside at 636 Castroville Road, San Antonio, Texas. Our mailing address is Route 9, Box 1, San Antonio, Texas. I am a widow. My husband was the late Miguel H. Flores who died on July 27, 1942, in San Antonio, Texas. For twenty years he was Superintendent of San Fernando Cemetery No. 2, in San Antonio, Texas. I am a citizen of the United States of America and so was my husband.

On November 18, 1942, I sent my children whose names I will give below, to a Barber Shop situated in front of the Edgewood School on the Cupples Road, in Bexar County, Texas, and which I understand is owned by one Gus Siebenniecker, and he refused to cut their hair stating that he did not cut the hair of persons of Mexican descent. The names of my children are as follows: Miguel R. Flores, 12 years of age; Jose A. Flores, 11 years of age; Delfino C. Flores, 10 years of age; and Arturo G. Flores, 8 years of age, and they were all born in San Antonio, Texas. My children are all attending school and they were all cleanly dressed when they called at said Barber Shop.

Further deponent sayeth not. Martina G. de Flores

Subscribed and sworn to before me this 23rd day of November, A. D. 1942.

Alonso S. Perales,
Notary Public in and for Bexar County, Texas.

THE STATE OF TEXAS, COUNTY OF BEXAR

My name is Elias A Cortinas. I am 31 years of age, married and have two children. I am a native born citizen of the United States of America. I reside at 1224 San Luis St., San Antonio, Texas.

About Monday or Tuesday, Oct. 26th or 27th, I saw an advertisement in the San Antonio Express in the name of the Opperman Realty Co., stating that there were three rooms for rent at 2813½ West Commerce Street. I telephoned the Office of the Opperman Realty Company and a lady answered the telephone. She gave me all the information I asked for regarding the rooms. Then she asked me what my name was and when I told her she said: "Sorry, but we cannot rent to Mexican people".

199

On November 4th 1942 I went to the office of the Opperman Realty Company, in the Travis Building, in San Antonio, Texas, and asked the lady in charge of the office who the owner of the rooms was and she said they could not give me that information.

Further deponent sayeth not.   Elias A. Cortinas

Sworn to and subscribed before me this 4th day of November, A. D. 1942.

Alonso S. Perales,
Notary Public in and for Bexar County, Texas.

THE STATE OF TEXAS, COUNTY OF BEXAR

My name is Juanita P. Sanchez. I am 38 years of age and reside at 202 Wingate Avenue, in San Antonio, Texas. I am married and have two children. My husband's name is George C. Sanchez. He is a member of the United States Army. He is in Company E, 104th Bn 22nd Med. Tng. Regt., Camp Joseph T. Robinson, Arkansas. He volunteered his services.

The names of our children are George Sanchez, Jr., who is 7 years of age, and Maria Marta Sanchez, who is 6 years of age.

Because my husband is in the United States Army it is necessary that I work in order to support myself and children. On October 5th 1942 I saw an advertisement in the San Antonio Light reading as follows:

WANTED — Women to drive milk trucks, $200 to $300 mo. Hours 7:30 to 4:30. Many other positions open. G-1807.. ALL-TRADES EMPLOYMENT, 131 5th."

I telephoned and asked them if that was the place where they employed women to drive trucks, and the woman who answered the telephone said to me: "Yes, but they do not want Mexicans or Spanish."

Further deponent sayeth not.   Juanita P. Sanchez

Sworn to and susbcribed before me this 7th day of October, A. D. 1942.

Alonso S. Perales,
Notary Public in and for Bexar County, Texas.

THE STATE OF TEXAS, COUNTY OF BEXAR

My name is Esperanza Esqueda. I am 14 years of age. I reside at 402 Runnels Street, in San Antonio, Texas. I am in the 9-A-2 grade at Emerson Junior High School.

On Sunday, May 12, 1942, about 3:30 P. M., some friends of mine and I went to Breeze Lake, at McQueeney, Texas. When we arrived there a girl friend of mine named Dea Vielman and I went to a stand there and we asked for some hamburgers. The girl attendant said that they did not sell anything to Latin-Americans and that we would have to leave the place. First she said they did

200

not have hamburgers and then we asked for ice cream, and it was then that she said that they did not sell anything to Latin-Americans and for us to leave the place. A little later two other girls members of our party got off our automobile and went to watch some boats that were cruising in the lake. Then the same girl that refused to sell us hamburgers and ice cream came to where the two girls were standing and told them that she had already requested them to leave the place, and that they should leave at once because that place was not for Latin-Americans and that Latin-Americans had their own park elsewhere.

We all left as requested.

Further deponent sayeth not.   Esperanza Esqueda

Sworn to and subscribed before me this 11th day of May, A. D. 1942.

Alonso S. Perales,
Notary Public in and for Bexar County, Texas.

THE STATE OF TEXAS, COUNTY OF BEXAR

My name is Bartolo Arriaga Cortez. I am 41 years of age, a citizen of the United States of America, and reside at 2412 El Paso Street, in San Antonio, Texas. I am employed as a sheet metal worker at Camp Swift, in Bastrop County, Texas. My employer is a private construction company. I began working there about March 23, 1942. I rented a room at the McLellan Hotel, at Elgin, Texas, about 15 miles from Camp Swift, and remained there four or five days. After I had been there four or five days Mr. Henry W. Hall, Owner-Manager of said Hotel, told me to move away from there because among some of his tenants there were people who had protested to him because he had rented a room to me in said Hotel. I complied with his request. Mr. Hall told me that the reason said tenants had protested against my living in said Hotel was that I was of Mexican descent.

There is a restaurant known as the Elgin Cafe, at Elgin, Texas, where I ate my meals for about two or three days. One evening the lady manager of the Cafe came and asked me what my nationality was and I replied that I was of Mexican extraction and she said that no Mexicans were served at said Cafe, and for me to go elsewhere.

There is a recreational club where they play billiards and dominoes, at Elgin, Texas, known as the _____. About April 27, 1942, Santos Rodriguez (a fellow-employee of mine) and I went to said place and we were told by the Manager, whose name I do not know: "I am sorry boys, but we do not allow Mexicans in this place. I don't want to cause you any trouble and don't want you to cause me trouble, so the best thing is for you to leave these premises." We left.

201

Further deponent sayeth not.   Bartolo Arriaga Cortez
Sworn to and subscribed before me this 2nd day of May, A. D.
1942.

Alonso S. Perales,
Notary Public in and for Bexar County, Texas.

THE STATE OF TEXAS, COUNTY OF BEXAR

My name is Ignacio Flores. I am 21 years of age and a citizen
of the United States of America. I reside 401 Mockert St., in San
Antonio, Texas.

This morning, March 30, 1942, I applied at Sears Roebuck
& Company, this city, for a position as Commercial Artist. I did
so in response to an advertisement which appeared in the San
Antonio Express of March 29, 1942. A young lady in the employment
office told me that she was sorry but that they could not employ
a Latin American because they wanted an American. I told her
that I was an American citizen of Latin American extraction. She
said that as far as she was concerned she was from the north and
did not have any prejudices against Latin Americans, but that
someone in the firm of Sears Roebuck & Company who had the
say so in the matter did not want a Latin American Commercial
Artist. I asked her to give me an application blank anyway in
order that I might fill it and return it and have a talk with that
"someone", whoever he is, and find out just why he does not
want to employ a Latin American Commercial Artist.

Further deponent sayeth not.   Ignacio B. Flores

Subscribed and sworn to before me this 30th day of March,
A. D. 1942.

Alonso S. Perales,
Notary Public in and for Bexar County, Texas.

THE STATE OF TEXAS, COUNTY OF BEXAR

My name is Antonio Valdez. I reside at 206 Camada Street, in
San Antonio, Texas.

On Sunday, March 29, 1942, about 5:30 P. M., I stopped at
the M A R I O N ' S   C A F E, 108 San Antonio Avenue, New
Braunfels, Texas, and asked for a cup of coffee. The attendant, a
man who appeared to be of German extraction, told me that there
was no coffee ready to be served. I asked him how long it would
be before he would have coffee ready to serve and he replied that
about fifteen or twenty minutes. I saw that he had coffee already
made. The glass percolator or coffee urn was about half full. I am
convinced that the real reason I was not served was that he saw
that I was of Mexican descent.

202

Further deponent sayeth not.   Antonio Valdez

Subscribed and sworn to before me this 30th day of March, A. D. 1942.

Alonso S. Perales,

Notary Public in and for Bexar County, Texas.

THE STATE OF TEXAS, COUNTY OF BEXAR

My name is Antonio Cardona. I am a native born citizen of the United States of America, twenty-one years of age and reside at 2414 San Luis Street, in San Antonio, Texas.

About five months ago Louis Cardenas, Joe Treviño and I went to the Legion Club, on Roosevelt Avenue. We had been there about an hour when Louis Cardenas walked up to the Orchestra Stand and stated that he wanted to make a dedication. Just then the floor walker came to Cardenas and asked him if he had made a reservation before coming to the Club and Cardenas said "No". Whereupon the floor walker said that we would have to leave the place because we did not have a reservation. Cardenas explained to him that we had a table just the same even though we had made no reservation, but the floor walker insisted that we leave the place so we left. While we were there several other people came in and took tables and they had not previously made any reservations, but they were of Anglo-American extraction. We are certain we were excluded because we are of Latin-American descent.

Further deponent sayeth not.   Antonio Cardona

Sworn to and subscribed before me this 18th day of March, A. D. 1942.

Alonso S. Perales,

Notary Public in and for Bexar County, Texas.

THE STATE OF TEXAS, COUNTY OF BEXAR

My name is Gilberto R. Longoria. I am a native born citizen of the United States of America and reside at 3114 North St. Mary's Street, in San Antonio, Texas. I am employed as an Agent for the Reliable Life Insurance Company, in this city.

On Wednesday, December 17, 1941, I told the Rental Service, Inc. (Real Estate Agency), at the National Bank of Commerce Building, in San Antonio, Texas, that I desired to rent a house situated at 1506 South Olive St., and which I had seen advertised for rent in the San Antonio Express. A man in the office of the said Rental Service by the name of Crouch told me that they could not rent the house to me because I was a Mexican, and that there are sections of the City of San Antonio where Mexicans may reside.

Further deponent sayeth not   *Gilberto R. Longoria*
Sworn to and subscribed before me this 18th day of December,
A. D. 1941.

Alonso S. Perales,
Notary Public in and for Bexar County, Texas.

THE STATE OF TEXAS, COUNTY OF BEXAR

My name is Amada B. Quesnot. I am a native born citizen of
the United States of America, and reside at 2518 Leal Street, in
San Antonio, Texas. I am married. My husband is Mr. Gus Quesnot,
who is a citizen of the United States of America and a veteran of
World War No. 1. We have a boy, Adrian Quesnot, in the United
States Army and is now stationed at Fort Bliss, Texas.

At the suggestion of Dr. O. S. Moore, of this city, on Thursday,
November 13, 1941, about noon, I took my child, Eugene Edward
Quesnot, who is 5 years old, to the M. & S. Clinic, 215 Camden
Street, San Antonio, Texas, for treatment. The lady in charge in
the Social Workers' Room asked me if I was a Latin American
and when I replied in the affirmative she stated that no Latin
American children were accepted for treatment at that Clinic.
She added that it applied to all children of French, Italian,
Spanish or Mexican extraction.

Further deponent sayeth not.   *Amada B. Quesnot.*
Sworn to and subscribed before me this 17th day of November,
A. D. 1941.

Alonso S. Perales,
Notary Public in and for Bexar County, Texas.

THE STATE OF TEXAS, COUNTY OF BEXAR

My name is Demetrio Gomez. I am 33 years of age and
married. I am a native born citizen of the United States of America
and reside at 539 Barclay, San Antonio, Texas. I am employed by
the United States Government at the San Antonio Air Depot,
Duncan Field, Texas.

On Saturday, September 20, 1941, about 2:30 P. M., I went
to a Barber Shop at 520 Cupples Road, in San Antonio, Texas,
and the barber-proprietor of the Shop asked what my nationality
was and I told him that I was a Mexican or Latin American, where-
upon he said: "I am sorry, but I cannot cut Mexican people's hair
because I am building this up as a white trade and if I cut your
hair then every Mexican will want to have his hair cut here and
that will hurt my business".

Further deponent sayeth not.   *Demeterio Gomez*
Sworn to and subscribed before me, this 23rd day of September,
A. D. 1941.

Alonso S. Perales,
Notary Public in and for Bexar County, Texas.

THE STATE OF TEXAS, COUNTY OF BEXAR

My name is Manuel Escobedo. I am nineteen years of age and a native born citizen of the United States of America. I was born, reared and educated in Gonzales, Gonzales County, Texas. I graduated from the Gonzales High School in May, 1941. I intend to enroll at the Texas Agricultural and Mechanical College, at College Station, Texas, on September 10, 1941.

On Saturday night, August 30, 1941, about 12:00 o'clock, Jose Portales, Jr., Vincent Patlan, Andrew Rodriguez and myself went into the Michelson Cafe, in Gonzales, Texas, and sat at the soda fountain table. We ordered some milk shakes. While we were waiting for the milk shakes to be served I got up and went to deposit a nickle in the nickleodium. When I returned to the table my companions above mentioned had already left. I went and asked one of the boys, who was at the door going out, what was the matter and they said they had left because we were not getting any service at all. I asked one of the waitresses why we did not get any service and she said I would have to talk to Mr. Lawrence Michelson, Manager, about that. I went and asked Mr. Lawrence Michelson why we could not get any service and he said he just could not explain why we could not get service. He would not talk to me and very reluctantly uttered the few words that he said.

The other young men above mentioned, to-wit, Portales, Patlan, and Rodriguez are also Gonzales boys, were born and reared there and are now attending the Gonzales High School, in Gonzales, Texas. We were all well dressed, we had just attended a Catholic reunion at Waelder, Texas (about 18 miles from Gonzales), were not intoxicated and we deported ourselves correctly when we went into said establishment.

The Greyhound Bus Station and the Western Union Telegraph Co.'s Office are situated in the same locale where the Michelson Cafe is.

Further deponent sayeth not.   Manuel Escobedo

Sworn to and susbcribed before me, this 1st day of September, A. D. 1941.

Alonso S. Perales,
Notary Public in and for Bexar County, Texas.

Lockhart, Texas,
August 12, 1941.

We, the undersigned citizens of the Republic of Mexico, were present at a dance sponsored by the Junior Chamber of Commerce of Lockhart, Texas, on July 4, 1941, when a representative, agent or employee of said Chamber of Commerce made, substantially, the following announcement:

"I have been asked to make this announcement: that all Spanish people gathered here must leave the block. Since this is an American celebration, it is for white people only." We left immediately.

NAME	ADDRESS	
Nemorio Quiroga	P. O. Box 875	Lockhart, Texas
Gumercindo Rojas	214 S. Commerce	ditto
E. Lopez	General Delivery	"
Harry Castilleja	P. Box 874	"
Refugio Villalobos	P. O. Box 627	"
Victor Hernandez	P. O. Box 945	"
Encarnacion Ruiz	P. B. Box 754	"
F. Prince Pruneda	P. O. Box 232	"
Lauro Maciel	Willow St.	"
Cresencio Mojica	R No. 3, Box 15	"
Pablo Guerra	P. O. Box 811	"
Gerardo Calderon	General Delivery	"

THE STATE OF TEXAS, COUNTY OF BEXAR

My name is Henry Meras. I reside at 1424 San Fernando St., in San Antonio, Texas. I am a native born citizen of the United States of America. I am a cement finisher by trade and employed at present, at Fort Sam Houston, Texas. I am 42 years of age, married and have nine children.

On or about the 29th day of July, 1941, my family and I went to Bastrop, Texas. A friend of mine named Esteban Hernandez and I went into a cafe (I could not see any name on it, but it is the Cafe situated on the north side of Main Street), and I told the Manager or owner, I do not know which, that we wanted to purchase some hamburgers, and he said: "We don't serve Mexicans". We thereupon left the place.

While in Bastrop I was informed by other persons of Mexican descent that persons of said racial lineage are not served at other business establishments in Bastrop such as soda fountains and beer parlors. In beer parlors Mexicans are served in the kitchen; that is, where the establishment is a combination of beer parlor and restaurant.

Further deponent sayeth not.   Henry Meras

Sworn to and subscribed before me this 21st day of July, A. D. 1941.

Alonso S. Perales,
Notary Public in and for Bexar County, Texas.

THE STATE OF TEXAS, COUNTY OF BEXAR

My name is Abdon Salazar Puente. I am 47 years of age, an American citizen, married, and reside in San Antonio, Texas.

I have a son by the name of Nieves Puente, who served in the United States Army in World War II.

206

On December 4, 1947, I purchased two and one half (2½) acres of land in Mayfield Park, in Bexar County, Texas, from Mr. Parry Jesse Humphreys. While I was getting ready to move into my newly acquired property, I. N. Clifton and Thurman Barrett filed suit against me seeking to restrain me from occupying said property on the ground that I am a person of Mexican descent. They allege that in the original deed there is a restriction to the effect that said property shall not be sold or leased to negroes or persons of Mexican descent.

The case is now pending in the 45th District Court of Bexar County, Texas, and is set for trial on April 12, 1948.

Further affiant sayeth not.   Abdon S. Puente

Sworn to and subscribed before me, this the 23rd day of March, A. D. 1948.

Alonso S. Perales,
Notary Public in and for Bexar County, Texas.

(On the 4th day of June, 1948, the Honorable S. G. Tayloe, Judge of the 45th District Court of Bexar County (San Antonio), Texas, rendered his decision in favor of the defendant Abdon Salazar Puente; whereupon the plaintiffs Thurman Barrett and I. N. Clifton gave notice of appeal to the Fourth Court of Civil Appeals, San Antonio, Texas, where the case is now pending. Submission date is October 13, 1948.)

THE STATE OF TEXAS, COUNTY OF BEXAR

My name is Ignacio B. Flores, and I reside at 401 Mockert street, San Antonio, Bexar County, Texas. I am a native born American Citizen, being born and raised in Bexar County, Texas. I am a Graduate of the Elementary and Junior High Schools and at present I am a Student of Commercial Art, at San Antonio Vocational & Technical High School.

On July 4, 1941, about 3 or 4 o'clock in the afternoon a party of individuals went to Camp Breeze, at Lake McQueeny, Texas, which included the following: Mr. and Mrs. Henry Flores, Miss Tony Garcez, Miss Olivia Cantu, Miss Esther Rios, Staff-Sargent John Benavidez, Mr. Edmund Flores, and myself.

We arrived at Camp Breeze, Lake McQueeny, Comal County, Texas, and after having refreshments, we decided to take a boat ride which we did. Then we decided to dance a few pieces of music in the pavilion and we did. When we went to our table a lady came up to us and said that she was sorry but we had to leave because they did not allow any Latin-Americans in the park. We asked her why and she said that the contract specified that no Latin-Americans were allowed on the premises. Then without arguing the matter further, we left.

Further deponent sayeth not.   Ignacio B. Flores

Sworn to and subscribed before me, at San Antonio, Texas, this 10th day of July, A. D. 1941.

Alonso S. Perales,
Notary Public in and for Bexar County, Texas.

THE STATE OF TEXAS, COUNTY OF BEXAR

My name is Henry Flores, and I reside at 2826 W. Poplar Street, San Antonio, Bexar County, Texas. I am a native born american citizen, being born in Bexar County, raised in Bexar County, Educated in Bexar County. I attended Elementary School in San Antonio, graduated from Brackenridge High School, graduated and went to St. Mary's University for a period of 3 years where I am pursuing the study of Law.

On July 4, 1941, at 4 o'clock p. m., a party consisting of four ladies and five gentlemen went to Camp Breeze, Lake McQueeny, Comal County, Texas; the people were Mrs. Henry Flores, Miss Tony Garcez, Miss Olivia Cantu, Miss Esther Rios, Staff-Sargent John Benavidez, Joe L. Gallardo, Mr. Edmund Flores, and Mr. Ignacio Flores and myself. We had been there about 45 minutes; we had danced and had refreshments, when a lady came up to us and told us that she was sorry but that we had to leave because they did not allow any Latin-Americans in the park. I asked why they did not allow any Latin-Americans in that place since we were just as American as they were. She repeated what she had said before, that we had to leave because we were Latin-Americans and the Contract of Camp Breeze specified that no Latin-Americans were to be admitted. I asked her who the owner of the place was and she declined and flatly refused to divulge the individual's name. The people there were mostly Germans and they being of Nazi descent, naturally they hated for us to be there. We left the place with a heavy heart and wondering if such places existed in our beloved United States, where all men are created equal!

Further deponent sayeth not.   Henry Flores

Sworn to and Subscribed before me, at San Antonio, Bexar County, Texas, this 9th day of July, A. D., 1941.

Alonso S. Perales,

Notary Public in and for Bexar County, Texas.

THE STATE OF TEXAS, COUNTY OF BEXAR

My name is D. R. Gutierrez. I reside at 113 Cecilia Street, in San Antonio, Texas, and am a native born citizen of the United States of America.

On Sunday, July 6, 1941, about 12:30 P. M., four couples went to Landa Park, in New Braunfels, Comal County, Texas. The party was composed of the following persons:

Mr. and Mrs. Pete Chavez, Miss Helen Aguirre and Mr. Olan Smith, Miss Dora Aguirre and Mr. John Zepeda, Miss Susie Zepeda and myself. We arrived there about 12:30 P. M. We took our own basket lunches and we ate there about 12:30 P. M. Then we took a walk in the Park and we played a few games of Box Hockey and Horse Shoe Rings. Then we walked to a dancing pavilion inside

208

the Park and we put a nickle in the nickleodium and we started dancing. We danced about four sets and then a man of German descent came and asked me if I was a Mexican from San Antonio. He was speaking Spanish. I answered in English that I was, and then I asked him why he asked me if I was a Mexican from San Antonio, whereupon he said: "That man over there (referring to a man at the soft drink stand) says Mexicans are not allowed in here". I asked him why and he said: "Well, he says so". Then I asked him if he would tell that to Uncle Sam, and he said he did not know anything about it. Then I told him to go and tell that man that he was referring to come and put me out. Then the man that I had sent word to come and put me out came toward me with a big stick in his hand and told me that that place was for whites only. I asked him what I was and he said: "You are a Mexican". He kept on telling me that they did not allow Mexicans there; that it was only for whites. Then I asked him about three or four times what I was and he kept on telling me that I was a Mexican and that I had better get out of there. Then I told him, "All right, we will go out". While he was telling me that no Mexicans were allowed he kept on swinging the stick he had in his hand.

I asked a clerk at the soft drink stand if he would go and put the United States Army Uniform on to fight for the United States and leave his job there, and he said that he did not know anything and that if I wanted any trouble to wait a while or go and see the manager; that he had nothing to do with this situation. We all left Landa Park.

Further deponent sayeth not.   D. R. Gutierrez

Sworn to and susbcribed before me this 7th day of July, A. D. 1941.

Alonso S. Perales,
Notary Public in and for Bexar County, Texas.

New Braunfels, Texas
June 29, 1941.

I, the undersigned Christino D. Perez, on the above date was present at the Hilltop Filling Station and Beer Joint at New Braunfels, Comal County, Texas, on the Austin Highway about 10 miles out of said City, where the said place is located.

After a stop on said place for a drink we observed after a good while in said place that we were paying more for our drinks than others that were in the same place who appeared to be German-Americans and were paying less than what we were paying for ours.

A simple question was asked by me. I, Christino D. Perez, asked one of the servants, "Why is it that we Latin-Americans have to pay more for our drinks than the Anglo-Americans on that table?" I pointed out to other tables where some men were sitting and who appeared to be German-Americans.

209

The servant's answer was that she had to obey the instructions of her boss and she had to follow them as she was instructed. And about that time the owner who was at a close distance from us came to answer the same question and said, "you belong over there pointing out to another room where at that time they were serving a good number of colored people. And when the owner said such thing with a certain manner that she appeared to be angry, and continued saying you smart man you don't deserve our service in this room, then I asked her for a package of cigarettes then the proprietress said you are not going to get nothing from here any more at no price and if you don't get out from here I will get the law for entering in a white people's place.

(Signed) Christino D. Perez

San Antonio, Texas,
June 28, 1941.

STATEMENT OF TOMAS RODRIGUEZ
923 Matamoros St.

My family and myself were humiliated the week before last at the Buck Horn saloon. We went in there and I asked for a root beer and one of the waiters told me there was not any; that I should go a little farther down the street on Flores Street, that there was where they served Mexicans; the waiter said I can sell to you here, but the truth is that it is very expensive, a soda will cost you 25c. Then I went to the coffee shop and the waiter there told me that the cup of coffee was worth 15c, and that they could not sell to us. Then I asked one of the Mexican clerks, and he told me that the Manager had the custom of not selling to Mexicans who were somewhat dark. Then we left the place. Those who went in there were my wife, myself and three children. We were clean and our appearance was all right.

I work for the San Antonio Public Service Company now and did at the time. I have worked for the Public Service Company about five years.

I reported the case to Mr. M. C. Gonzales, of the Mexican Consulate, and he said that there was nothing that could be done about it. Mr. Felix Gonzalez, of the Consulate, said that he was a Mexican and he was going to do something about it; for me to bring some witnesses.

THE STATE OF TEXAS, COUNTY OF BEXAR

My name is Avelino Peña, Jr. I am thirteen years of age and reside at 209 Lavaca Street, in San Antonio, Texas. I was born and reared in San Antonio, Texas. I am attending the Nelson Page Junior School. I am in the 6-A Grade.

Anglo-American boys have run me and other boys of Mexican or Spanish descent away from Roosevelt Park when we have gone

210

there to swim. *This has happened to us recently. We have been run away from there several times. The last time was the early part of June, 1941.*

They have run us away from the entire Park. They do not want us to use any part of it, not even the swings. They tell us: "Get out of here, Mexicans".

Further deponent sayeth not.   Avelino Peña, Jr.

Sworn to and subscribed before me, this 26th day of June, A. D. 1941.

Alonso S. Perales,
Notary Public in and for Bexar County, Texas.

THE STATE OF TEXAS, COUNTY OF BEXAR

My name is Jesus G. Valdez. I reside at 908 South Frio St., in San Antonio, Texas. I have a wife and four children all of whom are living with me at said address.

Up until Tuesday, June 24th 1941, I had been working for the General Supply Co., Inc., of San Antonio, Texas, on a construction project at Fort Sam Houston, Texas. We have been putting on tile roofs upon the warehouses already built there.

There are about seventy five or eigthy men of different races working on the project. The foreman, whose first name is Steve, but whose surname I do not know, marked the drinking water pails as follows: "For Whites"; "For Mexicans"; and "For Negroes". The water pails had their corresponding drinking cups.

On Tuesday morning, June 24th 1941, about eleven o'clock the water man came by and I drank water out of the pail marked "For Whites". Whereupon the foreman, whose first name is "Steve", as I said before, came to me and told me that he was going to discharge me because I had drunk water out of the pail marked "For Whites". I told him that I considered myself as white as he or any other white person. He then said substantially, the following: "You are discharged, and any other person of Mexican or African descent who drinks water out of the pails marked "For Whites" will be discharged also."

The foreman discharged me and I have not worked since. I have not been paid yet, but understand I will receive my pay next Friday.

Further deponent sayeth not.   Jesus G. Valdez

Sworn to and subscribed before me this 26th day of June, A. D. 1941.

Alonso S. Perales,
Notary Public in and for Bexar County, Texas.

THE STATE OF TEXAS, COUNTY OF BEXAR

My name is Beatrice Trujillo de Molinar. I am 23 years of age and married and reside at 1004 Lamar Street, in San Antonio,

211

Texas. My husband's name is Jesse Molinar, Jr. I am a native born citizen of the United States of America and have lived in San Antonio all my life.

On Saturday, June 7th 1941, about 11:00 P. M., my sister-in-law, Mrs. Rafaela Sanchez, her husband, Mr. Ignacio Sanchez, my husband, Mr. Jesse Molinar, Jr., and Mrs.   , the Anglo-American wife of Mr.   , who is a Sergeant in the United States Army, and I, went into a beer parlor known as the Three Stars Tavern, situated at 931 North New Braunfels Avenue, in San Antonio, Texas. We sat in a booth and ordered some beer. After we had been there about thirty minutes Mrs.   , the wife of Sergeant   , asked me to dance with her. I got up and started dancing with her. Then a man named Alfred Schaffer, who I believe is the Manager of the said beer parlor, came and tapped me on the shoulder and said for us to stop. I asked him why and he said that they would not allow any Mexicans to dance there. So I just stopped, walked to the booth, sat down for a minute and then left the said beer parlor.

Further deponent sayeth not. Beatrice Trujillo de Molinar

Sworn to and subscribed before me, this 9th day of June, A. D. 1941.

Alonso S. Perales,
Notary Public in and for Bexar County, Texas.

THE STATE OF TEXAS, COUNTY OF BEXAR

My name is Leopoldo Almanza Moreno. I am 30 years of age and a citizen of the United States of America. My home is at 808 South San Jacinto Street, in San Antonio, Texas. I voluntarily joined the United States Army on August 9, 1940, for a period of three years. I am a member of Troop A, Fifth Cavalry, and am stationed at Fort Bliss, Texas.

On Friday, April 11, 1941, I left Fort Bliss for San Antonio, Texas, on a furlough. I rode as a passenger on a travel bureau automobile. Travelling in the same car there were two Anglo-American ladies and three Anglo-American gentlemen, including the driver of the car. When we arrived at Fort Stockton, Texas, at about 1:30 A. M., Saturday morning, April 12th, we all went into the Hollywood Cafe. We all sat at the same table. A waitress came to our table and took the orders from all the Anglo-American folks, but refused to take my order, stating that Mexicans were not served in the dining room; that if I wanted something to eat I would have to go around the back and into the kitchen to be served there. I left the dining room and went and sat in my automobile. I was wearing the United States Army uniform at the time.

My Anglo-American fellow-passengers and the driver of the automobile disapproved of the incident and the driver said that

212

he was going to report the case to the proper officials in Washington.

Witness my hand at San Antonio, Texas, this 15th day of April, A. D. 1941.

(Signed) Pfc. L. A. Moreno

Sworn to and susbcribed before me this 15th day of April, A. D. 1941.

Alonso S. Perales,
Notary Public in and for Bexar County, Texas.

SOME OF THE PLACES WHERE MEXICANS ARE DISCRIMINATED AGAINST IN TEXAS EITHER BY DENYING THEM SERVICE OR BY SEGREGATING THEM FROM ANGLO-AMERICANS

ALICE, TEXAS. Mexicans are denied service in every Anglo-American Barber Shop. Mexican children are segregated from the Anglo-American children in the elementary schools of Alice.

ALPINE, TEXAS. Mexicans, including American soldiers of Mexican descent, are segregated from the Anglo-Americans at the theatre and are placed together with the Negroes. The owner of a pool hall refuses to permit American soldiers and sailors of Mexican descent to play there.

ANSON, TEXAS. Sommer's Cafe. Mexicans are denied service.

AUSTIN, TEXAS. Mexicans are segregated from the Anglo-American patients at the Public Hospital. There are several residential districts where Mexicans, irrespective of their position, are denied the privilege of residing.

BALMORRHEA, TEXAS. Mexicans are not admitted to the Public Park. Not even Boy Scouts of Mexican descent are admitted. Representative Borunda, of Ciudad Juarez, Chihuahua, Mexico, was denied service at a cafe.

BASTROP, TEXAS. There are several business establishments where Mexicans are not served. The owner of a cafe situated on Main Street very frankly stated: "We do not serve Mexicans." In some cafes Mexicans are served in the kitchen.

BEEVILLE, TEXAS. Gaun Rooming House. A war worker of Mexican descent was denied a room merely because he was of Mexican lineage. Three Anglo-American war workers went with the Mexican and applied for rooms at the same time. The three Anglo-Americans got rooms, but the Mexican did not.

BIG SPRING, TEXAS. Mexicans are denied service at the Cafes and are segregated from the Anglo-Americans at the theatres. At the U. S. Army Aviation Field there was a sign stating that any soldier who considers himself white shall not cross into the Mexican section of the city.—Pales Lunch Room, 104 Main St. Waffer Cafe, Quick Lunch, Main St., A. F. Lunch, 207 Main St. and Clover Grill Cafe.

BLUNTZER. TEXAS. Mexican Children are segregated from the Anglo-American children in the elementary school. The best building was assigned to the Anglo-American children while a filthy shack was assigned to the Mexican children.

BOERNE, TEXAS. Mexicans are segregated from the Anglo-Americans at the Cascade Theatre. Mexicans are denied admission to the Boerne Municipal Swimming Pool, which is owned by the City of Boerne.

BORGER, TEXAS. DeLuxe Barber Shop denies service to Mexicans.

BRADY, TEXAS. Service denied Mexicans at the E. Y. Barbecue Pit. At the Brady Public Park there was a sign reading: "This park is for whites. Negroes and Mexicans keep out." Mexican children are segregated from Anglo-American school children in the elementary schools. Mexicans, including American soldiers of Mexican descent, are denied service at restaurants and drug stores. The "Waffle Shop" is another place where Mexicans are not served.

CALVERT, TEXAS. The Robertson County War Price and Rationing Board refused to issue gasoline coupons to a farmer of Mexican descent notwithstanding that he was entitled to them. The complainant says the reason he was thus treated was that he is a Mexican.

CAMERON, TEXAS. Mexican children are segregated from the Anglo-American children up to the seventh grade in the public schools of Cameron. Mexicans are segregated from the Anglo-Americans in the theatre. In clothing stores Mexicans are not permitted to try on the clothes before they purchase same. Mexicans are denied service in several public business establishments.

CLEBURNE, TEXAS. Mexicans are segregated from the Anglo-American patients in every railroad company hospital. Mexicans are placed together with the Negro patients.

214

COLEMAN, TEXAS. Mexicans are seated with the Negroes at the theatres. The names of the theatres are Dixie, Gem and Howell. Ten Anglo-American restaurants are denying service to Mexicans.

COLORADO, TEXAS. Mexicans are denied service in several public business establishments.

CORPUS CHRISTI, TEXAS. A Chancellor of the Mexican Consulate was charged 10c for a soft drink that was worth only 5c at a Drive-Inn stand. When he inquired why he was told that because he was a Mexican. Persons of Mexican descent have been discriminated against in several other business establishments. Also there is opposition on the part of Anglo-Americans to persons of Mexican descent residing in districts intended for Anglo-American residents.

The City Council of Corpus Christi refused to pass an ordinance forbidding discrimination against Mexicans in local business establishments.

DEVINE, TEXAS. Gene's Grill, owner Mrs. Thelma Bohl. On August 14, 1943, two respectable Mexicans went in and sat at a table. An Anglo-American man was sitting at one end of said table. Just then the proprietress came to where the Mexicans were and said to them: "What are you boys doing sitting over here? Can't you boys see that a white man is drinking at this table? Don't you know the difference between a white man and you all?"

EDNA, TEXAS. Dahlstrom Eats. Ed's Cafe. Cozy Cafe. Runnel's Cafe. Two other Cafes. Mexicans, including American soldiers of Mexican descent, are denied service.

ELGIN, TEXAS. Mexicans are denied service in several business establishments. At cafes and restaurants they are told to go to the kitchen if they want to be served. American soldiers of Mexican descent are treated likewise. The Elgin Cafe and the McLellan Hotel refuse service to Mexicans.

FORT STOCKTON, TEXAS. Private First Class L. A. Moreno, Troop A, Fifth Cavalry, Fort Bliss, Texas, was denied service at the Hollywood Cafe at Fort Stockton, Texas. He was told that if he wanted something to eat, he would have to go around the back and into the kitchen. The Pecos Theatre. Mexicans are not admitted to the first floor, only in the balcony. Mexicans are not allowed to go into the Comanche Swimming Pool.

FORT WORTH, TEXAS. At a restaurant owned by M. A. Johnson, 114 E. Weatherford St., Fort Worth, Texas, Mexicans, including American soldiers of Mexican descent, are denied service. When asked why, the said proprietor answers that he does not serve Mexicans and that he does not have the time to explain any further.

FREDERICKSBURG, TEXAS. Downtown Cafe, 323 East Main St. On March 7, 1944, the following members of the Armed Forces of the United States were denied service. They were told that they could not be served in the front part of the Cafe, but they could be served in the kitchen. Jose Alvarez Fuentes, Seaman Second Class, United States Navy, Private Joe D. Salas, A. S. N. 38557190, Company B, 65th Battalion, M.R.T.C., United States Army, Private Paul R. Ramos, A.S.N. 38557007, Company B, 65th Battalion, M.R.T.C., United States Army, and Seaman Juan Garcia, United States Navy.

GANADO, TEX. Lee Konce Cafe, Macon Cafe. Mexicans are denied service in the dining room where Anglo-Americans are served. Mexicans are told to go into a room designated for Negroes.

GERONIMO, TEXAS. Mexican children are segregated from the Anglo-American children in the public schools.

GOLIAD, TEXAS. There is a restaurant that denies service to Mexicans. One day a Mexican asked the proprietor why he refused to serve Mexicans, and in reply the proprietor got out a pistol and told him to get out of the place.

GONZALES, TEXAS. Four well dressed young men of Mexican descent were denied service at the Michelson Cafe.

HAPPY, TEXAS. There is a restaurant that denies service to Mexicans.

HARLINGEN, TEXAS. A group of High School students, some of them of German and Japanese extraction, went to a public swimming pool and although we were at war with Germany and Japan nothing was said about them, but even though Mexico was our ally, our boys of Mexican descent were excluded.

HASKELL, TEXAS. Service is denied to Mexicans at Reid's Drug Store.

HONDO, TEXAS, Mexicans are segregated from the Anglo-Americans at the Ray Theatre. Mexicans are told that they cannot sit with the Anglo-Americans because Mexicans are not "Whites."

HUTTO, TEXAS. There is a restaurant where Mexicans are denied service in the front part of the establishment. They are told to go out to the rear door of the place. That is where Negroes are served.

JUNCTION, TEXAS. City Cafe, Manager John R. Kenard. Cozy Cafe, Manager Buddie Hunt. Mexicans are denied service.

LAMESA, TEXAS Mexicans are refused service in public business establishments. Bill's Cafe and the Blue Bonnett Cafe are two of them.

LITTLEFIELD, TEXAS. There is a soda fountain that refuses to sell to Mexicans, unless they are willing to eat the ice cream outside.

LOCKHART, TEXAS. On July 4, 1941, a number of Mexicans attended a dance which was being held on one of the main streets of Lockhart. About 11:00 P.M. the orchestra announcer made, substantially, the following announcement: "I have been asked to make this announcement: that all Spanish people gathered here must leave the block, since this is an American celebration."

LOLITA, TEXAS. Mexican children are segregated from the Anglo-American children in the public schools.

LUBBOCK, TEXAS. Mexican-American members of the Armed Forces of the United States, and persons of Mexican descent generally, have been denied service at the following business establishments: Ben's Cafe, 813 13th St. - 805 Broadway. Ben Kinard, Proprietor. Brown's Drug Store, Cafe Department, Broadway Ave. Luby's Cafeteria, Broadway Ave. Weis Motor Co., Texas Ave. Cammack Drug Co., Broadway Ave., Cafe Department. Jack-o-Lantern Cafe, 1220 Broadway Ave., F. W. Woolworth Co., Restaurant Department, Broadway Ave. Post Office Drug Store, Cafe Department, Avenue C. All Anglo-American Barber Shops. Mexicans are segregated from Anglo-Americans at the City Bus Station. Several hotels and apartment houses will not rent accommodations to Mexicans. Mexicans are denied the privilege of renting houses in certain sections of the city.

LULING, TEXAS. Cottage Inn. Owner: Gus Terrel. Mexicans are served in the kitchen only. Hi-way Inn Cafe. Owner: T. A. Landrith. Mexicans are served here, but they are segregated from the Anglo-Americans. Frenchy's Sandwich Shop. Mexicans are denied service. J. R. Mackey Drug Co., Owner: C. R. Mackey. Mexicans are not served inside the establishment. Ice cream is sold to them, but they must eat it outside. Mehner Drug Co., Owner: Geo. Mehner. Watkins Drugs, Owner: Bill Watkins. Green Cross Pharmacy. Owner: Dr. Clay Nichols. Mexicans are denied service in these drug stores also, but ice cream is sold to them and they have to eat it outside. Southern Cafe. Mexicans are denied service. Dr. J. T. O'Banion. He segregates the Mexicans from the Anglo-Americans in his office.

217

MASON, TEXAS. King's Cafe. Service denied to Mexicans.

MARATHON, TEXAS. A big sign "No Mexicans Allowed" was placed in front of a Cafe, and when the Mexican people protested, a bigger and better sign replaced it.

McALLEN, TEXAS. W. E. Hester, owner of the Broadway Service Station, refuses to permit Mexicans to drink water at said station merely because they are Mexicans.

McCAMEY, TEXAS. Club Cafe and three other Cafes. Mexicans are denied service. They are denied service also at the Anglo-American Barber Shops.

McQUEENEY, TEXAS. Mexicans are not permitted to visit Breeze Lake. They even refuse to sell them hamburgers at a stand there. American soldiers of Mexican descent have likewise been humiliated.

MELVIN, TEXAS. Children of Mexican descent are segregated from the Anglo-American children in the elementary schools.

A community center and Library Building built by the National Youth Administration has been denied several times to leaders of Mexican descent who have applied for the use of it for PTA meetings. Ladies of Mexican extraction have been denied the use of the rest room in said building.

MIDLAND, TEXAS. Persons of Mexican descent are segregated from the Anglo-Americans and required to sit in a section upstairs, which is reserved for Negroes, at the Yuca, Ritz and Rex Theatres. Mexicans are denied service at restaurants. The Ritz Cafe even had a sign reading NO MEXICANS ALLOWED. Five soldiers of Mexican descent were denied service there merely because of their racial lineage.

The civilian police are very hard on persons of Mexican descent. The following incident reflects their attitude toward persons of Mexican extraction. One day an American soldier of Mexican descent was walking down the street with a girl of German descent, and a policeman called her and told her not to go around with Mexicans, that it was a disgrace for "White" people to go around with Mexicans.

Children of Mexican descent are segregated from the Anglo-American children in the elementary schools.

NATALIA, TEXAS. Cox Place. Dick's Cafe, Owner W. R. Lay. Mexicans are denied service.

NEW BRAUNFELS, TEXAS. Ivey Green Cafe. Mexicans are denied service. Landa Park. Mexicans are denied admittance. South Americans have been segregated from Anglo-Americans.

218

They have been told: "Those tables over there are for South Americans." These are for "White people only." Marion Cafe, 180 San Antonio Avenue. Mexicans are denied service at this and other business establishments.

NEW GULF, TEXAS. Mexicans are refused service in public business establishments in New Gulf, Wharton, Boling and neighboring towns.

NIXON, TEXAS. Service is denied to Mexicans at the White Spot Cafe.

O'DONNELL, TEXAS. Persons of Mexican descent are denied service at the Middel S. Cafe.

OZONA, TEXAS. Hancock's Cafe. Ozona Drug Store, Ozona Hotel. Butler Cafe, Smith Drug Store. Mexicans denied service. Mexicans are segregated from the Anglo-Americans and placed with the Negroes at the Ozona Theatre. Mr. Alejos Lara, who has two sons in the U. S. Army and who were wounded in action, was denied service at the Ozona Drug Store. Mexican children are segregated from the Anglo-American children in the elementary and high schools of Ozona.

PANDORA, TEXAS. Mexicans are denied service in several public business establishments.

PECOS, TEXAS. Mexicans are denied service in Anglo-American Hotels, Cafes, Beer Parlors and recreational Centers. In the theatres they are placed together with the Negroes. In the Anglo-American stores Anglo-Americans are waited on first, e v e n if the Mexicans arrived first.

PEARLAND, TEXAS. Mexican children are segregated from the Anglo-American children up to the seventh grade in the public schools of Pearland, Brazoria County, Texas.

POST, TEXAS. Only one of the 5 Anglo-American restaurants serve Mexicans. The other four restaurants refuse to serve Mexicans and they have signs reading: "No Mexicans served" and "No Mexicans Wanted".

POTEET, TEXAS. At a 4th of July celebration on the public highway, a certain space was roped in "for white people to dance in" and the Mexicans present were told to go and dance elsewhere, as they were not welcomed there.

ROBSTOWN, TEXAS. Persons of Mexican descent denied service at the Steak House. At the Robstown Hospital owned by Dr. N. T. Gibson, persons of Mexican descent were denied admittance to a comfortably furnished waiting room intended for

219

Anglo-Americans, and instead were required to wait in a poorly furnished waiting room intended for colored people. Two of the persons actually evicted from the Anglo-American waiting room and requested to go into the waiting room for colored people were Rev. Jesus Rios, Pastor of the Robstown Baptist Church, and his wife. Mexican children are segregated from the Anglo-American children in the elementary schools of Robstown, Texas.

ROCK SPRING, TEXAS. In the month of August, 1944, Luis Gonzalez Jr., of Rock Springs, was denied service at Smith's Cafe. Several other American soldiers of Mexican descent have been denied service also. One of them is Trinidad Perez. Both Perez and Gonzalez were wearing the uniform of the United States Army at the time they were thus humiliated. Perez was wounded in action and is now discharged.

ROSCOE, TEXAS. Mexicans are denied service in every Anglo-American restaurant and barber shop.

ROSEBUD, TEXAS. At the public hospital Mexicans are segregated from the Anglo-Americans and are placed together with the Negroes. To go into the hospital they have to go through a rear door that has a sign reading: "Entrance for Negroes and Mexicans." Mexicans are denied service at the Imperial Cafe. The owner published an announcement in a local newspaper reading as follows: "Mexicans are not served at the Imperial Cafe." There is a dentist that segregates Mexicans from Anglo-Americans and does not permit the Mexicans to go through the same door that Anglo-Americans use. He wants Mexicans to go through a rear door into a room designated for Negroes and seats Mexicans upon the chair used by Negroes, and he charges Mexicans more for his services than he does Anglo-Americans.

ROTAN, TEXAS. City Barber Shop, Vittitow Barber Shop, Alton Parker Barber Shop. All these Barber Shops denied service to Sgt. Alexander Martinez, Paratrooper Frank Velez, Pvt. William Gonzalez and about fifty soldiers more. Mexicans are also denied service in restaurants and drug stores.

RUNGE, TEXAS. Manda's Cafe, owner: Miss Groos. Mexicans are denied service.

ROUND ROCK, TEXAS. There are two restaurants where Mexicans are denied service.

SAN ANGELO, TEXAS. Texas Grill, N. Chadbourne St., owned by George Wylie. Curry Drug Store. Coney Island Sandwich Shop, 214 S. Chadbourne St., Triple Gables. Woolworth's Coffee Shop. Manning Cafe, Chadbourne St., Wilson's Lunch, 125 N. Chadbourne St., Red Top Inn, 1302 N. Chadbourne St., proprietor: Ed. Motl. Mexicans are denied service.

SAN ANTONIO, TEXAS. Barber shop owned by Gus Siebenniecker, on Cupples Road. Mexicans are denied service. At Terrell Wells Swimming pool owned by H. E. Stumberg, Mexicans are denied admittance regardless of their social position. There are several other business places in the County of Bexar where Mexicans are discriminated against. Also, there are several residential districts where Mexicans, irrespective of their social position, are denied the privilege of residing.

SAN MARCOS, TEXAS. Mexican women are not permitted to use the rest room designated for Anglo-American women at the Court House in San Marcos, Texas. Mexicans are denied service in several restaurants and drug stores. Mexican children are segregated from the Anglo-American children in the public Schools.

SEAGRAVES, TEXAS. Mexicans are denied service at all of the Anglo-American cafes, and are denied admission to the theatre.

SEGUIN, TEXAS. A troop of American Boy Scouts of Mexican descent, carrying the national colors, were evicted from Starcke Park (a municipal park) because it is supposed to be "for whites only."

SEMINOLE, TEXAS. Mexicans are denied service at the Chuck Wagon cafe.

SINTON, TEXAS. Dodson Cafe, owner Mr. Dodson. Steak House Cafe. Mexicans are denied service.

SLATON, TEXAS. Mexicans are denied service in several public business establishments.

SNYDER, TEXAS. Mexicans are denied service at restaurants and barber shops. A Mexican is not even permitted to have his shoes shined in an Anglo-American barber shop. Dental Services were denied to the mother of a U. S. soldier of Mexican descent by Dr. J. G. Hicks. A young lady came out and informed the patient that Dr. Hicks did not work for colored people.

SPUR, TEXAS. Palace theatre. Mexicans segregated from Anglo-Americans. Hagan's Barber Shop, Spur Barber Shop, Cayce's Barber Shop, Johnson's Barber Shop, City Drug Co., Red Front Drug Store. Mexicans are denied service. The City Drug Store denied Pvt. Pedro Hernandez of the U. S. Army, a drink of water in the heat of last summer. There are two dentists at Spur, Texas, who have separate chairs for Mexicans.

STERLING CITY, TEXAS. There is a restaurant that refuses to serve Mexicans, unless they are willing to eat the food outside.

STRAWN, TEXAS. Mexicans are denied service at all Anglo-American barber shops, and they are segregated from the Anglo-Americans at the theatre.

SUDEN, TEXAS. Blondie Cafe, owner Blondie Puckett. On Oct. 7, 1944, he refused service to two men of Mexican descent who had gone into the restaurant accompanied by an Anglo-American friend of theirs. The Anglo-American invited them to have a cup of coffee with him. When they went in the owner of the Cafe asked the Mexican men if they were Mexicans and when they answered in the affirmative, he told them to get out.

SUGARLAND, TEXAS. Mexicans are mistreated by foremen in agricultural fields. Children are segregated in schools. Mexicans are placed together with the Negroes in the hospital.

TAHOKA, TEXAS. D. and E. Drugs - Luncheonette. Lee's Cafe. Owner: Lee Montadilen. Victory Cafe Owner: Joe T. Mosley. There are other places besides these ones.

UVALDE, TEXAS. Dinette Restaurant. On April 8, 1944, Pfc. Cruz M. Rodriguez and Pvt. Lydia Rodriguez, both members of the United States Army, were denied service. Mexicans, including American soldiers of Mexican descent, are denied service at all Anglo-American barber shops and at the following Anglo-American business establishments: Dinette Cafe. Newport Cafe. Owner: Mr. Midget. Shadowland Cafe and Beer Parlors, owner Robert Fullingwater. Walgreen's Drug Store, Owners: Spears Bros. Hanger Six Cafe. Palace Drug Store. Uvalde Candy Shoppe. Manhattan Cafe. Casey Jones Cafe and Beer Parlors, ower Casey Jones. Casal Cave, owner Henry Casal.

VICTORIA, TEXAS. Hi-way Cafe, S. Moody, Owner: E. H. Jay. Omas Cafe, 211 S. Main St. Rips Cafe, Port Lavaca Highway. Baker's Place, S. Main St. Round House Bar, 211 S. Cameron St. Mexicans are denied service. Service is also denied to American soldiers of Mexican descent.

WACO, TEXAS. Mexicans are placed together with Negroes in the County Jail of McClennan County, Texas.

WHARTON, TEXAS. Persons of Mexican descent are discriminated in several business establishments. Until recently, Americans of Mexican descent were not allowed to vote in Wharton County.

Horton, Richmond, Matagorda, Brazoria, Bay City, Angleton, Stanton, Amarillo, Greenville, Jacksonville, Cleveland, Braunfield, Levelland, and Shamrock, Texas. In all these towns and cities there are business establishments where Mexicans are denied service.

The Mexican children are segregated from the Anglo-American children in the public schools of nearly every town and city in Texas.

In nearly every town and city in Texas there are residential districts where Mexicans are not permitted to reside.

The purpose has been to keep the Mexican at arm's length and to treat him as an inferior.

The same situation exists in the States of Arizona, Colorado, California and a part of New Mexico.

WICHITA FALLS, TEXAS. Domestic Egg Plant, Inc., 1900 Bluff St., Wichita Laundry, 602 Austin St., Pond Laundry, 602 Ohio St. Wives and other relatives of United States soldiers of Mexican descent are denied employment merely because they are of Mexican lineage.

LETTERS

Rotan, Texas,
March 11, 1944.

Alonso S. Perales.
714 Gunter Building,
San Antonio, Texas.

Dear Sir:

We heartily endorse your efforts to stamp out discrimination against us. There are about six hundred Mexicans living in and about Rotan. We are barred from every barber shop, several beauty parlors, and one restaurant. Even soldiers are denied services. Here are some cases: City Barber Shop, Vittitow Barber Shop, Alton Parker Barber Shop, all of Rotan, denied services to Sgt. Alexander Martinez, Paratrooper Pancho Velez, Pvt. Rito Velez, Pvt. William Gonzalez and all the rest, some fifty soldiers. We telegraphed the Governor and he answered see the Mayor, and the County Officials. These replied: the Governor is only passing the buck.

It is worse in Jones County, where Mexicans are denied all barber shop, beauty parlor and cafe services.

At Spur, Texas, The City Drug Store would not give Pvt. Pedro Hernandez a drink of water in the heat of last summer.

The cases are innumerable in Nolan, Kent, Stonewall, King, Garza and Dickens Counties. Other discriminations are in movie houses and it often happens that a Mexican plows the land and sows and cultivates it without pay, being promised a portion of the harvest, but is kicked off before he gets it. They are trying to relegate us to the Pagan Negroes.

It would be a great pleasure to meet you. All of us read your articles with avidity. Our problems must and will be solved. We can send you many cases of people willing to testify in any court.

Sincerely yours,

(Signed)   Roberto Martínez.

B. 486

STATEMENT OF MR. FELIX R. GARZA
(formerly of Roma, Texas.)

About 5 years ago (Aug. 1939) I stopped at Pearsall, Texas, on the way to San Antonio, and went into an Anglo-American Barbershop. As soon as I went in and took off my hat, the barber told me: "I am sorry, but we do not work on Spanish people".

About March, 1941, in San Antonio, Texas, I went to a house on Buena Vista Street (Prospect Hill) and I asked a lady there if she was in charge of the apartment I wanted to rent (at the apartment I wanted to rent there was a sign saying that the interested party should call at the other address for further information), and she said: "I am sorry, but we do not rent to Spanish people." My wife was with me at the time.

Félix R. Garza.
2516 Saunders Ave.,
San Antonio, Texas.

McKinney, Texas,
P. O. Box 235,
February 8, 1944.

Lic. Alonso S. Perales,
San Antonio,
Texas.

Dear Sir:

I notice in the newspaper "La Prensa" dated February 6, 1944, that you advise that if any business houses discriminate against Mexicans, that this matter should be reported.

This is to advise you that some of the places in McKinney discriminate against the Mexicans. It is impossible for Mexicans to get their hair cut at any barber shop. Also the theatre "Texas" at McKinney will not permit the Mexicans to sit where the Anglo-American people sit, but force them to go up in the balcony to sit with the negroes.

Also, the drug store operated by W. B. Mitchell refuses to serve cold drinks at the fountain to Mexicans. My son was in his drug store in McKinney a few weeks ago with an Anglo-American boy and the Anglo-American boy ordered drinks for both of them, and the fountain boy and Mr. Mitchell served the drink to the Anglo-American boy, but refused to serve a drink to my boy because he was a Mexican.

I shall be glad if you will see about this matter and advise me what can be done, if anything.

Yours very truly,
M. R. Garza.

A Mexican Embarrassed By Refusal of Service in a Cafe, Asks Why Such Discrimination Persists in Texas.

Editor, The Press:

I WAS born in Fort Worth in 1907. I have a brother and three nephews in the armed forces now fighting at some front. I am a Mexican by birth and so is my brother and nephews.

Three friends of mine, all of Mexican origin, went to a cafe on East Weatherford St. and the waitress and the proprietor refused to serve them because they were Mexicans. They told me about it and I told them there must be some mistake and asked them to take me to the place and they did and again the waitress and the proprietor refused to serve us, and ordered us out. I would like to know, if such discrimination still exists in regard to our race, what our Mexican boys and men in uniform are fighting for? As I see it and have been told and read daily, we are supposed to be fighting for freedom from such discriminations as these and that our democratic form of government means such freedom. I would like to be enlightened by anyone who has authority to discuss this humiliating subject of discrimination.

Why is there such an extreme amount of discrimination against a Mexican? Wherever he travels, works, eats and even where he lives. I will say that your guess is as good as mine.

Before the war, a Mexican was supposed to have the privilege of travelling, residing, working, eating and attending all public places where the Anglo-American man went. At least this was the law on the surface and I mean on the surface only, because a

Mexican really has never had the right to exercise these privileges without being offended and humiliated. This has been brought to light in many instances all over the nation, not one time but many times, and especially here in the northern part of our State, Texas.

When travelling on buses or street cars, many times the Anglos have refused to sit by a person because he or she is Mexican. Many times at public swimming pools persons have not been allowed to go in because they are Mexicans. In many neighborhoods the landlords have refused to rent their properties to Mexicans, at many places jobs are refused Mexicans. If a Mexican is arrested for any reason he is not put in a cell with the Anglo-Americans.

There is good and bad in every race, but the extreme discrimination against most Mexicans is something for the intelligent minds of this country to consider and weigh and see if by any means this is right.

And I will add, without regret or remorse in my heart, that before the war the Mexican faced all the discrimination. So, will he face it after the war?

S. M. ZEPEDA.

Fort Worth, Texas.

1634 Fresno Drive,
San Antonio, Texas,
Oct. 28, 1941.

My dear Mr. Perales:

On this past nineteenth day of September, Mrs. Flores, an American neighbor, whose husband is of Mexican birth, and I, made an appointment for services at the Stahls Beauty Parlor, by telephone.

I spelled both our names to an attendant there, who in turn gave me the hour for our appointment.

Mrs. Flores and I presented ourselves at the appointed time, but as the place seemed crowded, we were forced to sit apart from each other. On the only chair available, were two cushions which I asked an employee, if I might move so as to be able to sit on that one chair. This employee, one Esther Lawson, answered me rudely, asking if I had made an appointment, and if so, to whom had I made it. I answered in the affirmative, stating the person on the opposite end of the line had given me no name. This employee was so brusque in her manners of inquiring that I immediately arose and told Mrs. Flores that I preferred to cancel my appointment, rather than be treated in such an insulting manner.

Mrs. Flores was at a loss as to why this employee was so rude to me, and asked me to wait until she called this to the attention of the owner, as Esther was merely an employee there.

226

In the meantime Mrs. Stahl and Esther were speaking to each other, apparently about our appointment. When Mrs. Flores called Mrs. Stahl to explain I had been the one who had made the appointment for both of us, Mrs. Stahl fumbled for words and meekly said there apparently was a mix-up in the appointment and that it was very likely that we would not be attended to for some time. She walked away and again spoke with Esther, beyond our reach of hearing.

After a moment, Esther called Mrs. Flores to a side and very firmly said, "Mrs. Flores, if you wish, we can take care of you, but we don't care for Mexican trade here!"

Mrs. Flores is a semi-invalid, and a mild tempered lady, and this so shocked her, that she could think of nothing but to tell this attendant she most certainly would not remain if I could not be attended, and to me she said, "come on, let's go Aurora."

I followed her out of the beauty parlor, but it was not until we reached the automobile that she told me what had been said to her.

You can imagine the deep humiliation I suffered, and the embarrassment of my friend.

Later that afternoon Mrs. Flores telephoned to Mrs. Stahl for an explanation, as I had been attended to, twice previously, on two different occasions. Mrs. Stahl admitted it must have been embarrassing to us, but said she had no knowledge or record of my having been attended to there, as she had decided from the very beginning, that they would not have a thing to do with Mexicans.

Mr. Perales, I am writing to you, hoping that in some way, I may be able to help you convince our city government, how un-American it is to encourage racial antipathy and discriminations, especially in these times, when so much has been said of the "true" friendship and unity between the peoples of the Americas. May you find success in your endeavors,

Sincerely,

Aurora Dávalos.

(Mrs. Rudolph A. Dávalos.)

P. S.

My address is 1634 Fresno Drive, and I may be reached at P-3471.

PART IV

ARTICLES AND COMMENTS

San Antonio, Texas,
November 24, 1947.

Honorable Watson Miller,
Commissioner of Immigration,
El Paso, Texas.

Dear Sir:

Referring to the labor conference which is being held between officials of the United States and Mexico with a view to entering into a new contract regarding migratory workers for this country, we deem it essential to clarify certain basic points in so far as the importation of such workers in Texas is concerned.

In the first place, it should be borne in mind that in Texas, for example, there are plenty of workers available, but these workers cannot work for twenty-five or thirty-five cents per hour due to the high cost of living. These workers, including the agricultural workers, should be paid a minimum of sixty cents per hour in order to subsist. The Government of the United States and the Government of Mexico should not, under any circumstances, permit employers to import workers who will come here to work for less money because this would compel the workers who are already here to migrate to Michigan, Colorado, Wyoming and other States of the Union in quest of more remunerative employment. This would not be fair either to the imported workers nor to the Texas citizens and inhabitants of the United States who have lived here for many years, have purchased homes, have their children in school and are permanent residents of this State.

In the second place, the Government of the United States and the Government of Mexico should exact from the proper Texas authorities the assurance that at the next session of the Legislature a law will be passed forbidding the humiliation of persons of Mexican descent in commercial establishments such as restaurants, theaters, drug stores, etc., simply because of their racial lineage. The interests of both Nations require that such a law be passed in Texas without further delay.

Leaders of both races are endeavoring to raise the standard of living of thousands of persons of Mexican descent in Texas, and to strengthen the bonds of friendship between the people of the United States, including the people of Texas, and the people of Mexico, but it is quite evident that their efforts will be in vain unless a living wage is paid to persons of Mexican extraction and an end is put to the shameful humiliations to which they are subjected in numerous towns and cities in this State.

Thanking you in advance for your earnest consideration to this our petition, we remain

Yours very truly,

COMMITTEE OF ONE HUNDRED.

THE LEAGUE OF LOYAL AMERICANS.

By Alonso S. Perales, Director General

Suite 308 International Trade Building,
510 W. Houston Street,
Oct. 29, 1947.

Honorable Joint Committee on Housing
of the Congress of the United States:

My name is Alonso S. Perales, an Attorney-at-law, with offices in Suite 308 International Trade Building, 510 West Houston Street, San Antonio, Texas. I represent the League of Loyal Americans, a civic and patriotic organization, chartered by the State of Texas in 1937. I am also appearing as State Judge Advocate of the Catholic War Veterans of America, Department of Texas.

The housing shortage in San Antonio, in so far as the veteran of Mexican descent is concerned has been seriously aggravated by the refusal of some real estate developers to sell them houses simply because of their racial ancestry. Attached hereto are copies of three affidavits which speak for themselves.

We do not believe that the Anglo-American veterans object to residing in the same neighborhood with Mexican-American veterans. In World War II these veterans learned not only to live together, but to fight together in defense of our country, precisely, to the end that Christianity and democracy might survive. We do not believe it is the Anglo-American veteran that is objecting to the presence of his Mexican-American buddy in his midst. It is the real state developers who insist upon segregating our people generally and now have the effrontery to attempt to segregate the defenders of our country, the very men who made it possible for them to con-

229

tinue to exist. Impelled by purely mercenary motives these real estate developers are establishing their so-called restricted additions thus fostering racial strife and undermining the very foundations of our Republic.

Our Federal Government can put a stop to these nefarious and un-American practices by serving notice upon the real estate developers that the Government will not guarantee any loan or grant priorities for the acquisition of critical materials in any real estate addition in which Mexican-American Veterans are denied the right to purchase a home simply because of their racial lineage.

COMMITTEE OF ONE HUNDRED
THE LEAGUE OF LOYAL AMERICANS
Alonso S. Perales, Director General.

EDITORIALS

FURTHER "INCIDENTS" WILL RUIN SONORA

The "incident" which occurred early last Saturday morning has serious implications in that, aside from being an effront to the peace and dignity of an individual and to our community, it could produce more such "incidents" which, fed by the flames of hate and prejudice, might easily undermine and destroy the peaceful, tolerant, Christian way of life which is our eternal ideal and which we have achieved to a great extent.

A full account of the occurrence is reported elsewhere in this edition but briefly here is what happened: A bus passenger, Francisco Ramirez, enroute from Fort Stockton to Eagle Pass, entered the Park Inn Cafe for a cup of coffee. When he left to return to the bus station he noticed three young men approaching him. He barricaded himself in the office of a filling station which adjoins the bus station. The men told him to come out and, fearing for his safety, he refused. The men came in after him and in attempting to defend himself he struck one of them across the chest with a tire tool. He was quickly beaten to the floor, but managed to regain his feet and make a dash for the draw behind the cafe. He was caught, knocked down again and given a thorough "treatment" which left him lying in the water in the bottom of the draw, his cheekbone smashed, his lips split, his head cut and bruised, a citizen of the United States, half crazed with fear and in a pitiful condition because he happened to be born in the wrong bed, and because he had accepted in good faith the bus company's information that it had a franchise with the cafe whereby the cafe agreed to serve food and drink to ALL bus passengers.

The three young men who provoked, administered and condoned the assault on Ramirez are not criminals, and this editorial is not published with the intention of hurling down a vitriolic denouncement against them. We feel that they acted out of ignorance, that they did not realize the terribleness of the thing they were doing, that they let blind prejudice void their sense of reasoning and humanity. We feel that all three sincerely regret their actions that night and will never again be guilty of an attack on another fellow being.

Sutton County is populated mainly with pioneers and their descendants, a free-thinking, broad-minded, independent people making up a part of the most independent state in the union. Although the majority is of Anglo-Saxon lineage there are living right here in this county today people whose ancestors were Czechoslovakian, Austrian, German, French, Mexican, Indian, Chinese, Italian, Dutch and Negro.

Together we have built schools, roads, a bank and many other things for the common good. Together we have thrived. Only by continuing to live and work together peacefully and tolerantly shall we continue to progress. And this applies not only to cooperation in our tiny spot on the globe but to the whole world—to our relations with the men of all nations. These, however, are only the practical aspects of the question.

Immeasurably greater is the moral issue involved. Are a man's flesh and soul more immune to pain because his skin is a different shade from mine? Are his inherent rights decreased? Is he a lesser being in the sight of God? If this is true, then the message of Jesus Christ and all His prophets, every war fought for the rights of man, every word of our American Constitution, is a mockery—every martyr since the world began was a fool who died in vain quest for a mere illusion.

The Devil's River News,
September 19, 1947,
Sonora, Texas.

TWO MEN FINED AFTER GUILTY PLEA TO ASSAULT CHARGE

Pleading guilty to charges of assault, two local men paid fines of $36 each Monday morning in Justice of the Peace George Barrow's court, following an altercation early Saturday morning in which Francisco Ramirez, Fort Stockton, was severely beaten.

The two men, Jim Martin and Leo Berry, were arrested Saturday morning by Deputy Sheriff Clyde Henderson and held in jail until Monday pending investigation of the extent of Ramirez' injuries. A third man, O. L. Richardson, Jr., who was present during the fray, was not arrested due to the fact that both Martin and Berry stated that he did not take part in the assault.

Ramirez told officers that he was a bus passenger enroute from Fort Stockton to Eagle Pass and that he stopped at the Park Inn Cafe about 2:30 o'clock Saturday morning for a cup of coffee. When he left the cafe, he said, three men approached him and tried to start a fight. He said he ran unto the office of the Humble Station and shut the door and that the men told him to come out. Refusing, they came in after him and knocked him down. According to his statement, he escaped from the office and ran behind the cafe toward the draw, but was caught and beaten by all three men. He was found lying in the draw about 3:30 o'clock by Jesus Gandar. He gave no reason for the attack.

According to Berry and Martin, Ramirez struck Berry across the chest with a tire tool when they entered the station office, and the fight ensued. They both reiterated that Richardson was present, but took no part in the fight.

The Devil's River News,
September 19, 1947.
Sonora, Texas.

RACIAL DISCRIMINATION CHARGED IN COMAL CO.
By Associated Press

AUSTIN, Aug. 5.—A university student of Latin-American descent Tuesday said he reported a case of racial discrimination against himself and five companions to the good neighbor commission. The student, Arnulfo Guerra of Roma, Starr County, said he and the five others were refused service in a New Braunfels restaurant Saturday night.

Guerra told reporters he was taking all possible action against a recurrence of "the humiliating incident".

"It was the first time in our lives for the six of us to have such a thing happen", he said. Guerra is a 20-year-old pre-law student. He saw service in Korea during the war.

He said he was awaiting the return to Austin of the Good Neighbor Commission's executive secretary, Mrs. Pauline Kibbe.

The university student said he also had sought expert legal advice about a possible suit against proprietors of the restaurant, but lawyers advised him there were no legal grounds for such a suit, there being no Texas statute prohibiting racial discrimination.

Guerra said a waitress at the New Braunfels restaurant told him the establishment did not serve Latin Americans, and when he asked the man in charge if this were so, the man said, "Get the hell out of here".

Guerra's two companions from the university were Ralph Carpinteyro, 22, pharmacy student from Cotulla, and Jesus Rodriguez, 23, geology student from Cotulla. All are veterans of overseas service during World War II.

Their dates were girls from Southwest State Teachers College at San Marcos, Guerra said.

(Taken from the San Antonio Express, San Antonio, Texas, Aug. 6, 1947).

DISCRIMINATION

Editor, The Star:

If Mrs. Mabel Lewis would swallow some of her high and mighty pride over wetbacks, I would like for her to lend an ear to this:

On June 25, 1941, a committee on Fair Employment Practice was set up by President Roosevelt in Executive Order 8802. He said: " . . . I do hereby reaffirm the policy of the United States that there shall be no discrimination in the employment of workers in defense industries or Government because of race, creed, color, or national origin, and I do hereby declare that it is the duty of employers and of labor organizations . . . to provide for the full and equitable participation of all workers in defense industries, without discrimination because of race, creed, color or national origin. . . . "

Luck, ability, and ambition, individually or together, are sometimes so strong a force that prejudice can't defeat them. Many of the states are outlawing discrimination in the job world, encouraging employers to disregard race and religion when they hire workers. Time will show how successful such laws are, once they have been put into practice. (That seems to be not true here, you see).

The information used here is from a book entitled, "Get The Job" by Willard Abraham.

Thank you.

Valdemar González.

(The Valley Morning Star,
Harlingen, Texas,
July, 1947.)

OUR OWN BACKYARD

Editor, The Star:

In reply to the letters of Mrs. Day and Mrs. Lewis regarding the stand I have taken in favor of educating the wetback children, evidently they have misconstrued the thought I tried to convey. Believe me, I am not trying to disparage my own people, but I realize that never before in our history have we needed neighborly understanding as we do now and where better can we start than in our own back yard? My convictions are to try and do unto others as I would have them do unto me.

Another thing. Who is he who doesn't pay taxes? Personally, I think it is a privilege and it is hard for me to understand why a grown person would begrudge a little child an elementary education. Again, I assure you that I feel it our duty to educate the wetback child if we are going to employ his parents. The Latin American pays his taxes the same as anyone else, therefore, why should we feel that the responsibility of educating these children falls entirely on our shoulders?

Regarding the statement that none other than the Anglo Saxon race had made any great contribution to world advancement - my dear Mrs. Day - perhaps you should review your Ancient History as any educated person knows that the Egyptians, Greeks Hindus, Italians, etc., contributed to world culture the fine arts we prize so highly. And the ones who say that Mexico has no advantages have in all probability never been past the border. Mexico City has fine schools and many beautiful churches. You may see the richest Mexican kneeling side by side with the poorest peasant. They are a very devout race and are loyal to one another. There is so much that we could learn from them. Why condemn any race? Jesus was a Jew, and who knows, Saint Peter may be a Latin.

> Mrs. Jimmy Haynes.
> Rt. 1 Stuart Place,
> Harlingen, Texas.

(The Valley Morning Star,
Harlingen, Texas,
July, 1947.)

VALLEY RACE DISCRIMINATION APPALLING AND SHAMEFUL

Editor, The Star:

I am not in habit of airing my views and opinions through the medium of the newspaper, but I feel that at times there are certain subjects that merit public attention.

234

Since arriving here in this very beautiful valley, I have been shockingly aware of the prevailing racial prejudice against our Latin American citizens. I find it almost impossible to believe that here in the United States such actions are allowed and practiced.

We recently completed a war against a nation steeped in racial prejudice against those who were not fortunate enough to be born a member of the so-called "super Nordic race". Thousands of our men and women gave their lives so that our American belief that "all men are created equal" might be practiced in other lands besides our own.

Yet in the face of this, it is an appalling and entirely shameful thing to discover that these same anti-American principles are being lived right here in the United States. Undoubtedly we should have swept our own doorstep first.

Fortunately, these so-called Americans are in the minority and millions of other citizens still retain their beliefs in the basic ideas used in the foundation of our country and the consequent forming of the constitution.

Do these people actually believe that they are a better race, and have the privilege of maintaining a superior attitude towards our good Latin American citizen?

There are certain business establishments here that bar Latin Americans for some un-American reason. If this practice is condoned, then it is a strange thing that these citizens do not erect concentration camps and such, so that they may be afforded the pleasure of practicing their disgusting beliefs according to a more complete interpretation of Hitler's "Mein Kampf".

Wayne Thomas,
Weslaco, Texas.

(The Valley Morning Star,
Harlingen, Texas,
    1947.)

DISCRIMINATION HERE SHOCKS VISITING VALLEY TEACHER

Editor, The Star:

I took 40 of the 7th and 8th grade pupils near the close of school to Harlingen for a skating party. I was shocked, humiliated and very unhappy to have to tell the pupils after talking to the manager of the skating rink that he did not let Latin-Americans on the floor to skate under any circumstances.

This situation must be faced by square-minded and liberal thinking people. Latin-Americans are a very fine race that respond beautifully to good treatment and fair dealings. I do know my Latin-American pupils and most of them come from very fine homes. Their parents are very civic-minded and they want their children to be fine American citizens and enjoy some of the finer things of life that probably they did not have while growing up, just like a lot of Anglos.

There were Latin-Americans on the bus that had lost members of their family in World War II. They died on various battlefields so that we could enjoy life in a land of plenty while many other countries today are starving to death. It seems to me that they inherited, as Latin-Americans, the right to fight our wars but not to enjoy the freedom for which they fought.

Did it ever occur to you that when these people are run over, receive underpaid salaries, etc., that the Anglo is setting the standard of living for himself? When the depression hits, and it always does after a war, your family will receive their low wages and will be glad to get it and will drop to a low standard of living. It is also undemocratic to segregate them in schools, and by helping them better themselves, you will help to make this wonderful Texas a better place to live.

It is my prayer that the Anglos will be awakened to the way they treat these people socially. I wish that all churches, Boy Scouts, and other civic organizations would try to do more to gain a better understanding of them. The United States will be trading with these Latin-American countries and it would certainly be to an advantage to any progressive person to understand them and to be able to speak their language.

Ava I. Humphreys.
Edcouch, Texas.

(The Valley Morning Star,
Harlingen, Texas,
July, 1947.)

THE WISHES OF GOD

Thanks, Mrs. Ava I. Humphreys, for your letter in the Star.

You are one of few who realize just how much the Latin American suffers to make his social life go through, amid a bunch of ingrateful Anglo-Saxons who call themselves Americans.

I could not fight the Germans or the Japanese, but both my brothers and sisters did, even knowing that most of the Anglo-Saxons hated us; knowing our rights and our neighbors, they went to fight for what you call democracy.

If they do not admit us in their establishments, I know very well it is because we are cheaply dressed, and because most of us Mexicans are farmers, hard workers, and very ignorant to fight for our rights.

Take an Anglo-Saxon: he is well fed, well paid, and even if he is not a hard worker, he makes more money, three times more, than a Latin American, thus, he can afford to be clean and live well, even if he does not know his arithmetic.

Why! Anglo-Saxons go to Mexico City, they eat Mexican food, they look to us for water and they are never refused or humiliated or embarrassed like they humiliate us here. We may be dirty, poor and disorganized, but we know it is best to be charitable, friendly and to work hard. I think that meets the wishes of God.

I know this, that this discrimination exists only in the Rio Grande Valley where we are supposed to be more friendly, but like everything else, the Anglo-Saxon wants to be number one in everything.

Remember what happened to Hitler because he wanted to own the world. And remember that we all have to make a living and we all have to sweat to make it. So why not let us have fun and be real friends? We are all Americans. We fight for the same reasons and ideals, so why not be real democrats?

George Esqueda.

(The Valley Morning Star,
Harlingen, Texas,
July, 1947.)

ALL CHIPS OFF SAME BLOCK, ALAMO FARMER POINTS OUT

Editor, The Star:

For quite a while I've been reading the letters of Latins and Anglos. I am a Mexican and very proud of it. American citizen? Yes. Proud of it? Yes. So what?

It really makes me mad, all this discrimination, especially on kids who go to school together with Anglos. I've heard of "being good neighbors". How can it be, when adults set the example? How do you think those kids felt? I can imagine. I know that it is bad and I am against it.

But as for adults, why! then, I know when I am not wanted, and if ever they don't admit me at their places, they can go and jump in the lake. My money is as good as theirs. If they don't want it, it's because it isn't needed. Otherwise you'd be surprised.

I am a farmer. Most of my friends are Anglos, and they are very nice. I try to get along with them. So let's all do our best. If not, well then, I've heard that this is a free country. As for democracy, what is democracy? Liberty? Brothers and sisters, when there is a war? I don't know . .

All I know is this: that we are chips off the same block, will be buried in the same earth. No discrimination in the eyes of God. So may God have mercy on all those who think as Hitler did.

As for me, I'll always be proud of being a Mexican, one hundred per cent, and believe in the Golden Rule.

Olivia Pérez,
Alamo, Texas.

(The Valley Morning Star,
Harlingen, Texas,
June 27, 1947.)

PROTESTS TO CONTINUE UNTIL DISCRIMINATION IS ENDED

Editor, The Star:

So Mrs. J. K. Collins of La Feria wants our letters scrapped, instead of published! Who is she to try to violate one of the four principles of our liberty, freedom of the press, as long as we are within the limits of our rights?

To stop telling the world our feelings because she does not like it and is fed up with it - the very idea! Of course, (truth is no sin, but it bothers - an old Spanish saying) all she cares is the work that the Mexicans do, as if they were animals, with no soul, no feelings, and no rights to defend themselves against stupid cruelties by unscrupulous persons that call themselves Americans but are everything but Americans.

Those children went to that skating rink because it was a school affair and anyone of dignity and pride should know and understand how they felt, humiliated the way they were in front of all the school children, being all of them of nice families.

The Mexicans and their work - yes, they are the blessed who with their strength and their strong arms have cleaned the brush mile by mile, have worked, built, helped construct every factory and business place to make this beautiful Valley what it is today. We all in gratitude should come out and strongly protest against all the injustices and insults done to them, and their race as a whole. Then the situation would change, I am sure, and we would cease reading letters of the kind.

But until then, I must inform all persons that disagree with our letters that we are going to keep it up, and not only are these letters sent to the Valley Morning Star, but to all the different towns of the Valley, San Antonio, Laredo, to the governor at Austin, and even to the President in Washington.

When something ails a child, he cries and cries and keeps crying, even if the whole house protests, until something is done to relieve his pain.

That is our case.

Mrs. Santos V. Lozano,
(Mrs. Francisca Pérez de Lozano)
Raymondville, Texas.

(The Valley Morning Star,
Harlingen, Texas,
June 19, 1947.)

EDITORIAL COMMENT

THE DAILY TEXAN,
Thursday, March 27, 1947.

THEIR BEST FRIENDS

In every country that the Communists have been successful, they have undermined the form of government in power by two main lines of attack. These are: (1) creating unrest among the working classes, and (2) fostering class hatreds. A divided people are at their weakest, the Communists realize, just as the Facists realized. Both groups capitalize on this weakness.

Therefore, rabble-rousers who encourage race and religious hatred in America are really the best friends the Communists have.

Some of these professional hate-mongers publicly state time and time again that they oppose Communism. Perhaps they say so in order to gain popularity and followers. Perhaps they really mean it. But at any rate, they, themselves, strengthen the cause of Communism in America far more than any Communist ever could.

A Communist openly trying to recruit Americans to his cause would not get very far. Most of us love our own democratic form of government very much, enough in fact to fight at the risk of our lives for it during the war.

So the only course left to these Marxists who would supplant our way of life with theirs is to bore from within, to sow discontent among us. Some Communists accomplish this purpose themselves, as well-trained cliques in many of our civic, industrial, and other organizations. But the greatest amount of unrest and discontent among Americans is instigated not by Communists, but, ironically enough, by men who loudly and longly proclaim their hatred of Communism.

If we listen to any professional peddler of hate against any minority, religious or racial, in America, then we too aid the Communistic cause. If we join or contribute to such traitors, then we pave the way for the internal discontent and bloodshed that will bring Communism to power in America.

IT CAN HAPPEN HERE

He walked up to the house and knocked. No one came to the door, so he entered the boarding house. Somewhere from the depths of the hall, a middle-aged woman appeared.

"Good morning", he smiled. "I would like to inquire about the ad in the paper for rooms for boys".

The woman's eyes flickered over him, seeing his dark eyes, neat mustache, slim brown hands.

"Yes", her answer could mean anything.

"Do you still have some vacancies?"

"Are you a Mexican?"

"Why, yes mam". His thoughts raced- no, not here; it won't happen here. She faced him with her arms on her hips.

"Well, I don't have any rooms for Mexicans".

He turned and went out; there wasn't anything else to do. He walked down the street while the woman stood on her porch - watching - until he was a block away.

And that actually happened at the University of Texas Wednesday morning. Not two blocks from the Law Building, while you were in your 10 o'clock class, this student was refused a room because he was a Mexican.

TEN RACES GET ALONG

Editor, The Star:

Discrimination. It isn't that I want to arouse what might better be forgotten. For the benefit of the so-called Anglo-American and the would-be Democratic people of these United States and for their own information, I happen to be one of Harlingen's native sons. I should be proud of the city of Harlingen, but at this very moment I am not.

It seems to me that people such as those that tolerate friction among themselves would be much better off if they would separate themselves from the people that want to be left with their kind.

I am a soldier stationed on the Island of Oahu, Territory of Hawaii. On that island are about ten races living together, without even looking to whom the best things should go. I can't see why, in the city of Harlingen, two different races which are so bound together can't get along as well as the ten different races do here.

It seems to me that at least we Latin Americans are way ahead of you Anglo Americans in your democratic teachings, as well as in culture and intelligence that you claim to have. If there were to be another war, I, as well as many of our boys that are now across the sea, would have to be the first to go into battle. Would I be fighting for that American soil which we all love? Or would we be fighting so that ruthless people may have the liberty of abusing our people?

Our nature is unquestionably strongly tinctured with pride. Because of some petty qualities of soul or body, which we may chance to possess, we strut about in silly vanity, expecting all who meet us on the way to pay high tribute to our imagined greatness. We pose as quite superior beings and look with pity or disdain upon our less favored fellow mortals. Is it not a stupid, childish thing to do?

I want everybody to know that during World War Two, my brother gave his life somewhere in France. Likewise many Latin Americans did. Is this what they fought for?

No! They fought so that the rest, like myself, would live free without being persecuted.

God did not say, "Let the white skins be kings, and the dark skins slaves! But He did say, "Love thy neighbor, for we are all brothers under the skin!"

Pfc. Joseph V. Delgado, Jr.,
348th Station Comp. Sq.
Oahu, Territory of Hawaii.

(The Valley Morning Star,
Harlingen, Texas, 1947.)

A WORD FOR MEXICO

Editor, The Star:

"Speak, that I may know you," says a proverb, Mr. San Benito Latin. Judging by your letter (that insures your bread and butter) we know more or less what kind of a person you are.

You should be thankful to the Lord, and to us, because you are doing good here, sure, but at least you could show a little more respect to your mother country. If you are a bad son, you can not possibly be a very grateful stepson. You certainly do not sound like a Mexican.

As for your parents not getting an education in Mexico, that depends on who your parents were and their ambition. Don't blame it on your country, just because you are ignorant of the fact that Mexico does have wonderful schools. One does not have to go very far into Mexico to find that out. While going from Reynosa to Monterrey you will find all kinds of beautiful school buildings, where all children can go and acquire a magnificent education from the first grade to the sixth. They cover what we cover here from the first to the 12th grade. When some of those children are sent here to school, all they have to do is learn the English language, and that they do in a year's time, and then they are ready to take up any study with the rest of the American kids. I have been among them; some of them graduated with me.

I wish more people of Mexican blood would visit Mexico and know its natural beauty and greatness. Then perhaps that would take out of their minds the inferiority complex that has developed among them.

Monterrey, for instance, is an industrial city of more than 600 factories, and all of them are directed and managed by intelligent, capable Mexican men. That road to the top of the Mesa del Chipinque (a mountain resort that is 1,500 metros high) is a masterpiece of engineering. Churches, theatres, municipal buildings beautifully decorated - one cannot help but admit that Mexico has an artist in each one of its sons.

Mexico has always produced professionals as competent as the best in the world, and don't think that all of them come from wealthy families. Some are of very poor people, but had ambition. Mexico is a free country like this, people are not forced to go to school. Not all American people take advantage of the wonderful opportunities that we have here. So why pick on the neighbor if we do not know them?

I am an American citizen and am very grateful to my Lord because He saw fit that I should be born here. This is my beloved country and I will stand and die for it, but I also have great love and respect for the rich Mexican blood that flows through my veins and heart, and that gives me a right to take up for them.

Mrs. Santos V. Lozano,
(Mrs. Francisca Pérez de Lozano)
Raymondville, Texas.

(The Valley Morning Star,
Harlingen, Texas, 1947.)

DISCRIMINATION SMACKS OF NAZIS, FIREMEN WRITE

Editor, The Star:

This is an account of what happened on the evening of Feb. 12 at a firemen's ball in Pharr. Please help us in this matter by publishing it.

On that date, the birthday of one of our most beloved Presidents, Abraham Lincoln, a firemen's ball was to take place at a club in Pharr honoring all Valley firemen. The Weslaco group was there with its department chief, as well as many other departments from neighboring towns.

As everyone was enjoying the party, three of the Weslaco firemen decided to go for a stroll. Upon their return they encountered opposition as they started to go in the door. They were told by an usher that their department head had an important message for them. To their surprise they found out that the message was that he had been instructed by the manager of the club to tell them that no Latin Americans were allowed on the premises. Naturally our pride was hurt. We thought that our chief was going to say something in our behalf, but no. We were really amazed by the action because only we three had to leave the club, and our chief had nothing to say about the matter.

Among us three Latin American firemen refused by the club was a World War Two veteran, a member in good standing of the Catholic War Veterans, Jose L. Garza Post No. 770 of Weslaco, a fast-growing organization which has the backing of over 800 American citizens of Latin American descent. This veteran has an honorable discharge, and a decoration, as he saved an Anglo-Saxon's life in an airplane crash. He did not stop to think of the race, color, or creed of the man in the burning plane, but risked his own life to save another's.

During the war emergency we were often called upon to donate our blood to help save a man's life, but never did the doctor stop to ask us our color, race, or creed. And we feel safe in saying that Latin American blood is flowing in some Anglo-Saxon's veins at this moment.

We know that we fought for democracy but sometimes we wonder if this is the type of compensation all of us Latin American veterans are going to get throughout the state. We always have been of the opinion that if we're good enough to donate our blood and shed it in the battlefields, we should be good enough to enjoy all entertainment provided for everyone.

For Hitler's Nazi super-race, all nationalities were considered far below the Nazis of Germany, or the super-race: In this melt-

243

ing pot of nations, the United States, why should anyone be permitted to introduce or continue Nazi principles?

Refugio Reyes - Fernando de los Santos.
Catholic War Veterans,
Post No. 770, Weslaco.

(The Valley Morning Star,
Harlingen, Texas, 1947.)

ALL KINDS OF PEOPLE

To Messrs. Refugio Reyes and Fernando de los Santos, Weslaco.

Gentlemen:

I read your letter published the 21st of February. I want to tell you boys that you should not feel so bad and discouraged about what happened to you at the ball the firemen were having at Pharr. Those things do happen, and will happen again and again.

Thanks to the Lord, there are all kinds of people in all races, and in this Valley of ours there are plenty of well-bred and highly educated people, both Anglo-Saxons and Latin-Americans, with whom you can associate and enjoy yourselves happily and peacefully.

As for us Latin Americans taking part in past wars, we have done it for generations, and will gladly do it again if necessary, as all other races born here have done, because this is our country, our very own, and we defend with our blood what is rightfully ours.

We did not fight for some one else, and we are not asking thanks from anyone. Gratitude comes from the heart. We love our country with our very souls, and our hearts thrill at the sight of our beautiful American flag, because this soil is sacred to us, land of our forefathers who were born in Texas, too. We feel as if we are product of this same soil, and are very proud of it.

We Latin-Americans will donate our blood again to save some one else regardless of color, creed or race because we love God and our country.

Mrs. Santos V. Lozano,
(Mrs. Francisca Pérez de Lozano)
Raymondville, Texas.

(The Valley Morning Star,
Harlingen, Texas, 1947.)

THE SEED IS STILL ALIVE

Another of those stupid and unnecessary cruelties which always result from racial prejudice cropped up in Harlingen a few days ago.

A teacher from the Edcouch school district decided to take forty of her seventh and eighth grade students for an outing to celebrate the end of the school year. The outing was to take the form of a roller skating party at a public rink in Harlingen.

When the teacher and her forty happy pupils arrived at the Harlingen skating rink, they got a rude shock. The manager of the skating rink informed the teacher that he did not permit Latin-Americans to skate on his rink.

Can you imagine the feeling of those pupils when they received this news? Isn't it wonderful to live in a nation which subscribes to the creed that all men are created equal?

Some of the kids in that school party had brothers who fought and died in the last war. They fought to preserve America and its cities, like Harlingen, so that children could grow up without the racial hatreds that had poisoned Europe.

It is easy to guess what the explanation of the skating rink manager might be for his anti-American policy. He probably would insist that he personally has no race prejudice but he must set up barriers against Latin-American kids or they "would take over his place" and ruin his business.

There is only one answer to this argument. It is that such a business, operating under such a policy, would be better ruined and closed up than allowed to go on operating.

That such a business, pursuing such an intolerably un-American policy, can exist and flourish in any Valley city today is not merely a reflection on the manager himself. The major reflection is on the citizens of the community which will tolerate its existence and on the city administration which will grant it a permit to operate.

There are those who try feebly to defend these instances of racial discrimination on the grounds that they are not really racial discrimination but merely social discrimination.

Such a defense, of course, is just so much meaningless balderdash. When an eighth grade student is barred from a skating rink because of his race, the question of social equality is not involved. If social equality were the issue, those Edcouch school children would have been admitted without question. By the mere fact that they came out of the same schoolroom where they had studied side by side for the past year they qualified as social equals.

Among school kids, social equality is an empty concept anyhow. Social standing, if any such criterion can truly be said to exist, can only be based on education and the size of an individual's bankroll. Since all eighth grade kids are on a par educationally, and since none of them have acquired bankrolls of any consequence, they are not afflicted with any social standing. Social standing is a disease from which only the adult of the species suffers.

Not only are such instances of discrimination in violent conflict with every tenet of American tradition and an unpardonable affront to hundreds of thousands of American citizens whose ancestors settled this country long before the first palefaced foreigner elbowed his way through the brush; but also this discrimination tion is a rank insult to the people of every nation south of the Rio Grande. More than this, it is a menace to the economic stability of the Valley.

We have only recently completed a pact with Mexico under which Mexican farm workers are permitted to enter legally for the first time. Until this pact was completed Mexico would not permit farm workers to enter this state because of the racial discrimination known to exist. We spent years assuring Mexico that discrimination was being stamped out and would not be tolerated wherever found.

And now, in the wake of all these fine assurances, we find a skating rink of all places throwing up the false and evil barrier of racial discrimination.

A skating rink is a small affair. Why make any fuss about it? Sure, we know a young man who in 1936 was told he could no longer play on the soccer team of the school he was attending in Mannheim, Germany, because he was Jewish. Just a small incident.

But five years later this same lad was thrown into a concentration camp while Hitler set about the chore of murdering six million Jewish men, women, and children.

No matter where it is found, racial discrimination is a deadly seed whose ultimate harvest is mass murder.

(Valley Evening Monitor,
McAllen, Texas,
June 8, 1947.)

ALL AMERICANS

Editor, the Corpus Christi Caller: Corpus Christi, Texas.

It seems to me that Louis W. Bryan, Jr. and C. G. surely hit the nail on the head in their letters on the question of class and social discrimination here in South Texas.

Recently, in reading the list of boys who gave their lives for our country during the past horrible war, I found the names of García, Toscáno and Ramón amongst the Joneses, Smiths and Kellys and others. Of all the races that make up the people of these United States, we all know that the Jap or German bullets did not discriminate when they were fired at our American boys.

It made no difference whether the boy was a Jones or a Ruiz. Yet so many of us here are so willing to insult and mistreat a people who really haven't been given a chance.

I recently was shown a picture of a grave of a boy from Robstown who gave his life after almost four years of service. In this American cemetery there wasn't any segregation for there were graves of other American boys of other races who had fought and died as he.

Many of our Spanish-speaking boys had a hard time at first in the service accustoming themselves to the food and discipline, but after a little time, we had from their group technicians of every type known to the service. Here in Robstown there is a good American mother who cannot speak English, yet she has a gold star in her window, for her son who went down with his flying fortress over Germany. To the present date his body has never been found, nor those of his companions.

So why not try to understand and help these good people? They want to be good Americans. Is it that some wish to keep them in a down-trodden state, so that cheap labor will be plentiful? Or have we Hitler's doctrine of a master-race in practice here?

I sincerely believe that a little Christian charity and common sense will help us to find that we can get along with each other here in this world.

For the first time here in Robstown we have many graduates from our Spanish-speaking families, and we are very proud of them. Given a chance and just a little encouragement we will have a larger class each year.

K. A. Dunne.
Robstown, Texas.

(Corpus Christi Caller,
May 17, 1947.)

CHEAP LABOR DOES NOT PAY IN THE LONG RUN, SAYS WRITER WHO TELLS OF PROBLEMS

Dear Editor:

I read with great interest your editorial of April 20th entitled, "Can We Afford Cheap Labor?".

The answer is no. We cannot afford cheap labor. It does not pay in the long run. Cheap labor ruins the health of workers, of their wives and children. It deprives the children of a school education.

When the married men who leave large families in Mexico work here, and they earn $12 a week, they live on a starvation diet in order to be able to send seven or eight dollars to their families. They either have to live on beans, potatoes or flour tortillas for their three meals. In other words, they must choose between beans, potatoes or flour tortillas.

Recently I knew a worker from Zacatecas, Mexico. That man lived on flour tortillas and black coffee for his three meals and worked hard all day in the field. He could not afford to buy an extra pair of work pants or shirt as most of his money was sent to his family. Day after day, he was seen with the same dirty clothes. No doubt this was one man who didn't have to do his washing on Sundays as some did. When he was ready to leave, he bought a pair of work pants and shirt, and from his smile, he felt as tho he had bought a hundred dollar suit. "This is good enough for me to get to my Zacatecas", he said.

How can a man be able to work and rest at night with the same dirty clothes? How can they survive on a starvation diet? Aren't these conditions almost as bad as the conditions of some of the war torn people of Europe? Why can't better wages be offered to the Mexican workers, the minimum of at least 40 cents an hour?".

We must bear in mind that cheap labor affects seriously another group of workers, that belong here, and who are not aliens, but Americans of Mexican descent. This group is forced to leave homes in the Valley by the hundreds every year, to harvest the crops of the Northern States where they can get better wages.

The U. S. is spending at present hundreds of dollars in helping Mexico to stamp out the mouth and hoof diseases. It is kind of our country to help Mexico, but shouldn't human beings come first? One good way we can help Mexico, is to help the working class who come to help us. We must see that they get decent wages, wages that would enable the workers to give their children an education.

The farmers claim that they don't make much money. However, most of them live in nice homes and have nice cars. But if the farmers don't get the money that they ought to get for their crops, then who gets the money? Then, why don't the farmers get together and demand good prices for their commodities?

Sometime ago I read an interesting writing by Clarence La Roche, entitled: "Billion Dollar Wetback" that pointed out the fact that millions of dollars were being deposited in Valley banks from Valley crops. If the farmers didn't get those fat bank rolls, then the shippers did.

248

The point is to help the Mexican workers get decent wages, for without their help, the prosperity of the Valley cannot longer be possible.

We have taken the lead in many of the problems of the world. This is one good way of helping a neighboring country. For in helping other people of America, we are helping ourselves. A better America, would mean a better and stronger United States.

Mrs. A. S. Vento.
San Juan, Texas.

(The Valley Morning Star,
Harlingen, Texas, 1947.)

"RACIAL ISSUE" ASSAILED IN WILLACY SCHOOL ELECTION

Editor, The Star:

Well, our situation in Raymondville will continue to be "taxation without representation", as seen by our tremendous defeat at the school board election.

It was the highest vote cast in the history of the county. Yes, and it was also the first time in the history of Raymondville that two Latin-Americans ran as candidates for trustees of the schools.

It is very obvious that it was made a racial problem, instead of what it really was, a "democratic election".

We, the Latin Americans of Raymondville, know and see the need of representation on the school board as an imperious necessity. We want to co-operate, not to "take-over". For more than 15 years, only our Latin American children have gone to school only half days; in other words, they have been getting only half a year of school. Year after year, we have appealed to the school board to see if something could be done about this problem, but we have been told that "there are too many Latin American children", that they are far more than the Anglo Americans, and they "didn't know what to do about it".

Now our town has grown so much and the number of children has increased, too; naturally our school problem is worse.

Dr. Sanchez of the University of Texas told 500 teachers at the convention in Corpus Christi the 14th of last March:

"It greatly aggravates the problem, of giving these children an adequate American education. The needs of these children are like those of all pupils, good schools, good teaching, and intelligent direction. No community can claim a good school system if it reserves its first rate education only for a selected population

249

group. The segregation of population is comparable to a concentration camp; trustees who uphold the practice are either ignorant of the damage they do to the state and nation, or are remiss in their obligation to community, state and nation".

We have a right to enjoy the privileges our country grants to all its citizens, or don't we? Fellow citizens and Anglo American friends, with one hand on your Bible and the other hand on your heart, answer me: Are we Latin Americans of Raymondville to be considered Americans only when citizens are called upon to fulfill their obligations and duties as such? Or are we the free people that can enjoy the liberty and justice granted by our constitution?

We Latin American people are descendants of a dignified and noble race of which we are very proud. Our bravery has been proven and can be better told by the buddies that slept, fought and died together in the battlefields of Germany and Japan.

We love our country, we like to live here, we have always kept in mind, with pride, the fact that Raymondville was named after a good and honorable man whose wife was Doña Juanita Raymond, a very respected and distinguished Latin American lady.

Our children were born here and we do not intend to move away. We have cooperated, donated and contributed with the best of intentions to the development and growth of this city. We also like to prosper and be happy among all citizens as is the right of all human beings. But we are very few, we need the cooperation and good will of all broad-minded and intelligent persons that are able to understand our problems.

We want education and to teach our children the real patriotism so that they will be better fitted to serve their country in the best way possible.

Mrs. Santos V. Lozano,
(Mrs. Francisca Pérez de Lozano)
Raymondville, Texas.

(The Valley Morning Star,
Harlingen, Texas, 1947.)

VETERAN'S WIFE RETURNING TO EDINBURG WANTS TOWN RETURNED TO AMERICANS

Dear Editor:

You being an American, I hope that you will be fair enough to print this where it will do the most good, in your paper. Please do, Sir: I am the wife of an American war veteran who was transferred away from Edinburg two years ago. Edinburg was formerly our home, and we returned with intentions of living here, and what do we find? We find that practically every available living space is occupied by a Mexican. In the two years we have been gone, Edinburg has become complete Mexican, - - - jobs, houses, everything.

I have heard several American veterans, and so many American home-owners here complain bitterly of this condition, which is growing worse all the time. They have taken our jobs for years, and now they are occupying our places to live. We want to start living here again, as before the war.

I say let them either be restricted or let them go back over where they were before the war. Give the American boys and their families a chance; they gave their best to us.

Sincerely,

Mrs. Charles Keller.
207 E. Samano St.

ABOUT THAT LETTER

"I may disagree with every word you say, but I'll defend unto death your right to say it," is a quotation from Voltaire. Those words have a lot behind them. They may be applied precisely to a letter which ran on this page under the "Letters to the Editor" column Tuesday morning

This newspaper disagrees with virtually every word that the letter writer uttered. We could go into the letter phrase by phrase and definitely disapprove and disagree with every statement. This, we feel, has been expertly done by other readers who submitted letters to the editor yesterday.

This newspaper has a column in which such letters, save those which are libelous, are printed. That column is open to anyone who wishes to use it. Such a system is used by all newspapers. Making the column available is imperative for any paper; not only because of custom, but in the sense of fairness.

There is only one column of this newspaper that is devoted to expressing the opinion of the editor—that is the one you are now reading. All other columns are devoted to a strict accounting of what other people—people who make news—say and do.

Into the "Letters" column go the ideas of the public with which you, nor the editor, may or may not agree. Anyone is at liberty as far as the paper is concerned to answer any letter that appears. He must not, however, write libelously and he must sign his name.

It is not the purpose of the Review to use the "Letters" column as a basis for editorial topics. A newspaper does not like to become

251

embroiled in the controversies of its readers.

The letter which appeared Tuesday is pretty sufficiently answered in this page today. Most of the answers have come from Americans who are World War II veterans. Most all of us, whether of Irish, German, French, Dutch, British, Scandinavian, or Mexican descent, probably had an answer in our minds, too. Technically a Frenchman or an Italian is just as much a Latin American as a Mexican who becomes an American.

It goes without saying that persons of Mexican extraction are as much American as any citizen of any other extraction.

As has been said in this same column many times, it is impossible to criticize a race. Only the individuals, the separate entities who make up the race, are capable of being criticized. The statement that all Irishmen have flat feet and are policemen or that all Frenchmen wear berets or that all Jews talk with their hands is just not true.

To be critical the statement must be specific. John Doe is a crack-pot, is one type of personal criticism; or, Richard Roe is not a good doctor, is another. But criticism must be direct at the individual to mean anything.

There aren't many men in Edinburg who did not, provided they were in the right age group, go out to defend their country. All Americans, regardless of extraction, did. Many Mexicans, and surely there is no need to say that by Mexican we mean a citizen of Mexico, came to this country and entered our army.

But who fought and who didn't and for whatever reasons is beside the point in this argument.

Some residents of Edinburg and the Valley, residents of Mexican descent, have lived here longer than any American of other origin. They were here first. So were the Spaniards. So were the French. The United States just expanded into the country. These Americans are proud that their forefathers were Mexicans just as others are proud theirs were English or Scotch or Australian or Canadian or South American.

What if the citizens of Mexican descent asked them to get out? They would think the request insane. With any group of any racial extraction removed from the Valley, there would be a distinct loss.

God put all races and all nationals here, and we expect He will keep us here. And maybe someday we'll gather enough intelligence into our heads to ask Him to help us live together as one family, one state, one country, and one world.

(Taken from "EDINBURG VALLEY REVIEW," February 11, 1947, Allan Engleman, Editor and Publisher.

Harry Quin, Managing Editor - James R. Ames, Advertising Manager.)

LETTERS TO THE EDITOR

Dear Editor:

It is regretful to read such letters as the one that appeared in your "Letters to the Editor" column of Feb. 11, 1947, written by Mrs. Charles Keller.

Her appeal may be justified in the fact that the housing situation is critical not only in Edinburg, but as far as I have been able to find out, anywhere in the United States.

Mrs. Keller was not the only one to leave a town to follow her husband wherever he would be stationted in the United States in order to be with him most of the time possible, as many other wives did during the war. Her husband was only doing his patriotic duty in serving his country to defend the rights that we so much praise.

My brother and many other relatives and Latin American friends fought in this war side by side with Anglo Americans and from the information I have been able to gather from them there were no restricted areas for them in the battle fields. Everybody was the same, used the same weapons, and fought for the same cause.

I am sure that Mrs. Keller has given her letter very much thought since it was published in your newspaper and feels that she has made a great mistake in having expressed her thoughts to the public before having considered this matter and discussed it with someone that is able to explain the logic of the present condition. I beg of Mrs. Keller or anyone that condones her feelings to please feel free to call on me to discuss any resentments that she or anybody may have toward the Latin American race. If I am not capable of answering your question, I will be able to find the answer within a reasonable time.

I am very much in favor of improving relations between the Anglo and Latin American people and though I may not be able to accomplish the whole mission myself, my contribution will certainly add to the efforts educated people are putting forth in reaching this goal.

Sincerely yours,
Mary L. Martínez.
Box 554, Mercedes, Texas.

* * *

Dear Editor:

It's a good feeling to know we are given freedom of speech,

253

press, etc., and I sincerely hope, dear Editor, that you will print my letter in the Review where it will do the most good. I feel that my husband has earned that recognition for me. What did Mrs. Keller expect after a war such as our nation suffered, to have things handed out to her on a silver platter?

I, too, am a veteran's wife with a child to remind me through the remainder of my life that his father gave his life trying to better living conditions, etc., for his little family; not only for us but for all the rest of the families at home. Did I squawk because I didn't find things just as they were after being away from Edinburg three years? After all, Mrs. Keller, a Mexican has a right to live as well as you. Who are you to say who should and who shouldn't live in Edinburg?

You write as if the American boy was the only one fighting the war; what was the capacity of the U. S. Army, were they all Americans? Mrs. Keller is to be sympathized with for her lack of supporting the "good neighbor policy". It's a shame that some of the Mexican property owners aren't dumb enough to move out and ask Mrs. Keller to occupy the place they have worked so hard for.

It's only common sense and every day life, Mrs. Keller, that to have anything one must work for it. Perhaps it's best that our good boys who gave their lives so freely, both Americans and Mexicans, didn't come back to find that since the war is over the Mexican should be culled from the American. Try doing something for yourself, Mrs. Keller, just as I knew I must do for my son and myself. A little effort will do more good than trying to push other people from what they have stayed at home and worked for. I, too, followed my husband when he was transferred, your husband came back to you, mine didn't.

I am doing my best I can alone, you should try helping your husband acquire something by a little hard work, no one gives away anything these days. I am only one from thousands of others, think it over, Mrs. Keller; should it be that you would happen to be one of the many you wrote about, would you like for someone to want to push you out of your home because you were not an American?

Thank you, Mr. Editor, I feel that by printing my letter just as you printed Mrs. Keller's, my husband has been done a great justice.

Mrs. Gene Whitmore.
Edinburg, Texas.

* * *

Dear Editor:

I would like to comment on a letter to the Editor appearing in the issue of this paper on Tuesday morning, Feb. 11, 1947, where a local citizen states: "Edinburg has become almost complete Mexican." I would like to bring up a few points that may give a clearer view of the situation concerning the "Mexican".

We understand that the so-called "wet backs" have migrated very densely into our country and especially to our valley cities, but the writer of Tuesday's letter doesn't specify whether the article referred to the "wet backs" alone. The word Mexican is used, and that, my dear readers, covers a lot of territory! Back to the laborers from south of the border, has the writer of Tuesday's letter considered the necessity of those workers in our country? During the bitter war days, every available man and women was busy in the armed forces or either in vital war work of some kind.

Who was to keep up our home front? Our fields needed hands, very, very many hands to raise our crops which were so vital to the winning of the war. Other large factories of different sources needed workers, any kind of workers as long as they could do the work. Our home front would have collapsed, probably. Without their aid, where were we to get all these workers? Oh, yes, we had a very big and powerful army and navy; we were sure to win the war.

We had to win the war but in Europe; and our home front? Was the writer of Tuesday's letter going out into the fields on cold and rainy days to toil and raise the much needed crops? Where could the labor be found? Right across the river where we get many other things we need. Cheap labor? Certainly! Very cheap labor, but the wet backs, need to work in order to exist. Was it their fault that the big rich owners of large farms and factories would give them jobs? Jobs which would probably keep them and their families from starving?

If one was very hungry and your bigger next door neighbor offered you relief if you'd do his washing, would you starve or wash? That is the real truth, people have to eat, and to eat you have to work. But why blame the poor immigrant who roams in search of a better place to live in. Don't we all? Didn't God make our country big enough where we can wander and find what we need?

No, the Mexican will not be restricted, if he was, many others of different nationalities would have to be restricted also. The Mexican is here to stay! Oh, yes you can put the wet backs across the river, etc., but the Americans of Mexican descent are still here, and no one can scare them to leave. My solution, or rather suggestion, to those who do not like the Mexican would be for them to pack their little bags and wander in search for greener pastures elsewhere because the Mexican is here to stay, and will be here as long as the world is to last.

Very truly yours,

Ramiro de la Garza.

Edinburg, Texas.

✿ ✿ ✿

Dear Editor:

It has been well said that he who sows the wind reaps the whirlwind. Mrs. Keller sowed what she thought was a gentle breeze and is now surrounded by a tornado. And she deserves it.

She's the wife of a veteran. I am a veteran. She complains about housing. I didn't. I bought a house. And I didn't have to stand in line nor elbow my way through a crowd of what she calls "Mexicans".

Maybe Mrs. Keller needs a little indoctrination in Americanism. A word to her. Many of the "Mexicans" she complains of have blood in their veins, descended from the peoples who lived here when Columbus set sail from Spain. Most have Latin blood - - - Columbus had that, de la Salle, Ponce de León, Coronado and many others had that too. Pretty good foundation blood for Americans, isn't it, Mrs. Keller? Rather intertwined with American history too, isn't it, Mrs. Keller?

In the army I dealt with many who were "Mexicans" according to her, and I never found duties handed out according to names, - - - Keller or Ríos, Smith or Rodríguez. They all had to do KP, stand guard, face the bullets. That's why the roster of World War II adds up to something that is really American.

Mrs. Keller thinks that the "Mexicans" are pushing her around, that she's evidently more "American". I don't feel that they have ever pushed me around and my ancestors fought beside George Washington.

As an Edinburg businessman, I feel it my duty to write as I have.

Yours sincerely,

Frank L. Fate.

✿ ✿ ✿

Dear Editor:

I've just read a letter in your paper by a certain Mrs. Keller, who seems to be quite aggravated at the horrid results she found upon her return to the city.

256

All right, so she is the wife of a veteran and cannot find a place to live. I am a sister of a boy who lost his life fighting for this country. If he was good enough to die for it, his family is good enough to live here also. What does she want us to do? Move out so that she may take over? And we are wondering where she is living now. It is a good thing we do not have a place for you. I am afraid there will never be a place in this part of the country for people like you, Mrs. Keller. Sure enough, it would be crowded then!

Miss Bertha Villarreal.
Box 1125, Edinburg, Texas.

* * *

Dear Editor:

Mrs. Keller's letter published in your edition of the 11th indicates that she's a bit desperate.

People native of this territory don't have to worry about homes, because one was passed on to them by their parents, who were pioneers here.

People who are well qualified don't have to worry about jobs being taken away from them.

My brother-in-law is a veteran with 27 months overseas. Sister stayed right here in her home and worked while he was gone three years. She had no trouble getting a job—she's well qualified.

Texas was formerly a part of Mexico and Mexico is part of the North American continent. So anyway you look at it, Mexicans whether U. S.-born or Mexico-born are Americans.

So—the Mexicans to Mexico, Germans to Germany, Poles to Poland, etc. Let's do give this land back to real Americans—the Indians and the Mexicans.

Simple, isn't it?

Robert Rodríguez.
518 E. Lovett.

* * *

The following citizens also answered Mrs. Keller and their letters were published in the same newspaper: Fadrique H. Barrera, Julia Anzaldúa, Frank Trudo, Edinburg; José Jesús Herrera, Miss Aurora Rutledge, Edinburg; Isaura Ríos, L. Flores, Pharr; Conrado Garza, Edinburg; Ignacio Rodríguez, Jr., María Vásquez, María Herrera, Alberto García, Mission, and Rafael Rodríguez, McAllen.

Hon. Martin Kessler,
Commander Post No. 26,
The American Legion,
Uvalde, Texas.

Dear Commander Kessler:

We are in receipt of a letter from Mr. David M. Ortiz, Commander of "Tomas Balle Post No. 479" of The American Legion, Uvalde, Texas, to the effect that recently two members of said Post went into the Hangar VII Grill, at Uvalde, and ordered two cups of coffee, and it was denied to them because they were of Mexican descent. The owner, Mr. W. W. Moore, told them that he was sorry, but that Mexicans were not served there, that if he did so, he would lose all his Anglo-American customers; that if the two Legionnaires mentioned wanted to be served, he had a place for them in the rear of the establishment.

To-day we received a complaint from Mr. Robert Canales, of 115 Alazan St., San Antonio, Texas (he is a nephew of Judge J. T. Canales, of Brownsville), also a Veteran of World War II. He served three and one-half years in the United States Army, one year of which he spent overseas. He says that he and his brother, Mr. Andrés Canales, went into said restaurant on Tuesday, Dec. 10, 1946, and they were denied service for the same reason.

We are reliably informed that the following other business establishments in Uvalde also deny service to persons of Mexican descent, including Veterans: Dinette Cafe, Newport Cafe, Shadowland Cafe, Walgreen's Drug Store, Palace Drug Store, Uvalde Candy Shoppe, Manhattan Cafe, Casey Jones Cafe, and Casal Cave.

We are wondering whether you could do something to persuade the owners of these establishments to cease to discriminate against Veterans of Mexican descent. It is so humiliating and disappointing to all Americans of Mexican or Hispanic extraction. Do you know of anything that might be done to solve this problem in Uvalde at least? If the Anglo-American people of Uvalde are the ones responsible for the attitude of the proprietors of these business places, what might be done to change the attitude of the people of Uvalde? Forty-four men from Uvalde died in World War II. Twenty-two of them were Americans of Mexican descent.

Thanking you in advance for anything you may do to put an end to this shameful situation, and awaiting your reply, we remain
Yours very truly,

THE LEAGUE OF LOYAL AMERICANS
(A Civic and Patriotic Organization)
By Alonso S. Perales - Director General.

Identical letters were sent on the same date to Mr. Bertram E. Giesecke, State Commander of the American Legion, Austin, Mr. John N. Garner, Uvalde, and Mr. H. P. Horby, Editor, Uvalde Leader News, Uvalde.

ESSAYING EDUCATION IN INTERRACIAL RELATIONS

The University of Tampa (Florida) is trying an interesting experiment toward scientific eradication of inter-racial friction. As announced by its president, Dr. Ellwood C. Nance, a new department concerned with education in interracial relations - particularly the domestic phase of that problem - will be directed by Dr. William G. Neiderland, who, significantly, is a professor of medical psychology.

Unreasoning race prejudice, causing shameful intolerance and violence, is something more than a social problem which ordinary education may combat with success. Certainly in the worst cases it becomes a form of mental sickness, impervious to the usual impact of educational facts and logic, but perhaps susceptible to the more scientific treatment accorded generally recognized psychopathy.

At any rate, the Tampa plan appears to be a practical approach. The new department will direct research into the causes of racial prejudices and interracial frictions, and then endeavor to devise aggressive educational methods with which to combat them. At first the courses are planned as advanced instruction for teachers, social workers and clergymen, but in time the department's scope will cover all university levels.

Purposing to carry the programs directly to the people, as well, the department's plans call for special conferences, sponsorship of radio programs, adult evening classes, and a speakers' bureau to provide lecturers for the State's churches, schools and civic clubs. "Trouble-shooters" will be sent to sore spots of interracial tension, both to study causes and lend a hand in quieting the friction. The department also aims to reach parents with its effort to encourage tolerance—instruction in the home, where environmental effects on children tend to perpetuate racial prejudices which long since ceased to have any rational motive.

As Dr. Neiderland reminds, the greatest menace to Western civilization is the fact that its progress in technical matters has far outrun its progress in human relations and social organization. That is true, he reasons, because the latter involves irrational and harmful emotional influences largely absent in science and engineering problems. Further, it is the responsibility of education—assisted by the knowledge developed by the science of psychology - to mitigate those retarding emotional influences. One of the worst is racial prejudice. That, briefly, is the justification for Tampa University's new inter-racial relations department, the first of the kind in the South.

Educators generally should watch the Tampa experiment closely. It holds promise of worthy results. The experiment itself merits emulation. Certainly, if future experience shall prove its expected benefits, the program should be extended to educational institutions wherever racial problems exist.

(San Antonio Evening News.
October 2, 1946.)

RACE ISSUE HIT AGAIN IN MEXICO
By Barry Bishop.

Mexico City Bureau of the News

MEXICO CITY, Jan. 5. Another campaign of criticism against racial discrimination practices in the United States, especially as they concern treatment of Mexicans in Texas, has begun here.

The newspaper "El Universal" carried a long front-page story under the headline "Discrimination Grows in Texas." "As soon as the war was over hatred grew against Mexicans."

"Equals in war, equals in civil life," the article began. "Such is the motto of several Mexican organizations in the southern part of the United States, especially in Texas, where as soon as the war was over, the Mexicans started to feel even with more intensity, the racial and economic discrimination which they have suffered since long ago, even against the wishes of the Federal Government of North America that has tried in many ways to help the Mexicans that live in the States of California, Arizona, New Mexico, Colorado and Texas.

SCHOOL SEGREGATION CITED

"Although for nearly five years that the war lasted the offensive against them quieted down, the complex of race superiority has been reborn and our countrymen find themselves ousted from restaurants, barbershops, amusement places and other sites, according to information given us by "Lulac" - an organization of Latin-American citizens in the United States.

The story said discrimination is not confined to adults but cites segregation in schools in New Braunfels, Midland, Brady, Sugarland and other places.

More than 200 Texas cities practice discrimination in all its aspects, the story charged.

"All the efforts of the Mexican consulates have been in vain, so have been the efforts of Texas authorities", the story said. "The present Governor is a friend of the Mexicans, the civic organizations and even the Federal Government also have tried with no success as it is very hard to change the Saxon mentality, and its ideas of employer and other social sectors."

Segregation in residential districts of Texas cities, with Mexicans unable to buy property freely, was criticized.

SOME EFFORTS PRAISED.

Special criticism was made of segregation signs aimed at Mexicans and said to have been seen in such places as Big Spring, in a park at Brady, in a hospital at Rosebud, and in such places as Post, Bastrop and Marathon.

Alleged inability of Mexicans to get service in restaurants in many places and even to obtain medical and dental aid was attacked.

"In this way it can be said that the South of the United States of America is a hell for 4,000,000 persons of Mexican descent who live in those border states," the story added.

The story concluded with a good word for efforts of some Texas cities to provide good, low-cost housing for Mexicans, and for work of various groups in trying to help the people. It predicted more results will come from efforts now getting better organized in the United States.

Dallas Morning News.
Dallas, Texas,
January, 1946.

THE FACTS ABOUT JOB DISCRIMINATION.

The Negroes are not the only group in the United States which suffers from job discrimination. Hence, the language of President Roosevelt's order was deliberately and wholesomely comprehensive. It specifies: "No discrimination because of race, creed, color or national origin", thereby providing for the first time in history the beginning of a federal court of appeal for over one-sixth of the United States.

THE MEXICANS

In New Mexico, Texas and Louisiana, 37 per cent; and in California, Nevada and Arizona 22 per cent of the FEPC cases involved Spanish-Americans. Discrimination against Spanish-Americans—the majority of whom are of Mexican origin—takes the following forms: (1) refusal to hire; (2) refusal to train; (3) refusal to upgrade; (4) payments of lower wages. A few examples, based on sworn statements, will show the trend.

Gilbert E. Lujan was employed in May, 1942, as a furnace helper and slag brakeman on his claim that he was of French-Italian ancestry, and was paid $6.08 a day. When it was learned that he was actually a Mexican-American, he was demoted to common labor and paid $4.20.

Alfredo Cerda started work as a common laborer at $4.20 a day. He was promoted to the copper-refining department, where the wages are $4.60. He continued to receive $4.20.

According to Dr. Carlos E. Castañeda, FEPC Regional Director for Arizona, New Mexico and West Texas, Mexican-Americans have been barred from employment in semiskilled jobs in all industries, with the possible exception of such war industries, as are specially influenced by the FEPC. The Chamber of Deputies of Mexico, corresponding to our House of Representatives, has recently set up a committee whose function it is to focus attention on job discrimination against Mexican-Americans in the United States.

THE JEWS

Close to 9 per cent of the complaints handled by the President's Committee on Fair Employment Practice between July 1943 and July 1944 involved Jews.

An investigator for a Jewish organization in New York City applied personally for 100 jobs as stenographer, secretary, accountant or auditor. In 91 interviews, she was told a Jew not acceptable. The same organization examined the records of 400 business firms making up the clientele of an important employment agency. Eighty nine per cent of these firms noted that they preferred Christians.

A survey of 179 American universities showed that 36 had no Jews on the faculty, 62 schools had 1.8 per cent or less, while 87 schools had not over 2.2 per cent of Jews on their teaching staffs. A group of Catholic schools proved more liberal than the general run of American universities, having 3.1 per cent of Jews among their 1,883 teachers.

In general, the Jews find it difficult to get jobs in industry, commerce, finance, scientific research engineering, and the professions. Discrimination exercised against them in New York City banks, insurance companies, and public utilities are striking. The National City Bank, 100,000 of whose 400,000 depositors are Jews, has six Jewish employees. One per cent of the 4,200 home office employees of the Equitable Life Insurance Co., are Jewish. Of the 1,500 persons employed in other types of insurance beside life, 1.4 per cent are Jewish. There are only a handful of Jewish employees of the Consolidated Gas Co., and the 60,000 employees of Western Electric.

THE CHINESE

As immigrants of the islands of the Pacific, the Chinese were for centuries successful as traders and businessmen. Their experience in the United States has proved different. Accepted on their arrival in 1849 without prejudice, some prospered in the gold mines, the abalone fisheries and other Pacific Coast industries. But economic greed soon reared its head. Driven from the gold mines by Vigilantes, nine-tenths of the Chinese are today in city Chinatowns, where they engage in such non-competitive businesses as running restaurants, curio shops and laundries. The foreign-born Chinese are proud and bitter; the native-born generation are completely American; but confined to a ghetto life from which they find little escape. In California, Ph. D.'s have had to take jobs as cooks and waiters. World War II has provided the first crack in the American wall of job discrimination. Because they were our allies, war industries hired them as stenographers, welders, carpenters, shipyard and aircraft workers. Whether this advance will survive the war remains to be seen.

"Fraternidad" Magazine.
Mexico, D. F., Sept. 1st 1945.

Aug. 1, 1945.
Editor,
New Braunfels Herald,
New Braunfels, Texas.

Dear Sir:

In the column entitled "Rambling Around" which appeared in the issue of your newspaper of July 27, 1945, you state, among other things, the following:

"Society, like water, has a way of seeking its own level. All the laws conceived by man cannot succeed in forcing friendships or undesired associations. Hence, Rambler is not at all perturbed, excited, or insulted with this news release from Mexico City appearing in the daily press of Monday.

(Here you quote an Associated Press Dispatch from Mexico City to the effect that the Mexican Committee against racial discrimination has just listed Spur, Snyder, Melvin, New Braunfels and Pecos, Texas, as five towns where Mexicans are discriminated against in business establishments).

263

"Rambler has been to Mexico City and to various other places in Mexico, several times. I have seen the 'discrimination' practiced between classes in that country, over and over. Eating together in cafes, patronizing the same stores, shops and 'Barber Shops', or congregating in the same 'parks' simply isn't done. I have seen, many times, members of one 'class' step off the sidewalk to permit a member of another 'class' to pass.

"People who live in glass houses shouldn't throw stones."

"Rambler's observation is that any so-called 'discrimination' practiced in Texas is based, not on race, but on cleanliness, sanitation, behavior. Segregation is not discrimination. Laws pass the limits of freedom when they attempt to force any individual to serve or associate with another against the natural laws of society, the law of water seeking its own level. True associations and mingling one with another can come only with education, development, understanding. Force can only retard the movement, nothing more."

In view of your statements, Mr. Editor, that "any so-called discrimination practiced in Texas is based, not on race, but on cleanliness, sanitation, behaviour", we should like to ask you whether uncleanliness or mishaviour was the reason why the Honorable Adolfo G. Dominguez, Consul of Mexico in Houston, was denied service in a restaurant in New Gulf, Texas, a short time ago; and whether that was the reason Senator Eugenio Prado, Chairman of the Permanent Commission of the Mexican Congress, was denied service in a restaurant in Pecos, Texas, about three months ago; and the reason why several Venezuelan aviators, who were training at Randolph Field, not so long ago, were segregated at Landa Park, in your own New Braunfels, Texas? In the case of the aviators the management of Landa Park asked them where they were from and when they replied that they were aviators from Venezuela, South America, they were told that "those tables over yonder are for South Americans; these tables over here are for 'white people' only."

Was it because the Mexican Consul, the Mexican Senator and the South American Aviators were unclean or because of their misbehaviour that they were discriminated against? No, Sir; they were thus humiliated simply because they were Latins and for no other reason, and you know it as well as we do, Mr. Editor.

No, Mr. Editor, you will have to agree with us that the basis of the discrimination practiced in Texas, which by the way is going on *not in five* but in at least *one hundred and fifty* towns and cities in Texas, most of which are German communities, is

264

based upon RACE AND RACE ONLY, and not upon cleanliness or behaviour.

Yours truly,

THE COMMITTEE OF ONE HUNDRED.
THE LEAGUE OF LOYAL AMERICANS.
(A Civic and Patriotic Organization).
By Alonso S. Perales, Director General.

March 29, 1945.

Mr. Guy Walker,
President Pecos Chamber of Commerce,
Pecos, Texas:

Dear Sir:

Mr. Alfonso Orozco, of your city, has requested me to write to you and explain what occurred in your city recently that has caused so much resentment and unfavorable comment. Recently Senator Eugenio Prado, President of the Permanent Commission of the Mexican Congress, and members of his party, were denied service in a restaurant in Pecos, Texas, merely because they were Mexicans. I am enclosing herewith a copy of a telegram received from Mexico City regarding the incident.

We are reliably informed that Mexicans are denied service in Anglo-American hotels, cafes, beer parlors and recreational centers. In the theaters they are placed together with the negroes. In the Anglo-American stores Anglo-Americans are waited on first, even if the Mexicans arrived first.

We believe that if the Pecos Chamber of Commerce wants to end this shameful situation, you can do so by prevailing upon the proprietors of all these places to cease discriminating against Mexicans. Also, there is now pending in the Texas Senate what is known as the Spears Anti-Discrimination Bill, sponsored by Senator J. Franklin Spears of San Antonio. Your Chamber of Commerce could get behind this Bill and thus help to make it unlawful for anyone to humiliate Mexicans in Texas just because they happen to be of Mexican blood. We are sure, your Senator, the Honorable H. L. Winfield, will be glad to furnish you a copy of said Bill. If not, it will give us pleasure to send you one.

Yours very truly,

COMMITTEE OF ONE HUNDRED.
THE LEAGUE OF LOYAL AMERICANS.
By Alonso S. Perales, Director General.

P. S. We are sending you the address of Dr. González Martínez and the Committee, in case you wish to telegraph him. If you do, please send us a copy.

265

PRESS STATEMENT OF ALONSO S. PERALES, DIRECTOR GENERAL OF THE COMMITTEE OF ONE HUNDRED AND THE LEAGUE OF LOYAL AMERICANS.

"We are sure that the discriminatory act perpetrated upon Senator Eugenio Prado, President of the Permanent Commission of the Congress of Mexico, will make every right thinking and fair-minded American blush with shame.

"In our judgment, the anti-discrimination bill introduced by Senator J. Franklin Spears this week will, if enacted into law, go a long way toward strengthening the bonds of friendship between the peoples of the United States and the people of the other American nations, particularly Mexico.

"During my travels in Hispanic America, I have observed that the discrimination in Texas and other states of our Union against persons of Mexican or Hispanic descent is deeply resented by our neighbors to the South. That there is need for such a law in Texas, and in fact throughout the Southwest is beyond question. Now, then, if the Texas Legislature enacts a law at this time, it will mean improved relations with Mexico and the other Latin-American nations immediately. Their reaction would be most beneficial to the United States, particularly Texas. Within 30 days after the enactment of such a law, we would see our friends from Mexico coming into Texas to help us harvest our crops and further the war effort. They are most willing to assist us. What is holding them back is that they have not been able to obtain from our government the assurance that Mexican nationals will not be humiliated anywhere in the future on account of their race.

"Likewise, it would be a splendid gesture toward the quarter of a million soldiers of Mexican descent now in all the battle fronts.

"Doubtless it would strengthen their faith in our form of government. Statistics show that from fifty percent to seventy-five percent of those who are falling on the firing line from SOUTH TEXAS are soldiers of Mexican descent. They are happy and proud to make the supreme sacrifice for our country. The question is: what are we willing to do for them?"

Perales was born in Alice, Texas. He has served in the diplomatic service of the United States in Mexico, Central and South America and the West Indies.

March, 1945.

266

HE WAS GOOD ENOUGH IN A TURRET

On a warm summer evening last July in Mission, a thousand or more citizens gathered at an open-air meeting to greet and acclaim a young soldier who had just returned from England.

This young soldier had been a turret gunner in a B-17 bomber crew. His squadron had participated in the first aerial raids on Germany.

On his first raid, this young gunner had been wounded. But the wound was slight and after a short stay in a hospital the gunner went back to his turret. Twenty-four more times he rode through the deadly air over Europe on bombing raids.

This boy wasn't any more of a hero than thousands of his fellow soldiers who are fighting for democracy and against the "super race" which preaches and practices with the sword that false and hateful doctrine holding some races of men superior to others. This boy wasn't a hero. He was just doing his part as decent people everywhere in the world today are doing theirs—and dying.

After his twenty-fifth bombing mission, this young gunner from Mission was sent back to the United States to train other gunners. While he wasn't any special hero, they did pin a few medals on his chest before he sailed for home. He brought back the Air Medal with three oak leef clusters and the Distinguished Flying Cross and the Purple Heart.

At the open-air meeting in Mission, this young gunner was lauded for his exploits by fellow citizens and presented with a fine watch. Then he went off to Sioux City, Ia. to be a gunnery instructor.

Last week the young gunner from Mission came back for another visit. This visit had a very special purpose. He came back to claim himself a bride.

Turret gunners and their brides, like any newly married couple, are happy people and like to kick up their heels on a well-polished floor to the strains of good music. So the gunner and his bride, together with two other young couples, betook themselves down to the Blue Moon between Pharr and San Juan, thinking to enjoy an evening of dancing which is one of the many privileges enjoyed by citizens of this enlightened and democratic nation.

The Blue Moon, it might be pointed out, is not exactly comparable with the Rainbow Room in Rockefeller Center nor do its patrons expect their social pedigrees to be enhanced by being seen there, but as Valley night spots go it is a fair average.

Anyhow, the young gunner and his wife and the two other

young couples entered the Blue Moon and proffered their money for admission to the dance floor.

The place was not crowded and the money they proffered was not counterfeit. But the young gunner and his wife were not admitted. They could not qualify, the doorman explained, because "we do not permit Mexicans in here."

The gunner and his wife, of course, are not Mexicans. They are citizens of the United States—much better citizens, it might be added, than the doorman of the Blue Moon. But they were turned away because the Blue Moon is operated on the same despicable racial policies that have made Nazi Germany the scourge of the civilized world. It so happens that one of the three couples in the young gunner's party belonged to the group commonly referred to as Anglo-American, but naturally the entire party departed after learning the club's policy, as any self-respecting American citizens would.

Questioned later about the policy of his club, the manager stated that his establishment did not bar soldiers in uniform and would have admitted the young gunner, providing he had left his wife outside. Such restrictions were necessary, the manager further explained, "to avoid trouble."

A lot of people here in the Valley don't like to read about such incidents as this story of the turret gunner and his wife. And this newspaper certainly doesn't enjoy recording them.

But as long as this is the United States of America and as long as the Constitution sets forth its declarations of equality among all citizens, to say nothing of the instincts of common decency and reason which govern the behavior of all good men, it is not possible to keep silent in the face of such bigoted behavior, even considering the source.

If there is any place in the nation where two so-called races (actually both Latin and Anglo-Americans are of the same race) of people should live in harmony and understanding and mutual appreciation it is here in the Valley. If there is any ethnological basis for showing preference to any group here in the Valley, that preference lies in the favor of our Latin-American people whose ancestors rightfully called this soil home centuries before the paleface knew of its existence.

Any individual unwilling to accord to the Latin-American population of the Valley the same courteous and equitable treatment enjoyed by any other individual because of any so-called racial distinction is a hostile influence both to the Valley and to this nation.

While we are engaged in fighting to the death against similar

268

hostile influences abroad, how can we tolerate them right under our noses here at home?
(VALLEY EVENING MONITOR,
Thursday, March 30, 1944.)

RACE ISSUE AROUSES IRE OF MEXICANS

By Curtis Vinson.

Staff Correspondent of The News.

MEXICO CITY. Oct. 23. Alleged racial discrimination in Texas against Mexicans and citizens of Mexican blood has been accorded much attention in the Mexico City press in recent weeks.

The subject is by no means a new one. Bitter charges of racial discrimination in the United States against Mexican blood have been expressed from time to time over a long period in the Mexican press. Regions and states other than Texas have been cited as localities fostering such discrimination.

The episode of the zoot suiters in California some time back lighted the fuse of excited public expression here. Alleged examples of discrimination against Mexican workers who have gone to the United States Government contracts to help harvest crops as a part of the war effort have been headlined from time to time, particularly by certain sectors of the Mexican press. However, alleged abuses and discriminations suffered by people of Mexican blood in Texas have inspired the major note of condemnation sounded by the Mexican press.

Certain public officials of Mexico, notably Ezequiel Padilla, Minister of Foreign Affairs, have repeatedly decried any tendency, particularly at this time, calculated to create friction between partners in the United Nations war effort. During the past summer Padilla took occasion to voice a warning that Axis fifth column activities stress the inciting of racial friction between supporters of the United Nations cause.

"The Nazi-Fascist powers have lost the initiative on the battlefield but they appear not to have lost it on the field of fifth columnism and espionage", he said. "Strikes, agitation, racial incidents, diplomatic conflicts that in reality lack deep roots, widespread or overt propaganda, all are testimony that fifth columnism is continuing to spread its subtle or invisible work."

OIL ON TROUBLED WATER.

Texas' own Gov. Coke Stevenson, on his visit here for the Mexican Independence celebration during September, took cognizance of the repeated Mexican charge of discrimination in Texas by stressing the existence of personal ties of friendship between the people of Mexico and the United States by declaring that

269

racial prejudice in Texas was at a minimum. Previously, in an official proclamation in Texas, he had declared the good-neighbor policy of Texas, had called for the cessation of any practice that might be interpreted as discriminatory against Mexicans.

Climaxing all reports, however, is the lengthy philippic in a recent issue of the magazine "Mañana", a new weekly publication of imposing format, under the heading of "We Are Also Gentlemen and Not the Servants of the Continent." In launching a biting criticism against "the Nazis of Texas" for alleged racial discrimination, "Mañana" quotes a communication allegedly sent the past September by a Houston lawyer of Mexican blood to the Spanish text newspaper "La Prensa" of San Antonio. In this letter, as quoted, the lawyer set forth that he was a United States citizen and secretary of the League of United Latin-American Citizens of Houston. According to the quoted letter, the attorney declared that he, the Mexican Consul in Houston and another man were refused service in a restaurant at New Gulf in Wharton County. The three were invited to enter the kitchen if they wished service, the lawyer was quoted as having said.

MEXICANS ALSO VICTIMS.

The "Mañana" editorialist, among other things, wrote: "The Nazis of Texas" are not political partisans of the Fuehrer of Germany nor do they desire his triumph; but indeed they are slaves of the same prejudices and superstitions. Hitler hates the noses of the Jews, and his correligionists in Texas view with the same profound aversion the black skin, the thick lips and the fuzzy hair of the descendants of the enslaved race. And not only the offspring of Africa are viewed with humiliating disdain; Mexicans also become the victims of ignorant rabble who see in blond hair and blue eyes their pretended racial superiority . . .

"It is monstrous that in depriving our blood brothers of the right of social equality, the obligations which they owe to the state are not reduced in the same proportion. They are thrown out of restaurants but they are not freed from the obligation of serving in the Army . . . .

"President Franklin D. Roosevelt is the first to recognize that justice is due us, and in many speeches he has recommended to his compatriots that they reject all ethnic prejudices. Those who have seconded this noble recommendation are the dynamic wife of the President, Secretary of State Hull, and Ex-Presidential Candidate Wendell Willkie . . . Finally, the Governor of Texas, Coke Stevenson, in a memorable proclamation, exhorted his fellow citizens to establish no more insulting differences against the Mexican race."

(The Dallas Morning News, Dallas, Texas, Sunday, October 24, 1943.)

PART V

CORRESPONDENCE AND COMMENTS

(Appropriate and special letters were written about discrimination of Latin-Americans to President Franklin Delano Roosevelt; to Mrs. Roosevelt, and to various departments of the Federal Government, and to my satisfaction, and the satisfaction of those who look ahead for a better understanding among all the peoples of this great country of ours, regardless of creed, religion or social standing, due attention was given to our petitions, and we sincerely hope that the problem of discrimination will soon be solved placing our nation in the place that it rightfully reserves among the democracies of the world.)

TRUMAN WANTS CIVIL-RIGHTS LAWS IMPROVED
By Associated Press

Washington, June 29.—President Truman said Sunday if democracy is to win over totalitarianism in war-torn nations the United States must put its own "house in order" by improving its laws on civil rights.

He declared there is much that state and local governments can do in "providing positive safeguards for civil rights," but that the nation "cannot any longer await the growth of a will to action in the slowest state or the most backward community."

"Our national government must show the way," he said, adding federal laws and administrative machinery must be improved and expanded.

The Chief Executive spoke to an outdoor audience at the Lincoln Memorial—the closing session of the 38th annual conference of the National Association for the Advancement of Colored People.

"Many of our people," he said, "still suffer the indignity of insult, the harrowing fear of intimidation, and, I regret to say, the threat of physical injury and mob violence. The prejudice and intolerance in which these evils are rotted still exist. The conscience of our nation, and the legal machinery which enforces it, have not yet secured to each citizen full freedom from fear."

(San Antonio Express, June 30, 1947.)

271

TRUMAN PROMISES BATTLE AGAINST RACIAL DISCRIMINATION

Washington, June 29—(UP)—President Truman, decrying race prejudice and discrimination, Sunday pledged the national government to "show the way" to backward states and communities which fail to safeguard the civil rights of all Americans.

Speaking at Lincoln memorial to the thirty-eight annual conference of the National Association for the Advancement of Colored People, Mr. Truman said the nation no longer can afford "the luxury of a leisurely attack" on prejudice and discrimination.

He was joined in his denunciation of such practices by Mrs. Franklin D. Roosevelt and Senator Wayne Morse (R., Ore.).

Noting that many peoples of the world are now making a choice between democracy and totalitarianism, Mr. Truman said that "our case for democracy should be as strong as we can make it."

It should rest, he warned, "on practical evidence that we have been able to put our own house in order."

The President said there was much that state and local governments can do to protect American citizens from "the indignity of insult, the harrowing fear of intimidation, and . . . the threat of physical injury and mob violence."

"But", he added, "we cannot, any longer, await the growth of a will to action in the slowest state or the most backward community. Our national government must show the way."

He acknowledged that this was a "difficult and complex" problem and said that federal laws and administrative machinery must be improved and expanded.

"Our immediate task is to remove the last remnants of the barriers which stand between millions of our citizens and their birthright. There is no justifiable reason for discrimination because of ancestry, or religion, or race, or color," he said.

Mr. Truman listed the basic rights, which he said each citizen should enjoy in a truly democratic society, as "the right to a decent home, the right to an education, the right to adequate medical care, the right to a worthwhile job, the right to an equal share in the making of public decisions through the ballot, and the right to a fair trial in a fair court."

"Recent events in the United States and abroad have made us realize that it is more important today than ever before to insure that all Americans enjoy these rights," he said. "And when I say all Americans, I mean all Americans."

272

He said that mob violence and intimidation continue because the "prejudice and intolerance in which these evils are rooted still exist."

"The conscience of our nation, and the legal machinery which enforces it, have not yet secured each citizen full freedom from fear.

"We cannot wait another decade or another generation to remedy these evils. We must work, as never before, to secure them now. The aftermath of war and the desire to keep faith with our nation's historic principles make the need a pressing one."

(The Houston Post.
June 30, 1947.)

San Antonio, Texas,
Feb. 8, 1946.

His Excellency
Harry S. Truman,
President of the United States of America,
The White House,
Washington, D. C.

Excellency:

Again permit us to congratulate your Excellency for your splendid work in behalf of the minority and forgotten groups in our country.

We sincerely hope the necessary two thirds vote in favor of cloture may be available Saturday afternoon, January 9th, and that the F.E.P.C. Bill may be approved by the Senate without further delay.

We are certain we voice the sentiments of three million Americans of Mexican descent in this matter.

Your Excellency's courageous leadership in this fight is a source of encouragement and inspiration to all real Americans throughout the length and breadth of our land.

May the Lord bless you and yours always.

Sincerely,

COMMITTEE OF ONE HUNDRED.
By Alonso S. Perales, Chairman.

273

CONGRESS OF THE UNITED STATES
House of Representatives
Washington 25, D. C.

November 6, 1945.

Mr. Alonso S. Perales, Director General
Committee of One Hundred
Suite 714, Gunter Building
San Antonio, Texas.

My dear Friend:

This has further reference to our correspondence as to the classification of Americans of Mexican descent as non-white, with particular reference to the case of Jesús Solís.

I send you herewith a letter which I have received from Major General Edward F. Witsell, Acting the Adjutant General, in this connection. This is self-explanatory.

If there is anything further I can do in this matter, feel free to call upon me.

Sincerely yours,

Paul J. Kilday, M. C.

WAR DEPARTMENT
The Adjutant General's Office
Washington 25, D. C.

AGCH-P 291.2 (21 Sep 45)   24 October 1945.
Honorable Paul J. Kilday
House of Representatives.

Dear Mr. Kilday:

This is in response to your letter of 17 October 1945 requesting clarification of War Department instructions regarding the racial classification by the Army of Americans of Mexican or Latin American descent and citing the case of Jesús Solís, Army serial number 38418353.

In my letter dated 10 October 1945 it was stated in substance that the discharge certificates were designed to facilitate the keeping of statistics in the most practical manner and that entries thereon regarding the race or nationality of an individual is not in any sense intended to be discriminatory.

Plans for the demobilization of the Army were prepared far in advance and have progressed to such an extent that it is considered impracticable to make any change in the tremendous supply of separation forms which have been printed and distributed

274

to the numerous separation points. Problems of procurement and distribution of new forms would seriously delay the demobilization, not to mention that a very considerable expense would be involved.

Permit me to point out that the separation form racial classification relates only to the individual separated and, therefore, no inference should be drawn that it is applicable to the people of a nation as a whole. The information upon which the entry is made regarding race or nationality is furnished initially by the individual concerned and accepted by the War Department without question. The entry under "Other" is intended to s h o w nationality.

For the reasons given above, therefore, it will be necessary for the nationality of citizens of countries other than the United States to continue to be shown under the heading of "Other".

In view of the factors involved, I trust you will understand and appreciate the position of the War Department in this matter.

Sincerely yours,

EDWARD F. WITSELL

Major General

Acting The Adjutant General.

San Antonio, Texas,

Nov. 16, 1944.

Commanding General,
Eighth Service Command,
United States Army,
Santa Fe Building,
Dallas, Texas.

Dear Sir:

We are pleased to enclose herewith a list of more than one hundred cities and towns in which American soldiers of Mexican descent are humiliated in public establishments such as restaurants, barber shops, theaters, etc., merely because of their Mexican lineage. In said list you will also find the names and addresses of the establishments, and in some cases the names of the proprietors also. This situation is typical of conditions existing in the rest of the Southwest.

We will appreciate it very much, Sir, if you will take the necessary steps *immediately* to protect these worthy servants of our country against further humiliations by anyone due to their racial lineage.

We thank you in advance, Sir, for a prompt reply.

Respectfully,

COMMITTEE OF ONE HUNDRED AMERICAN CITIZENS OF MEXICAN DESCENT.
LEAGUE OF LOYAL AMERICANS.
Alonso S. Perales, Director General.

Enclosures: 1

DEPARTMENT OF JUSTICE
Washington, D. C.
May 8, 1944.

Mr. Alonso S. Perales, Director General
Committee of One Hundred,
League of Loyal Americans
Suite 714 Gunter Building
San Antonio, Texas.

Dear Mr. Perales:

This will acknowledge the receipt, by reference from the White House, of your letter to Mrs. Roosevelt dated April 15 and requesting an interview with President Roosevelt for representatives of the Committee of One Hundred, League of Loyal Americans. Since writing that letter, you will have received the reply of April 14 to your letter of March 31, suggesting that you make an appointment with me at which we may discuss the matters of which you write.

I am writing now to assure you of my readiness to make such an appointment at any time you suggest and to renew my suggestion that you also present any material that you may have concerning discrimination against Americans of Mexican origin to the Civil Rights Section of the Criminal Division of the Department of Justice. This section is in charge of matters relating to discrimination on grounds of race.

Respectfully,

For the Attorney General,
TOM C. CLARK,
Assistant Attorney General.

San Antonio, Texas,
April 15, 1944.

Honorable Clare Boothe Luce,
Member of the U. S. House of Representatives,
The Capitol,
Washington, D. C.

Dear Representative Boothe Luce:

On March 21, 1944, the "San Antonio Evening News," published an Associated Press Dispatch to the effect that you had proposed a resolution that the house set up a seven member special Committee to investigate whether discrimination exists against minority groups in the armed services. We believe the idea is excellent, and we should like to know whether the Committee has been named and is now functioning.

Also, we should like to know whether said Committee could be charged with the duty of investigating whether or not soldiers are being distributed throughout the battlefronts impartially, without regard to race, color or creed. In other words, we Americans of Mexican descent, for example, would like to make sure that racial prejudice is not carried to the battlefronts in such a manner that our soldiers of Mexican extraction are sent to the firing line first and in great numbers and in preference to others of other racial lineages. Please do not misunderstand us. We are more than glad to do our part, and, in fact, we are already very well represented in all the battlefronts, but the point we are making is that our honest opinion is that all the Races which compose our great cosmopolitan Nation should be on an equal footing on the firing line, and that no advantage should be taken by anyone of any of these Races. This is something our National Congress can very well make sure of by appointing the Committee you have proposed.

Wishing you success, and awaiting your reply, for which we thank you in advance, we remain

Very truly yours,

COMMITTEE OF ONE HUNDRED.
THE LEAGUE OF LOYAL AMERICANS.
By Alonso S. Perales, Director General.

CONGRESS OF THE UNITED STATES
House of Representatives
Washington, D. C.

April 20, 1944.

277

Mr. Alonso S. Perales, Director General
The League of Loyal Americans
Suite 714 Gunter Building
San Antonio, Texas.

Dear Mr. Perales:

This will acknowledge your letter of April 15th concerning my Resolution 476 recently introduced by me in the House to set up a Committee to investigate whether discrimination exists against minority groups in the armed services.

Your letter has been read with considerable interest, and I am grateful for your views.

For your information I am enclosing copy of my Resolution.

Sincerely yours,

CLARE BOOTHE LUCE.

Enclosure

San Antonio, Texas,
March 31, 1944.

His Excellency
Franklin Delano Roosevelt,
President of the United States of America,
The White House,
Washington, D. C.

Excellency:

This will confirm our telegrams dated the 10th and 17th instant with reference to discrimination against persons of Mexican and Hispanic descent generally, including members of the armed forces of our country, in Texas, California, Colorado, Oklahoma, New Mexico, and other States of the Union.

To-day we are writing Your Excellency to request an audience for the purpose of presenting concrete evidence of said discrimination. We have no objection to submitting such evidence to the members of both Houses of the Congress of the United States also. We are willing to make the trip to Washington at our own expense. Or, if it is preferred to send a Congressional Committee to investigate the situation, we are ready to furnish the information right on the ground of the events.

Referring specifically to the State of Texas, we are going to show that discrimination exists against persons of Mexican and Hispanic descent generally, including members of the armed forces of our Nation, in two hundred and forty nine out of the two hundred and fifty four Counties of the State, and that said discrimination consists not only of slights and humiliations in restaurants, theaters, barber shops and other public places of business, but also segregation in public schools and residential districts. Not only persons of Mexican lineage are victims of such discrimination. Venezuelans, Hondurans and Argentinians, some of them members of the Armies of said countries, have also been discriminated against.

We are also going to prove that there is discrimination in the economic field. There are public establishments where persons of Mexican and Hispanic descent generally are not employed, and where they are employed they are not paid the salary or wage that Anglo-Americans receive for the same services. The Committee on Fair Employment Practice created by Your Excellency has relieved the situation in Government camps and in factories and shops where work is being done for the Federal Government, but in establishments, factories and shops over which said Committee has no jurisdiction, the situation remains the same.

The evidence which we intend to present to Your Excellency includes statements signed, under oath, by the victims of said humiliations, as well as the testimony, in the form of articles and lectures, of eminent North American citizens, such as His Excellency Robert E. Lucey, Archbishop of San Antonio, Texas, Messrs. Sumner Welles, Ex-Undersecretary of State of our country, William P. Blocker, United States Consul General in Ciudad Juarez, Chihuahua, Mexico, Jack Danciger, prominent business man of Fort Worth, Texas, Malcom Ross, Chairman of the Committee on Fair Employment Practice, the Editor of TIME Magazine, and the Editor of the New York Herald Tribune.

For the past four years we have been asking the Texas Legislature to pass a law forbidding the humiliation of Mexicans and Hispanic peoples generally in this State, but it has absolutely refused to do so. Among the Legislators who have actively opposed the enactment of such a law are Senator R. A. Weinert, of Seguin, and Representative Frank B. Voight, of New Braunfels. Seguin and New Braunfels are two German-American communities of Texas that have always distinguished themselves for their anti-Mexicanism.

There are some people who opine that the solution of this problem rests in waging an educational campaign among the Anglo-American elements designed to show them the merits and qualities of the Mexican and of the Hispanic Race generally, but the majority of us contend that in addition to such an educational program there is need for a federal law prohibiting the humiliation of Mexicans and persons of Hispanic descent generally in any part of our country. The law is necessary in order to put an end to this painful situation immediately. The educational program is useful, but it is very slow, and we have no time to lose. We are at war and in order to win it we need unity among the peoples of the Americas. The best way to show all the inhabitants of Hispanic America that they are respected in our country is to pass a law making it unlawful for anyone to humiliate them here. The citizens of Venezuela, Honduras and Argentina feel just as deeply hurt as the citizens of Mexico when they learn that there are places in the United States where members of their Race, and above all their fellow-citizens, are humiliated; more so at this moment when more than a quarter of a million soldiers of Mexican descent are giving their blood for democracy. The resentment of these sister Republics of ours has reached the point where Mexico, for example, has become quite firm in her resolve not to send more workers to Texas until and end is put to these humiliations.

As regards the thousands of American citizens of Mexican descent who are fighting in the battle fronts, the best way to encourage them to continue fighting with enthusiasm is to pass a law that will assure to them that our Federal Government does not intend to permit anyone to humiliate them or any member of their families, either in Texas or in any other State of the Union, merely because they are Mexicans by blood.

Awaiting a prompt reply, we remain, with all due respect and consideration, Your Excellency's most obedient servants.

THE COMMITTEE OF ONE-HUNDRED MEXICAN-AMERICAN CITIZENS.

THE LEAGUE OF LOYAL AMERICANS.

Alonso S. Perales, Director General.

TELEGRAM

San Antonio, Texas,
March 10, 1944.

HIS EXCELLENCY
Franklin Delano Roosevelt,
President of the United States of America
The White House
Washington, D. C.

Seaman José Alvarez Fuentes and Juan García, United States Navy, and Privates Joe I. Salas and Paul R. Ramos, United States Army, all wearing uniform were denied service at the Downtown Cafe, three twenty three East Main Street, Fredericksburg, Texas, on March Seventh merely because of their Mexican lineage. Proprietor told them they could not be served in front and that they would have to go to the kitchen. Such occurrences are common in Texas. There are over one hundred towns and cities where Mexicans and nationals of other Latin American countries are discriminated against.

In each of these towns there are from two to eight public places of business or amusement where Mexicans and other Latin Americans are humiliated. We are reliably informed such discrimination exists also in California, Colorado, New Mexico, Oklahoma and other states. For the good of our nation we respectfully suggest that Your Excellency ask Congress to enact legislation immediately forbidding such tactics; first, because they are un-American, and, secondly, because they are contrary to Your Excellency's Good Neighbor Policy. The Texas Legislature has refused to pass such a law. Please advise whether our Federal Government will act to remedy this situation.

THE LEAGUE OF LOYAL AMERICANS.

By Alonso S. Perales, Director General.

San Antonio, Texas,
March 17, 1944.

His Excellency,
Franklin Delano Roosevelt
President of the United States
The White House
Washington, D. C.

Our commendations and thanks to your Excellency for splendid work of your Committee on Fair Employment Practice. Three million Americans of Mexican descent anxiously await relief through Federal Legislation as requested in our telegram of March 10. Discrimination against Mexicans and Latin Americans in public places of business is undermining morale of our men in the armed forces. Conditions are intolerable. Humiliations suffered by our men in uniform affect temper of our men in armed forces and may lead to unnecessary bloodshed. We urge action or statement from your Excellency that Latin Americans and Mexicans must not be denied service at public places.

THE LEAGUE OF LOYAL AMERICANS.

By Alonso S. Perales, Director General.

San Antonio, Texas,
January 1st 1943.

Honorable Voorhis,
Member of the U. S. House of Representatives,
The Capitol,
Washington, D. C.

Dear Sir:

Our League, a civic and patriotic organization composed of American citizens of Mexican descent, desires to commend you most sincerely upon your determination to see that the people of Mexico are accorded proper recognition for their collaboration with our country in this war. The statement made by you appeared in The San Antonio Light of December 10, 1942, and we want you to know that you are absolutely correct, and that we are ready to cooperate with you to the fullest extent to the end that our Government may have all the facts. Unquestionably, there is a great deal of discrimination going on in practically every field of endeavor. We have many affidavits revealing the true situation in Texas, and shall be delighted to place same at your disposal. Also, we shall be very glad to come to Washington to testify before any interested Congressional Committee. We are fully convinced that in order to unite the peoples of the Americas we shall have to cast aside any petty prejudices which we may have had in the past and to treat each other with the respect and consideration to which we all are entitled.

The enclosed copies of letters will give you an idea of what is going on in Texas. There are many, many cases like these.

You will be rendering a great service to our Nation, the United States of America, if you go through with your plan, and we want to cooperate with you one-hundred-percent.

Kindly let us hear from you with reference to this matter at your earliest convenience, as we are profoundly interested.

Thanking you in advance, and again congratulating you upon your good work, we remain

Respectfully yours,

THE LEAGUE OF LOYAL AMERICANS.

By Alonso S. Perales, Director General.

Enclosures: 2

PART VI

RECORD OF MEXICAN-AMERICANS IN WORLD WAR II.

San Antonio, Texas,
November 24, 1944.

Honorable Paul J. Kilday,
Member of the U. S. House of Representatives,
The Capitol,
Washington, D. C.

Dear Congressman Kilday:

Please ascertain from our War Department why is it that from fifty per cent to seventy-five per cent of the casualties from South Texas are soldiers of Mexican descent. The population of Texas is estimated at six million. Of these about one-half million are inhabitants of Mexican extraction. This being the case, it would seem that our share of representation in the Armed Forces should be one American soldier of Mexican descent to six American soldiers of other extractions. We are referring to Texas only. Now, please do not misunderstand us. We are not complaining about the very liberal representation we have on the battle fronts. On the contrary, we are quite proud of the opportunity afforded us to defend our country on the firing line, but we want to ascertain for sure whether the circumstances that fifty to seventy-five per cent of the casualties from South Texas are of Mexican descent is due to the fact that there are not sufficient soldiers of other extractions in South Texas to defend our country on the battle fields, or whether it is because some individuals who are prejudiced against the Mexican people are rushing our boys to the battle fronts in order that they may be the first to get killed and get rid of them that way. I once heard a Texas Anglo-American remark that he wished we had a war and that one-half of the Mexicans in Texas would get killed. As you well know, Congressman Kilday, there is a great deal of prejudice against Mexicans in Texas, and said prejudice has found its way to our military camps in Texas, and also to industries engaged in work for our Federal Government. The result has been that our people have been underpaid and grossly discriminated against. Fortunately, President

Roosevelt put a stop to it when he created his Committee on Fair Employment Practices. Our people have fared much better since then. Again we say, we are not afraid to die; on the contrary, we are very proud and happy to have the privilege of serving our country at any time and anywhere. We just want to make certain that our Boys are marching to the firing line in the proper and fair proportion in so far as the population and fighting manpower of South Texas are concerned, and that they are not the victims of foulplay on the part of individuals who, hating our race, may now be in a position to satisfy their prejudices.

Thanking you in advance for a prompt reply, we remain

Sincerely yours,

COMMITTEE OF ONE HUNDRED.

LEAGUE OF LOYAL AMERICANS.

By Alonso S. Perales, Director General.

NOTE: Same letter as the above was sent to the Honorable Milton H. West, Representative for the 15th Congressional District of Texas.

EVERY DAY DURING WORLD WAR II WE WOULD SEE PUBLISHED IN THE TEXAS PRESS LISTS OF CASUALTIES SUCH AS THIS:

SIX SAN ANTONIO MEN ARE REPORTED KILLED

25 South Texans Dead, 67 Others Named As Wounded, Missing or War Prisoners

Six San Antonio men and 25 South Texans have been reported killed in action on the latest army-navy casualty list released by the office of war information. In addition, 14 San Antonians and 38 others from this area are listed as wounded in action. One San Antonio sailor and one South Texas sailor are missing in action. Two San Antonians and 11 South Texans are reported to be prisoners of war in Germany.

KILLED

From San Antonio:

Pfc. Lynn B. Shannon, U.S.M.C.R., husband of Mrs. Lynn B. Shannon, Dinero; son of Mr. and Mrs. Lawrence S. Shannon, 521 Madison St.; **Pvt. Alvaro S. Flores,** son of Mrs. María S. Flores, 1005 Ruiz St.; **Lt. Col. Leonard D. Peterson,** husband of Mrs. Mildred

284

S. Peterson, 1314 W. Woodlawn Ave.; **Pfc. Daniel Martínez,** husband of Mrs. Carolina C. Martínez, Route 8, Box 282.; **Tech. Sgt. Salomé L. Gonzáles,** son of Mrs. Eulalia Gonzáles, 308 Chestnut St.; **Pfc. José Rodríguez,** son of Jesús Rodríguez, 2526 El Paso St.

From South Texas.

Pfc. Preston C. Clark, U.S.M.C.R., Buda; **Pfc. Adrian E. Hull,** U.S.M.C.R., Aransas Pass; **Pfc. Jack S. Lipscomb,** U.S.M.C., Austin; **Pvt. Jessie M. Lozano,** U.S.M.C., Flatonia; **Cpl. Cecil B. Penn,** U.S.M.C.R., Moore; **Pfc. Aurelio G. Chapa,** Alice; **Pvt. Guadalupe Esquivél,** Divot; **Tech. Sgt. James H. Evans, Jr.,** Wharton; **Pfc. Herman G. Keseling,** Cuero; **Pvt. Meyer F. Morris,** Hondo; **Pvt. José M. Yáñez,** Elsa; **Pfc. Lonnie F. Creech,** Somerset; **Pfc. Gregorio Gonzáles,** Brownsville; **Pvt. Everardo López,** Laredo; **Cpl. William D. Spurlin,** Lampasas; **Pfc. Elmore J. White,** Austin; **Pfc. Horace D. Campbell,** Bishop; **Cpl. Israél J. Cisneros,** Raymondville; **Capt. Edward W. Prove,** Lockhart; **Pfc. Leonardo Sosa,** Encinal; **Pfc. Santos S. Zamarripa,** Round Rock; **Second Lt. Arthur D. McKinney, J.,** Corpus Christi; **Pfc. John W. Montgomery,** Junction; **Pfc. Ross M. Morales,** Laredo and **Pfc. Francisco G. Ybarra,** Hondo.

WOUNDED

From San Antonio:

Cpl. Refugio L. Avila, husband of Esperanza L. Avila, 813 Austin St.; **Pvt. Félix Ortíz,** husband of Mrs. Gudelia F. Ortíz, 816 S. Pecos St.; **Pfc. Robert Persyn,** son of Mrs. Mary A. Persyn, Route 9, Box 167; **Pfc. Louis H. Estrada,** son of Mrs. Irene C. Estrada, 349 Hawthorne St.; **Tech. 5th Gr. Francisco Q. García, Jr.,** son of Mrs. Andres Q. García, 1409 Guadalupe St.; **Tech. Sgt. Robert J. Heath,** husband of Mrs. Maxine L. Heath, 1311 W. Agarita St.; **Staff Sgt. Kurt B. Kleefeld,** son of Gisela C. Bauer, 1610 W. Texas Ave.; **Pfc. Isaac J. Lara,** son of Seferino Lara, 201 Henry St.; **Pfc. Mike M. Martínez,** son of Mrs. Natalia M. Martínez, 2212 San Fernando St.; **Pfc. William Norman Pegg,** USMCR, son of Mr. and Mrs. William F. Pegg, 310 Barret Pl.; **Pfc. James Erler,** son of Mrs. E. Erler, 635 Thompson Pl.; **Pvt. Rodolfo P. Mendiola,** son of Mrs. Mónica P. Mendiola, 1307 Vera Cruz St.; **Tech. 4th Gr. Francisco V. Soriano,** son of Mrs. Baslica V. Soriano, 1608 Chihuahua St.; **First Lt. Carrol P. Sullivan,** husband of Mrs. Cora Lee Sullivan, 819 W. Lubbock St.

From South Texas:

Cpl. Marvin L. Kerr, USMCR, La Feria; **Second Lt. Eugene Lawrence McCarthy,** USMCR, Corpus Christi; **Pfc. John G. Peters,** USMCR, New Braunfels; **Pvt. Dewey M. Pickens,** USMCR, Round

Rock; **Sgt. Marvin A. Heinecke,** La Grange; **Tech. Sgt. William H. Lester,** Austin; **Pvt. Raymon Marquardt,** Sisterdale; **Pvt. Alfredo C. Mata,** Marfa; **Pfc. Gaylon F. Urban,** Goliad; **Staff Sgt. Hilario P. Vargas,** Carrizo Springs; **Pvt. Jesús G. Villa,** Hondo; **Pfc. Raúl C. Villarreal,** Brownsville; **Pvt. Jesús A. Arreóla,** Schertz; **Tech. 5th Gr. Fred D. Binion,** Austin; **Pfc. Refugio M. Caunder, Jr.,** Pearsall; **Pfc. Alfred A. Harrison,** Brownsville; **Sgt. Manuel A. Jáime,** Falfurias; **Pfc. Estéban N. Martínez,** Harlingen; **First Sgt. Emil E. Matula,** Granger; **Pfc. Wenferd E. Morgan,** Hallettsville; **Pfc. Guadalupe V. Naránjo,** Beeville; **Pfc. Robert A. Nava,** Corpus Christi; **Pfc. Milton H. Rivera,** Corpus Christi; **Pfc. Israél Sauceda,** Sejita; **Pvt. Edward W. Scheible,** Devine; **Pfc. John M. Silvas,** Gonzáles; **Pfc. Manuel Vásquez, Jr.,** Marion; **Pvt. Ignacio L. Canales,** Baytown; **Pfc. Alonso Z. García,** Corpus Christi; **Tech. 5th Gr. Jesús R. García,** San Diego; **Pfc. Wilfrido Marroquín,** Corpus Christi; **Pfc. George J. Migl,** Flatonia; **Pfc. Howard A. Poth,** Pleasanton; **Pfc. D. Ryon,** Seguin; **Pfc. Cleménte Salinas,** Laredo; **Pfc. Lúcas Sandovál,** Edinburg; **Sgt. Manuel H. Strong,** Dilley and **Pfc. Ramón S. Villarreal,** Laredo.

MISSING

From San Antonio:

Antonio Rivera Mejía, Seaman 2nd. cl., U.S.N.R., son of Mr. and Mrs. Gregorio Mejía, 115 El Paso St.

From South Texas:

Leopoldo Peña, Seaman 1st cl., U.S.N.R., Elsa.

PRISONERS

From San Antonio:

Pvt. Simón M. Cárdenas, husband of Mrs. Petra S. Cárdenas, 614 Brazos St.; **Pfc. Alonzo V. Forshee,** husband of Mrs. Eunice M. Forshee, Route 7, Box 568.

From South Texas:

Pvt. José A. Flores, Corpus Christi; **Sgt. Cantú García, Jr.,** Edinburg; **Staff Sgt. Frank E. Kocurek,** Schulenburg; **Pfc. Johnny Loesch,** Rosenberg; **Pvt. Benno J. Matocha,** Cistern; **Sgt. Carlton E. Mueller,** Runge; **Pfc. Barney E. Wade,** Georgetown; **Pvt. Juan D. Zamora,** Robstown; **Pfc. Lee R. Best, Jr.,** Flatonia; **Pvt. Frank Guzmán,** Kingville, and **Pfc. Fidel Regalado,** Christine.

(Taken from "San Antonio Express," San Antonio, Texas, April 5, 1945.)

ARMY RETURNS REMAINS OF SOUTH TEXAS HEROES FOR BURIAL IN CEMETERIES NEAR HOMES

(Herewith a partial list of patriots who did not return alive. This, and the foregoing sample general list of casualties, give us an idea of the proportion in which the Mexican-American made the supreme sacrifice for our country. It should be borne in mind in this connection that the inhabitants of Mexican descent of Texas are at most one-sixth of the entire population of the State.)

The remains of 5,864 Americans who lost their lives during World War II have been returned to the United States from Europe aboard the U. S. Army Transport Lawrence Victory, the Department of the Army announced. The Army said each next-of-kin was notified in advance of the vessel's arrival, and would be notified again after arrival of the remains at the regional distribution centers of the American Graves Registration Service. Of the 259 remains being returned upon instructions of next-of-kin residing in Texas, 25 are being sent to San Antonio and 65 are being returned to the San Antonio area. Following is a list of remains being returned to this city and the names of next-of-kin:

San Antonians

Pvt. Juan R. Castañón, Army, Hipólita A. Castañón, 713 Stafford St.; Pfc. Eduardo Cavazos, Army, Crisanto Cavazos, 137 Gould St.; Pfc. Joe L. Esqueda, Army, Anselmo Esqueda, 415 Torreon St.; Pvt. Antiro G. Fierros, Army, Noe Fierros, 913 Rip Ford St.; Staff Sgt. Frank U. Flores, Army, Isabel G. Flores, 111 Rosita Place; Pfc. Harry E. Geissler, Army, Martha L. Geissler, 2042 Kentucky Ave.; Pfc. Alvino C. Hernández, Army, Mrs. Catarina Hernández, 127 Sharp St.; Pvt. Manuel A. Hernández, Army, Benigno Hernández, 916 Durango St.; Pfc. Basilio G. Herrera, Army, Juanita V. Herrera, Route 7, Box 284-A; Second Lt. Ralph E. Hodges, Jr., Army, Mrs. Betty Lee Hodges, 251 Primera Drive; Pvt. J. C. Keith, Army, Mrs. Bobbye L. Keith, 506 W. Mrytle St.; Pfc. Agustín C. Larios, Army, Valentín Larios, 2010 Saunders Ave.; Pfc. Juan S. Martínez, Army, Lupe H. Martínez, 1415 W. Commerce St.; Pfc. Joe L. Matjeka, Army, Edward J. Matjeka 1701 Virginia Blvd.; Pfc. Willie E. McKimmy, Army, Margaret McKimmy, 1301 Burnet St.; Pfc Joe V. Méndez, Army, Catalina P. Méndez, 2505 Monterrey St.; Tech. (4th. gr.) Ewald F. Morgenroth, Army, Theresa Morgenroth, 1136 W. Rosewood Ave.; Pfc. Fernando Noin, Army, Mrs. Genara Noin, 1 Elmira Alley; Pfc. Roy Núñez, Army, José Núñez, 1520 Delgado St.; Staff Sgt. Clarence O. Peavler, Army, Mrs. Melba G. Whitcomb, 305 Jim St.; Sgt. Guadalupe San Miguel, Army, Victoria P. Muriel, 3811 W. Salinas St.;Sgt. Joe Soriano, Air Force,

Gregorio Soriano, 129 Reichert St.; **Pfc. Eugene E. Wenzel, Army,** Ottmar J. Wenzel, Route 3, Box 156; **Pvt. William D. Wicker, Army,** Owen Wicker, 1214 Sacramento St.; **Sgt. Carl E. Young, Army,** Robert E. Young, 220 Southwest Military Drive, and **Sgt. Joe G. Zepeda, Army,** Manuela G. Sánchez, 201 Hidalgo St.

From this Area

Following is a list of remains being returned to the San Antonio area with the names of next-of-kin:

Staff Sgt. J. C. Andrews, Air Force, John T. Andrews, San Angelo; **Pfc. Feliberto C. Atkinson, Army,** Miss Juanita C. Atkinson, Rio Hondo; **Pvt. Daniel Barrera, Army,** Jesús Barrera, Laredo; **Pfc. Roberto Beltrán, Army,** Alfredo Beltrán, Kingsville; **Pvt. Arturo Bermea, Army,** Santos Bermea, Harlingen; **Staff Sgt. Joseph E. Bradshaw, Air Force,** Mrs. Elma Bradshaw, Mission; **Pfc. Wilmer O. Bridges, Army,** Cleveland Bridges, San Benito; **Pvt. Jack T. Calhoun, Army,** Dan Calhoun, Goliad; **Pfc. Manuel N. Cuéllar, Army,** Virginia Nieto, Corpus Christi; **Pvt. James H. Cummings, Army,** J. D. Cummings, San Marcos; **Pvt. Luther W. Davis, Jr., Army,** Luther W. Davis, Sr., Rockport; **Second Lt. Allan H. De Berry, Air Force,** Allan M. De Berry, Austin; **Pfc. Joseph W. Du Bose, Army,** Mrs. Frona Du Bose, Cuero; **Pfc. Juan R. Flores, Army,** Mrs. San Juana G. Flores, McAllen; **First Lt. William A. Forbes, Air Force,** Eugene D. Forbes, Edinburg; **Staff Sgt. Conrado Gamboa, Army,** Mrs. Diamantina L. Gamboa, Laredo; **Pfc. Guillermo M. Gámez, Army,** María Gámez, Placido; **Pfc. Carlos R. García, Army,** Polo R. García, Raymondville; **Pvt. Faustino Garza, Army,** María C. Garza, Laredo; **Pfc. Félix R. Gómez, Army,** Mrs. Ramona P. Gómez, Mission; **Pvt. Francisco C. González, Army,** Martina C. González, Mercedes; **First Lt. George W. Goss, Army,** Florence E. Goss, Menard; **Staff Sgt. Manuel Guzmán, Army,** Lucía Guzmán, Bay City; **Pvt. Milton E. Hartmann, Army,** Alma Hartmann, Floresville; **Pvt. Rodolfo Hernádez, Army,** Fernando Hernández, Sinton; **Pfc. Wayne D. Howard, Army,** V a u g h n Howard, Uvalde; **Pvt. Santos Ibáñez, Jr., Army,** Esperanza Ibáñez, San Diego; **Pvt. Leroy E. Jubela, Army,** Charles Jubela, Seguin; **Tech. (4th gr.) Herbert L. Kainer, Army,** Mrs. Wilhelmia Kainer, Schulenburg; **Pvt. John F. Kozelsky, Army,** John J. Kozelsky, Moulton; **Pfc. Serafín C. López, Army,** Antonia Martínez, Cotulla; **First Lt. Almer J. Mann, Army,** Gullee Mann, Laredo; **Pvt. Julio Martínez, Army,** Juan Martínez, Laredo; **Pfc. Saturnino H. Martínez, Army, Mrs.** Abrana H. Martínez, San Marcos; **Pvt. Salvador Mascorro, Army,** Mercurio Mascorro, Laredo; **Pvt. James S. McCall, Army,** Johnnie O. McCall, San Angelo; **Pvt. John N. McCoy, Army,** John D. McCoy, Natalia; **Second Lt. Everett R. McCulloch, Air Force,** Frank S. G. McCulloch, Von Ormy; **Sgt. Alvin B. Miller,**

Army, Mrs. Josephine Miller, Laredo; **Pvt. Homóbono Moroles, Jr., Army,** Mrs. Manuela M. Moroles, Donna; **Pvt. Gerónimo S. Muñoz, Army,** Juanita A. Muñoz, Sonora; **Pfc. Gumescindo G. Nájar, Army,** Sixto Nájar, Llano; **Pvt. Glenn W. Northcutt, Army,** Anna N. Joiner, Corpus Christi; **Tech. Sgt. James O. Perry, Army,** Florence L. Perry, Austin; **Staff Sgt. David B. Pursch, Air Force,** August E. Pursch, Tilden; **Pfc. Rogelio G. Ramírez, Army,** Crisanto C. Ramírez, Kingsville; **Sgt. Benito Rangel, Army,** Agustina H. Rangel, San Benito; **Pfc. Domingo Sáenz, Army,** Bernabé Sáenz, Laredo; **Pfc. Alfredo Salazar, Army,** Abelardo Salazar, Jourdanton; **Pvt. Abelardo Saldaña, Army,** Mrs. María A. Saldaña, Brownsville; **Pvt. Manuel C. Sánchez, Army,** Arcadio Sánchez, Del Rio; **Pvt. Raymond W. See, Army,** Mrs. Irma See, Seadrift; **Pvt. Federico G. Soto, Army,** Andrés Soto, Laredo; **Pvt. Arthur S. Spies, Army,** Fannie M. Spies, Yorktown; **Pfc. Lee R. Strown, Army,** John B. Strown, Seadrift; **Pvt. Pablo Tórres, Army,** Juan A. Tórres, Sabinal; **Pfc. F. S. Treviño, Jr., Army,** Federico Treviño, Sr., Victoria; **Tech. (5th gr.) José M. Treviño, Jr., Army,** José M. Treviño, Sr., San Diego; **Pfc. Robert L. Treviño, Army,** Mrs. María Treviño, San Diego; **Pvt. Antonio F. Valle, Army,** Salomé S. Valle, Uvalde; **Tech. (5th gr.) Avelino Vera, Army,** Vera C. Domingo, Devine; **Pvt. Santos G. Verástigue, Army,** Ben Verástigue, Austin; **Pvt. Daniel C. Veselka, Army,** Cyrill W. Veselka, El Campo; **Sgt. Joseph F. Wick, Army,** Emil A. Wick, Rio Hondo; and **Pfc. Paulíno S. Zamora, Army,** Mrs. Berta P. Zamora, Brownsville.

(Taken from "San Antonio Express", August 22, 1948).

CITATIONS TO THE CONGRESSIONAL MEDAL OF HONOR FOR SIX LATIN AMERICANS OF THE STATE OF TEXAS.

Sergeant José M. López.

"Sergeant José M. López, (then Private First Class) 23rd Infantry, near Krinkelt, Belgium, on December 17, 1944, on his own initiative carried his heavy machinegun from K Company's right flank to its left, in order to protect that flank which was in danger of being overrun by advancing enemy infantry supported by tanks.

"Occupying a shallow hole offering no protection above his waist, he cut down a group of ten Germans. Ignoring enemy fire from an advancing tank, he held his position and cut down 25 more enemy infantry attempting to turn his flank. Glancing to his right he saw a large number of infantry swarming in from the front. Although dazed and shaken from enemy artillery fire which had crashed into the ground only a few yards away, he realized that his position would be soon outflanked.

"Again, alone, he carried his machinegun to a position to the right rear of the sector; enemy tanks and infantry were forcing a withdrawal. Blown over backwards by the concussion of enemy fire, he immediately reset his gun and continued his fire. Single-handed, he held off the German horde until he was satisfied his company had effected its retirement. Again he loaded his gun on his back and in a hail of small arms fire he ran to a point where a few of his comrades were attempting to set up another defense against the onrushing enemy.

"He fired from this position until his ammunition was exhausted. Still carrying his gun, he fell back with his small group to Krinkelt. Sergeant López' gallantry and intrepidity, on seemingly suicidal missions in which he killed at least 100 of the enemy, were almost solely responsible for allowing K Company to avoid being enveloped, to withdraw successfully, and to give other forces coming up in support time to build a line which repelled the enemy drive".

Staff Sergeant Macario García.

"Staff Sergeant Macario García, (then PFC), Infantry, while an acting squad leader of Company B, 22nd Infantry, on November 27, 1944, near Grosshau, Germany, singlehandedly assaulted two enemy machinegun emplacements. Attacking prepared positions on a wooded hill, which could be approached only through meager cover, his company was pinned down by intense machinegun fire and subjected to a concentrated artillery and mortar barrage. Although painfully wounded, he refused to be evacuated and on his own initiative crawled forward alone until he reached a position near an enemy emplacement. Hurling grenades, he boldly assaulted the position, destroyed the gun, and with his rifle, killed three of the enemy who attempted to escape. When he rejoined his company, a second machinegun opened fire and again the intrepid soldier went forward, utterly disregarding his own safety. He stormed the position and destroyed the gun, killed three more Germans and captured four prisoners. He fought on with his unit until the objective was taken and only then did he permit himself to be removed for medical care. Private García's conspicuous heroism, his inspiring, courageous conduct and his complete disregard for his personal safety wiped out two enemy emplacements and enabled his company to advance and secure its objective".

Private First Class Cleto L. Rodríguez.

"Private First Class Cleto L. Rodríguez was an automatic

290

rifleman with Company B, 148th Infantry, on February 9, 1945, when his unit attacked the strongly defended Paco Railroad Station during the battle for Manila, Philippine Islands.

"While making a frontal assault across an open field, his position was halted one hundred yards from the station by intense enemy fire. On his own initiative, he left the platoon, accompanied by a comrade, and continued forward to a house sixty yards from the objective.

"Although under constant enemy observation, the two men remained in this position for an hour, firing at targets of opportunity, killing more than thirty-five hostile soldiers and wounding many more. Moving closer to the station and discovering a group of Japanese replacements attempting to reach pillboxes, they opened heavy fire, killed more than forty and stopped all subsequent attempts to man the emplacements. Enemy fire became more intense as they advanced to within twenty yards of the station. Then, covered by his companion, Private Rodríguez boldly moved up to the building and threw five grenades through a doorway, killing seven Japanese, destroying a 20-millimeter gun and wrecking a heavy machinegun.

"With their ammunition running low, the two men started to return to the American lines, alternately providing covering fire for each other's withdrawal. During this movement, Private Rodríguez' companion was killed.

"In two and one-half hours of fierce fighting the intrepid team killed more than eighty-two Japanese, completely disorganized their defense and paved the way for the subsequent overwhelming defeat of the enemy at this strongpoint.

"Two days later, Private Rodríguez again enabled his comrades to advance when he singlehandedly killed six Japanese and destroyed a well-placed 20-millimeter gun. By his outstanding skill with his weapons, gallant determination to destroy the enemy and heroic courage in the face of tremendous odds, Private Rodríguez on two occasions, materially aided the advance of our troops in Manila".

Staff Sergeant Lucian Adams.

"For conspicuous gallantry and intrepidity at risk of life above and beyond the call of duty on October 28, 1944, near St. Die, France. When his company was stopped in its effort to drive through the Mortagne Forest to reopen the supply line to the isolated 3rd battalion, Staff Sergeant Adams braved the concentrated fire of machineguns in a lone assault on a force of German troops. Although his company had progressed less than ten yards and had lost three killed, six wounded, Sergeant Adams charged forward dodging from tree to tree firing a borrowed BAR from

291

the hip. Despite intense machinegun fire which the enemy directed at him and rifle grenades which struck the trees over his head showering him with broken twigs and branches, Sergeant Adams made his way to within ten yards of the closest machinegun and killed the gunner with a hand grenade. An enemy soldier threw hand grenades at him from a position only ten yards distant; however, Sergeant Adams dispatched him with a single burst of BAR fire. Charging into the vortex of the enemy fire, he killed another machinegunner at 15 yards range with a hand grenade and forced the surrender of two supporting infantrymen. Although the remainder of the German group concentrated the full force of its automatic weapons fire in a desperate effort to knock him out, he proceeded through the woods to find and exterminate five more of the enemy. Finally when the third German machinegun opened up on him at a range of 20 yards, Sergeant Adams killed the gunner with BAR fire. In the course of the action he personally killed nine Germans, eliminated three enemy machineguns, vanquished a specialized force which was armed with automatic weapons and grenade launchers, cleared the woods of hostile elements and reopened the severed supply lines to the assault companies of his battalion".

Private First Class Silvestre S. Herrera.

"Private First Class Silvestre S. Herrera, Company E, 142d Infantry Regiment, advanced with a platoon along a wooded road near Mertzwiller, France, on March 15, 1945, until stopped by heavy enemy machinegun fire. As the rest of the unit took cover, he made a one-man, frontal assault on a strongpoint and captured eight enemy soldiers.

"When the platoon resumed its advance and was subjected to fire from a second emplacement beyond an extensive minefield, Private Herrera again moved forward, disregarding the danger of exploding mines, to attack the position. He stepped on a mine and had both feet severed; but, despite intense pain and unchecked loss of blood, he pinned down the enemy with accurate rifle fire while a friendly squad captured the enemy gun by skirting the minefield and rushing in from the flank.

"The magnificent courage, extraordinary heroism and willing self-sacrifice displayed by Private Herrera resulted in the capture of two enemy strongpoints and the taking of eight prisoners".

Private First Class Alejandro R. Ruíz.

"Private First Class Alejandro Rentería Ruíz, Company A, 165th Infantry, on April 28, 1945, on Okinawa, when his unit was stopped by a skillfully camouflaged enemy pillbox, displayed conspicuous gallantry and intrepidity above and beyond the call of duty. His squad, suddenly brought under a hail of machinegun fire and a vicious grenade attack, was pinned down. Jumping to his feet, Private Ruíz seized an automatic rifle and lunged through the flying grenades and rifle and automatic fire for the top of the emplacement. When an enemy soldier charged him, his rifle jammed. Undaunted, Private Ruíz whirled on his assailant and clubbed him down. Then he ran back through bullets and grenades, seized more ammunition and another automatic rifle, and again made for the pillbox. Enemy fire now was concentrated on him, but he charged on, miraculously reaching the position, and in plain view he climbed to the top. Leaping from one opening to another, he sent burst after burst into the pillbox, killing 12 of the enemy and completely destroying the position. Private Ruíz' heroic conduct, in the face of overwhelming odds, saved the lives of many comrades and eliminated an obstacle that long would have checked his unit's advance".

GONZALEZ, TEXAS HERO, TALKS, BUT NOT ABOUT SELF.

By Graham Hovey

NAPLES, May 2.—(INS)—Said Lieut. Even J. MacIlraith of Evanston, Ill.

"Come along to the hospital and meet him. I think you can understand him okay now, but he didn't speak a word of English when he joined the army."

I asked, getting into the jeep:

"What did you say his name was?"

Mac said:

"González, Manuel S. González, He's from somewhere in West Texas near the Mexican border- some spot where they don't speak anything but Spanish. He's a Staff or Tech Sergeant now, I think, and he was a regular "Commando Kelly" in combat.

"This guy was such a terrific soldier all the way that I have trouble recalling his individual exploits, even though he was in my company. A wonderful squad leader. He'd volunteer for anything, any time, and at Salerno, when his squad was practically wiped out, he fought a one-man battle against the Germans for 24 hours.

"All of what he did there will never come out - the number of Germans he killed, for instance - because nobody saw him do it and he won't talk about it. But we know he knocked out an 88mm. gun nest with a hand grenade. That was really wrecked.

293

I saw it. He must have hit an ammunition pile. Got some machine-gun nests, too.

"But he really got shot up on Mt. Castellone, and I guess he's all through with combat. They'll probably ship him home."

COT EMPTY

We found Ward 7-B in the hospital, but González' cot was empty.

Mac said:

"That's funny. Let's go down to the ward office."

We did - and found González, a big, bronze man with a tremendous shock of black hair, dressed incongruously in combat boots and a blue bathrobe. He had been chatting with an army chaplain. As he saw MacIlraith, his thick lips parted in a huge smile and dimples which looked like miniature foxholes appeared on the big, copper-colored face. He said, pumping Mac's hand:

"I'm glad to see you, Lieutenant. I'm glad you come today because I go back to company tonight."

Said MacIlraith:

"Sergeant, you're amazing. Back to company! I thought they'd put you on limited service this time."

Said González:

"No, sir. I don't want limited service. I want to go back to company. I've got too much friends there. I don't want to miss this. I want to get back to company."

A. W. O. L. DENIED

He took MacIlraith by the arm, still grinning, and we strolled back to his bunk, where we sat down.

Mac asked:

"Well, how did it go this time, sergeant? Didn't go A. W. O. L. this time, did you?"

MacIlraith explained to me that González once ran away from an army hospital before being discharged to rejoin his company during a tough fight. González said:

"No, sir, sir. I never really went A. W. O. L. since I've been in the army."

I had three operations this time and the second one kept me in bed 36 days and I lose too much weight. I'm weigh 160 pounds now but I used to weigh 215 pounds."

Mac said:

"That's nothing to worry about. You used to be too fat. You could hardly move around."

WOUNDING TOLD

González grinned again, showing large, irregular white teeth, and as he rocked back on the cot, I could see an American flag tatooed on his left arm. He said:

"No, sir, sir. I could always move."

"How did you get hit?"

MacIlraith answered for González.

"Got three machine pistol slugs in his groin when he attacked on Castellone the last day of January. Went back under his own power after he got hit and reported at the aid station still on his feet. He wouldn't tell you that himself."

González grinned:

"But I'm feeling good now. Major Carney, he's a pretty good doctor, boy, he saved my life."

Mac told him:

"Tell him about getting the Distinguished Service Cross from General Clark on Christmas day. I think you're going to get some more medals soon, too."

Said González, embarrassed:

"No, sir, sir, I don't want no more. No, sir, sir, no more medals. But I wish my mother would get that one. She hasn't gotten it yet."

Mac answered:

"She'll get it all right. If she doesn't, I'll see that you get another one to send her."

LEARNS ENGLISH

González' mother, Mrs. Cármen Mendoza, and his wife both live in Fort Davis, Texas, where the 27-year old sergeant worked in a cement works prior to the war. His father, Angel González, lives in El Paso.

González said:

"Everybody speaks Spanish at Fort Davis. I just learn American language in the army. The boys in the company teach me at night. They're pretty good boys."

Said MacIlraith:

"Tell him what you did at Salerno. Knocked out some German tanks there, didn't you?"

"No, sir. I threw some hand grenades at those tanks but it was no good. They just kept on coming."

Mac said::

"It's no use, He won't talk about himself.

295

"He won't tell you how he fought the Germans alone or how he volunteered for patrols or how he came right back into the line after being ruptured and having 'flu' and malaria and getting wounded."

I asked:

"What do you think of the Germans?"

Said González:

"I think they are good but I think we are better. We don't holler 'kamerad' but they do. They give up too easy but we don't."

I asked:

"How was MacIlraith as a company commander?"

González grinned again and slapped Mac on the back:

"The best. He was the best commander and we'd like to have him back but we can't help it because they won't let him."

WHO'S HERO?

I asked:

"González, you've seen a lot of combat. They say you're slated for rotation home. Why don't you take it?"

The grin vanished. He said:

"No, sir, sir, I don't like rotation because they might send me to a new outfit. I want to stick with my company. When the war is over I want to rotate home for good, but I don't want to get far from my company until then."

Outside the hospital, MacIlraith gave me the fish eye. He said:

"What's the idea, asking him about me? The idea was to interview González."

"I can't find out anything about González from González and I can't find out anything about MacIlraith from MacIlraith. You've never yet told me how you got the Silver Star."

Said Mac:

"Guys like González got it for me. It's a cinch to be a hero when you're commanding guys like González."

(Taken from "San Antonio Light," San Antonio, Texas, May 2, 1944.)

TABLE OF CONTENTS

297

The Mexican American

An Arno Press Collection

Castañeda, Alfredo, et al, eds. **Mexican Americans and Educational Change.** 1974

Church Views of the Mexican American. 1974

Clinchy, Everett Ross, Jr. **Equality of Opportunity for Latin-Americans in Texas.** 1974

Crichton, Kyle S. **Law and Order Ltd.** 1928

Education and the Mexican American. 1974

Fincher, E. B. **Spanish-Americans as a Political Factor in New Mexico, 1912-1950.** 1974

Greenwood, Robert. **The California Outlaw:** Tiburcio Vasquez. 1960

Juan N. Cortina: Two Interpretations. 1974

Kibbe, Pauline R. **Latin Americans in Texas.** 1946

The Mexican American and the Law. 1974

Mexican American Bibliographies. 1974

Mexican Labor in the United States. 1974

The New Mexican Hispano. 1974

Otero, Miguel Antonio. **Otero:** An Autobiographical Trilogy. 1935/39/40

The Penitentes of New Mexico. 1974

Perales, Alonso S. **Are We Good Neighbors?** 1948

Perspectives on Mexican-American Life. 1974

Simmons, Ozzie G. **Anglo-Americans and Mexican Americans in South Texas.** 1974

Spanish and Mexican Land Grants. 1974

Tuck, Ruth D. **Not With the Fist.** 1946

Zeleny, Carolyn. **Relations Between the Spanish-Americans and Anglo-Americans in New Mexico.** 1974